Sheikh Abdullah

Sheikh Abdullah

Series Editor

Dr. M.H. Syed

Editor

R.K. Singh **P.K. Choudhry**

Himalaya Books Pvt. Ltd.

'Ramdoot', Dr. Bhalerao Marg, Girgaon, Mumbai - 400 004
Tel : (022) 23863863, Fax : (022) 23877178
Email : himpub@vsnl.com

Edition : 2014

Published by : **H.B.P.L.**
"Pooja Apartment", 4-B, Murari Lal Street, Ansari Road,
Darya Ganj, New Delhi-110 002
Phones : 23270392, 23278631 Reliance : 30180392 to 396
Fax : 011-23256286 Email : hphdel@vsnl.com

Sole Distributers : **HIMALAYA PUBLISHING HOUSE PVT. LTD.**

Branch Offices :

Mumbai : "Ramdoot", Dr. Bhalerao Marg, Girgaon, Mumbai - 400 004.
Phone: 022-23860170/23863863, Fax: 022-23877178
E-mail: himpub@vsnl.com; Website: www.himpub.com

Nagpur : Kundanlal Chandak Industrial Estate, Ghat Road, Nagpur - 440 018. Phone: 0712-2738731, 3296733; Telefax: 0712-2721216

Bengaluru : No. 16/1 (Old 12/1), 1st Floor, Next to Hotel Highlands, Madhava Nagar, Race Course Road, Bengaluru - 560 001.
Phone: 080-22286611, 22385461, 4113 8821, 22281541

Hyderabad : No. 3-4-184, Lingampally, Besides Raghavendra Swamy Matham, Kachiguda, Hyderabad - 500 027.
Phone: 040-27560041, 27550139

Chennai : 8/2 Madley 2nd street, T. Nagar, Chennai - 600 017.
Mobile: 09320490962

Pune : First Floor, "Laksha" Apartment, No. 527, Mehunpura, Shaniwarpeth (Near Prabhat Theatre), Pune - 411 030.
Phone: 020-24496323/24496333; Mobile: 09370579333

Lucknow : House No 731, Shekhupura Colony, Near B.D. Convent School, Aliganj, Lucknow - 226 022.
Phone: 0522-4012353; Mobile: 09307501549

Ahmedabad : 114, "SHAIL", 1st Floor, Opp. Madhu Sudan House, C.G. Road, Navrang Pura, Ahmedabad - 380 009.
Phone: 079-26560126; Mobile: 09377088847

Ernakulam : 39/176 (New No: 60/251) 1st Floor, Karikkamuri Road, Ernakulam, Kochi – 682011. Phone: 0484-2378012, 2378016;
Mobile: 09387122121

Bhubaneswar : 5 Station Square, Bhubaneswar - 751 001 (Odisha).
Phone: 0674-2532129, Mobile: 09338746007

Indore : Kesardeep Avenue Extension, 73, Narayan Bagh, Flat No. 302, IIIrd Floor, Near Humpty Dumpty School, Indore - 452007 (M.P.).
Mobile: 09303399304

Kolkata : 108/4, Beliaghata Main Road, Near ID Hospital, Opp. SBI Bank, Kolkata - 700 010, Phone: 033-32449649, Mobile: 7439040301

Guwahati : House No. 15, Behind Pragjyotish College, Near Sharma Printing Press, P.O. Bharalumukh, Guwahati - 781009, (Assam).
Mobile: 09883055590, 08486355289, 7439040301

Printed at : M/s. Aditya Offset Process (I) Pvt. Ltd., Hyderabad. On behalf of HPH.

Preface

Biography, is now a form of literature, very much in vogue. In fact, biography is a description or account of someone's life and the times, which is usually published in the form of a book. A biography is more than a mention of personal facts (life, education, work, relationships and death), it also portrays the subject's experience of events. Technically speaking, a work is biographical, if it covers, all of a person's life. Biography writing has a long history. A biography is real. Ancient Greeks developed the biographical tradition, which we have inherited, although until the 5th century AD, when the word 'biographia' first appeared, in Damascius' "Life of Isodorus," biographical pieces were called simply "lives". It is quite likely that the Greeks were drawing on a pre-existing eastern tradition. Certainly Herodotus' "Histories" contains more detailed biographical information on Persian kings and subjects. The earliest surviving pieces, which we would identify as biographical are Isocrates' "Life of Evagoras" and Xenophon's "Life of Agesilaos," both from the fifth century BC. "Parallel Lives" by Plutarch, a Greek writing under the Roman empire, is a series of short biographies of eminent men.

The Golden Age of English biography emerged in late eighteenth century, the century in which the terms "biography" and "autobiography" entered English lexicon. The classic works of the period were Samuel Johnson's "Critical Lives of the Poets" and James Boswell's "Massive Life of Johnson". Generally American biography followed English model. By World War I, cheap hardcover reprints had become popular. The decade of the 1920s witnessed a biographical 'boom'. Later, biographical writings developed a lot and today biographies are written and compiled in the finest form of the genre. In India too, biography, as a form of literature has been evolved, cultivated and polished over the years. Here is an effort to promote this tradition further.

This series of biographies of great men, great women and celebrities in all walks of life is an adventurous academic endeavour, in its own right. A team of researchers and compilers has worked for a good period of time to accomplish the project. For this purpose, hundreds of books by eminent authors and editors have been consulted and referred to. We have benefited from various works, liberally, in order to illustrate and enrich this effort of ours. Present book is devoted to the great personality of Sheikh Mohammed Abdullah.

Sheikh Mohammed Abdullah, known as Sher-e-Kashmir' (the Lion of Kashmir) was one of the most important political figures in the modern history of Kashmir. Sheikh Abdullah was a charismatic leader, and had the following of a huge majority of Kashmiris. Sheikh Abdullah became the Prime Minister of Jammu and Kashmir, soon after its accession to India. He represented India's case on Kashmir in UN. Sheikh Abdullah made an important speech in the shrine of Hazratbal in 1949. He lost power in 1953, but successfully came back as Chief Minister of J&K in 1975. He held this position till his death. No doubt, the Sheikh was the tallest figure in Kashmir's political and social life. He is still respected in the state, as the builder of modern Kashmir. Sheikh Abdullah redefined freedom in a manner that appeared refreshingly new and revolutionary even, today in the 21st century.

This is a compact and comprehensive account of the above mentioned great life, which is bound to attract the attention of scholars, researchers, students and the general readers, alike. Let's hope this humble effort would receive a warm welcome and due applause.

— ***Editors***

Contents

1

An Illustrious Life

Introduction

- *Sheikh Mohammed Abdullah, Sher-e-Kashmir (the Lion of Kashmir) (December 5, 1905 – September 8, 1982), was one of the most important political figures in the modern history of Jammu and Kashmir. In 1933 he married Akbar Jahan, the daughter of Michael Harry Nedou, the European proprietor of a chain of hotels in India, including Nedous Hotel in Srinagar and his Kashmiri wife Mirjan. Michael Harry Nedou was also the proprietor of a hotel at the tourist resort of Gulmarg.*
- *Sheikh Abdullah agitated against the rule of the Maharaja Hari Singh, and urged self-rule for Kashmir. He was the Prime Minister of Jammu and Kashmir State after its accession to India in 1947, and was later jailed and exiled. He again became the Chief Minister of the state, following the 1974 Indira-Sheikh accord and remained in the top slot till his death.*

Early Life

[The most important source of Sheikh Abdullah's early life is his official biography Atish-e-Chinar (In its foreword Sheikh Abdullah says,

it should be considered as his memoirs) and the main facts regarding it as given in Atish-e-Chinar (Urdu) are detailed below.]

Sheikh Mohammed Abdullah was born in Soura, a village on the outskirts of Srinagar, just eleven days after the death of his father Sheikh Mohammed Ibrahim, a middle class manufacturer and trader of Kashmirishawls. In his own words he was born an orphan. Sheikh Ibrahim like poet Iqbal was the descendant of a Hindu Kashmiri Pandit named Ragho Ram Koul, who was converted to Islam in 1722 by the saint Rashid Balkhi and after conversion changed his name to Sheikh Mohammed Abdullah. Thus Sheikh Abdullah was the namesake of the progenitor of his family branch.

His step brothers mistreated his mother and his early childhood was marked by utter poverty. His mother was keen that her children should receive proper education and so as a child he was first admitted to a traditional school or Maktab where he learnt the recitation of Holy Quran and some basic Persian texts like Gulistan, Bostan, Padshanama, etc. Then in 1911 he was admitted to a primary school, where he studied for about two years. His elder step brothers then stopped his further education and he was first set to work in the family workshop, embroidering shawls and later asked to sit on a grocers shop as a sales boy.

However, their family barber Mohammed Ramzan prevailed upon his uncle to send him back to school. He had to walk the distance of ten miles to school and back on foot but in his own words, the joy of being allowed to obtain a school education made it seem a light work. He passed his Matriculation examination from Punjab University in 1922.

Higher Studies

After matriculation he obtained admission in Sri Partap College the leading college of Kashmir. Because of extreme poverty he had to walk the distance of about fifteen miles from Soura to S.P.College and back and so developed Cardiomegaly (perhaps an early sign of beriberi brought about by malnutrition and severe exertion.) He was admitted to the Mission Hospital, where under the treatment of the famous Neve brothers he recovered completely. His elder brother Sheikh Maqbool was moved by his illness and agreed to pay for his stay in the college hostel, from where he passed his intermediate (F.Sc.) examination.

He obtained admission in Islamia College Lahore, from where he completed his B.Sc. degree. After that he obtained admission to the M.Sc. Chemistry course in Aligarh Muslim University and obtained Masters degree in Chemistry on 12 April 1930. He was the first Kashmiri Muslim to have obtained a Master's degree in Chemistry.

In Political Arena

As a student at Aligarh Muslim University, he came in contact with and was influenced by persons with liberal and progressive ideas. He became convinced that the feudal system was responsible for the miseries of the Kashmiris and like all progressive people of the world Kashmiris too should have a democratically elected government.

Muslim Conference Formed

Sheikh Abdullah and his colleagues were greatly influenced by the lectures of a Kashmiri polymath and lawyer Molvi Abdullah. Molvi Abdullah's son Molvi Abdul Rahim, Sheikh Abdullah and Ghulam Nabi Gilkar were the first three educated Kashmiri youth to be arrested during the public agitation of 1931.

Kashmir's first Political Party, the Muslim Conference with Sheikh Abdullah as President, Chaudhary Ghulam Abbas as General Secretary, and Molvi Abdul Rahim as Secretary was formed on 16 October 1932.

In his presidential address, Sheikh Abdullah categorically stated that the Muslim Conference had come into existence to struggle for the rights of all oppressed sections of the society and not Muslims alone. It was not a communal party and would struggle for the rights of the oppressed, whether Hindu, Muslim, or Sikh, with the same fervour. He reasserted that the struggle of Kashmiris was not a communal struggle.

In March 1933 the Muslim Conference constituted a committee, which included Molvi Abdullah and nine other members for the purpose of establishing contacts with non- Muslim parties and exploring the possibility of forming a joint organisation. According to Sheikh Abdullah, this effort was not successful because of the unfavourable reception of the idea by the non-Muslim parties. Sheikh Abdullah later changed the name of the Muslim Conference to National Conference, under the influence of Jawaharlal Nehru.

Formation of Praja Sabha (Legislative Assembly)

As a result of the 1931 agitation the Maharaja appointed a Greviances Commission with an Englishman B.J. Glancy as President which submitted its report in March 1932. Subsequently a Constitutional Reforms Conference also presided over by B.J. Glancy recommended the setting up of an elected Legislative Assembly (Praja Sabha). Consequently a Praja Sabha with 33 elected and 42 nominated members selected on the basis of separate electorates for Hindus and Muslims was established in 1934). Women and Illiterate men without sufficient property, or title, or annual income of less than Rupees four hundred did not have the right to vote. Roughly less than 10 per cent (According to Justice Anand only 3%) of the population were enfranchised. Even after the formation of Praja Sabha in 1934, as recommended by the Commission real power continued to remain in the hands of the Maharaja.

Meeting with Nehru

Sheikh Abdullah was introduced to Jawaharlal Nehru in 1937 and as he too as a leader of the Indian National Congress was demanding similar rights for people of British India and had formed 'The All India States Peoples Conference' for supporting the people of Princely States in their struggle for a representative government, the two became friends and political allies.

Muslim Conference Renamed as National Conference

Sheikh introduced a resolution in the working committee of the Muslim Conference for changing its name to National Conference on 24 June 1938 to allow people from all communities to join the struggle against the autocratic rule of the Maharaja. Meanwhile he along with his liberal progressive friends, many of whom were not Muslims like Kashyap Bandhu, Jia Lal Kilam, Pandit Sudama Sidha, Prem Nath Bazaz and Sardar Budh Singh drafted the National Demands the forerunner of the famous Naya Kashmir (New Kashmir) Manifesto, which was a charter of demands for granting a democratic Constitution committed to the welfare of the common people of Kashmir.

He presented these demand to the Maharaja in a speech on 28 August 1938. The Maharaja of course was not willing to accept these demands and so he along with many of his companions was arrested for defying prohibitory orders and sentenced to six months imprisonment and a fine. His arrest provoked a public agitation in which volunteers called Dictators (so called because they had the authority to defy laws that was forbidden for normal law abiding party members) courted arrest. This agitation was called off on the appeal of Mahatama Gandhi. He was released after serving his sentence on 24 February 1939 and accorded a grand reception by the people of Srinagar on his return. Speeches were made at the reception, stressing the importance of unity among Hindus, Muslims and Sikhs. Subsequently the resolution for changing the name of Muslim Conference to National Conference was ratified with an overwhelming majority by the General Council of the Muslim Conference on 11 June 1939 and from that date Muslim Conference became National Conference.

Quit Kashmir Agitation

In May 1946 Sheikh Abdullah launched the Quit Kashmir agitation against Maharaja Hari Singh and was arrested and sentenced to three years imprisonment, but was released only sixteen months later on 29 September 1947.

Head of Emergency Administration

Following an attack by Pakistan, Hari Singh appealed to Lord Mountbatten, the Governor-General of India for Indian military aid. In his Accession Offer dated October 26, 1947, which accompanied the Instrument of Accession duly signed by him, Maharaja Hari Singh wrote: "I may also inform your

Excellency's Government that it is my intention at once to set up an interim Government and ask Sheikh Abdullah to carry the responsibilities in this emergency with my Prime Minister".

Lord Mountbatten accepted the accession after a meeting of the Defence Committee on October 27, 1947. In accepting the accession unconditionally he wrote "I do hereby accept this Instrument of Accession. Dated this twenty seventh day of October, nineteen hundred and forty seven".

In the covering letter to Hari Singh, he wrote "In consistence with their policy that in the case of any State where the issue of accession has been the subject of dispute, the question of accession should be decided in accordance with the wishes of the people of the State, it is my Government's wish that, as soon as law and order have been restored in Kashmir and its soil cleared of the invader, the question of the State's accession should be settled by a reference to the people". Also in his letter to the Maharaja Lord Mountbatten wrote "My Government and I note with satisfaction that your Highness has decided to invite Sheikh Abdullah to form an Interim Government to work with your Prime Minister."

In fact, the support of Mahatma Gandhi and Jawaharlal Nehru, the Prime Minister of India was a key factor in getting Sheikh Abdullah appointed as Head of the emergency administration by the Maharaja.

As a consequence, Sheikh Abdullah was appointed head of an emergency administration by an order issued by the Maharaja, which was undated except for the mention October 1947 in place of the date. He took charge as Head of the Emergency Administration on 30 October 1947. After assuming the charge of the Head of the Emergency Administration, he addressing his first meeting with the government officers said "Pakistan is not our enemy and we have the same respect for Mr. Jinnah that we had previously. We want the Kashmir issue to be settled by dialogue and if for this purpose I have to go to Karachi to meet Mr. Jinnah I am willing to go there".

He raised a force of local Kashmiri volunteers to patrol Srinagar and take control of administration after the flight of the Maharaja along with his family and Prime Minister Meher Chand Mahajan to Jammu even before the Indian troops had landed. This group of volunteers would serve as the nucleus for the subsequent formation of Jammu and Kashmir Militia. This Sheikh Abdullah hoped would take over the defence of Kashmir after the Indian army was withdrawn.

This was articulated in his letter to Sardar Patel dated 7 October 1948 in which he wrote, "With the taking over of the State forces by the Indian Government, it was agreed that steps would be taken to reorganise and rebuild our army so that when the present emergency is over and the Indian forces are withdrawn, the State will be left with a proper organised army of its own to fall back upon". (Sheikh Abdullah has alleged that most of the Muslim soldiers of the Militia were either discharged or imprisoned before his arrest in 1953. The Militia (dubbed as Dagan Brigade) was converted from a State Militia to a regular unit of the Indian Army on 2 December 1972 and re-designated the Jammu and Kashmir Light Infantry.

First Democratic Elections

In 1951; the government of Kashmir with Sheikh Abdullah as Prime Minister held elections to a Constituent Assembly on the basis of universal adult suffrage. Sheikh Abdullah's Government had been accused of rigging in these elections to the Constituent Assembly. Nonetheless, due consideration should be given to the quantum leap in moving from elections with 10 per cent of enfranchised population to universal adult suffrage and that too just after a cease fire from an active war.

Prime Minister of Kashmir

Sheikh Abdullah took oath as Prime Minister of Kashmir on March 17, 1948. It was a saga that was like a Bollywood film. A poor orphan boy, set to work by his stepbrothers, embroidering shawls and selling groceries, allowed to go to school only on the pleading of a kind hearted barber, nearly dying of malnutrition and overexertion, getting his applications for grant of scholarships rejected time and again by a heartless aristocracy which heeded only those who had the backing of the rich and the powerful, had been appointed to an office to which only the most powerful landlords of the Maharaja or the highest ranking mandarins of the British administration would dare to aspire Fate in one of its more munificent moods had once again replayed the drama of poor Dick Whittington.

Arrest and Release

On 8 August 1953, he was dismissed as Prime Minister by the then Sadr-e-Riyasat (Constitutional Head of State) Dr. Karan Singh son of the erstwhile Maharaja Hari Singh on the charge that he had lost the confidence of his Cabinet (not the house) He was denied the opportunity to prove his majority on the floor of the house and his dissident Cabinet minister Bakshi Ghulam Mohammed was appointed as Prime Minister. Sheikh Abdullah was immediately arrested and later jailed for eleven years, accused of conspiracy against the State in the infamous "Kashmir Conspiracy Case".

According to Sheikh Abdullah his dismissal and arrest were engineered by the Central government headed by Prime Minister Nehru. He has quoted B.N. Mullicks' statements in his book "My Years with Nehru" in support of his statement. A.G. Noorani writing in 'Frontline' supported this view, as according to him Nehru himself had ordered the arrest. On 8 April 1964, the State Government dropped all charges in the so called "Kashmir Conspiracy Case". Sheikh Abdullah was released and returned to Srinagar, where he was accorded an unprecedented welcome by the people of the valley".

After his release, he was reconciled with Nehru. Nehru requested Sheikh Abdullah to act as a bridge between India and Pakistan and make President Ayub to agree to come to New Delhi for talks for a final solution of the Kashmir problem. President Ayub Khan also sent telegrams to Nehru and Sheikh Abdullah with the message that as Pakistan too was a party to the Kashmir dispute any resolution of the conflict without its participation would not be acceptable to Pakistan. This paved the way for Sheikh Abdullah's visit to Pakistan to help broker a solution to the Kashmir problem.

Sheikh Abdullah went to Pakistan in spring of 1964. President Ayub Khan of Pakistan held extensive talks with him to explore various avenues for solving the Kashmir problem and agreed to come to Delhi in mid June for talks with Nehru as suggested by him. Even the date of his proposed visit was fixed and communicated to New Delhi. On 27 May, while he was *en route* to Muzaffarabad in Pakistani Occupied Kashmir, news came of the sudden death of Nehru and the Sheikh after addressing a public rally at Muzaffarabad returned to Delhi. On his suggestion President Ayub Khan sent a high level Pakistani delegation to take part in the last rites of Jawaharlal Nehru.

After Nehru's death in 1964, he was interned from 1965 to 1968 and exiled from Kashmir in 1971 for 18 months. The Plebiscite Front was also banned. This was allegedly done to prevent him and the Plebiscite Front which was supported by him from taking part in elections in Kashmir.

Indo-Pakistan War and Creation of Bangladesh

In 1971 an insurrection broke out in erstwhile East Pakistan, and subsequently a war broke out between India and Pakistan, which ended in the creation of Bangladesh. Sheikh Abdullah watching the alarming turn of events in the subcontinent realised that for the survival of this region there was an urgent need to stop pursuing confrontational politics and promoting solution of issues by a process of reconciliation and dialogue rather than confrontation.

Realising this he started talks with the then Prime Minister Indira Gandhi for normalising the situation in the state and came to an accord, called 1974 Indira-Sheikh accord, by giving up the demand for a plebiscite in lieu of the people being given the right to self-rule by a democratically elected Government (as envisaged under article 370 of the Constitution of India) rather than the puppet governments which till then ruled the State.

Chief Minister of the State

Sheikh assumed the position of Chief Minister of Jammu and Kashmir. Unfortunately the Central Government and the ruling Congress Party withdrew its support so the State Assembly had to be dissolved and mid term elections were called.

The National Conference won an overwhelming majority in the subsequent elections and re-elected Sheikh Abdullah as Chief Minister. He remained as Chief Minister till his death in 1982. During his brief tenure as Chief Minister, he tried to develop close ties between the three regions of the State namely Jammu, Kashmir and Ladakh. He also attempted to promote infrastructural development in the State and built the prestigious Sher-e-Kashmir Institute of Medical Sciences and a Convention Centre built to international standards so as to promote Medical and Business tourism in the valley.

Abdullah, described as a six feet four inches tall man, was fluent both in Kashmiri and Urdu. His biography in Urdu entitled *Atish-e-Chinar* was written by the noted Kashmiri author M.Y. Taing and published after Sheikh Abdullah's death. It is often referred to as his autobiography as Taing claimed that he only acted as an amanuensis. It is based on extensive interviews that Taing had with Sheikh Abdullah and provides valuable information on Sheikh Abdullah's family background, early life, ringside glimpses of happenings in Kashmir at a crucial juncture in its history, and his viewpoint about the political events in Kashmir, in which he himself played a central role.

After his death his eldest son Dr. Farooq Abdullah was elected as the Chief Minister of the State. Omar Abdullah who is the son of Farooq Abdullah has also emerged as an important political leader of the National Conference. He is the present chief minister of Jammu and Kashmir.

Demise and the Aftermath

The political situation in J&K remained stable for the next few years with Sheikh Abdullah as the Chief Minister, and the NC maintaining cordial relations with the Central Government and furthering the ideals of democracy and secularism in the State. However, the Congress started making efforts to stage a comeback in the State and expand its following. This led to a confrontation with the NC to an extent that it contributed towards Sheikh Abdullah, allegedly, indulging in anti-Centre fulminations.

Sheikh Abdullah died in September 8, 1982 and his son, Dr. Farooq Abdullah took over the leadership of the NC. This succession led to a bitter conflict with his brother-in-law G.M. Shah, emerging as a rival aspirant. The June 1983 Assembly elections again returned NC under Dr. Farooq Abdullah to power, but the internal quarrels had not dissipated. Defection of the G.M. Shah group from the NC led to the fall of Dr. Farooq Abdullah's government on 2 July 1984 and G.M. Shah (NC-K) assumed power with the support of the Congress, from outside. This ushered in a period of unprecedented communal violence and misrule in the State

Lion of Kashmir (Brief Life Sketch)

Jawaharlal Nehru called him Sher-e-Kashmir, ('the Lion of Kashmir'), before freedom from foreign rule, and the people of Kashmir joyously took up the chant after the freedom dawned. He led the struggle of Kashmiris for freedom from the King's rule, and became the symbol of Kashmiri nationalism; but he stood for the merger of Kashmir with India. He was arrested and imprisoned for years by Nehru himself; but he became first the Prime Minister and then the chief minister of Kashmir under Congress rule.

Abdullah, born in 1905 in Saura of Kashmir, to Sheikh Muhammed Ibrahim who died just days before the birth of the child, was influenced in his early days by the history of Islam and poets like Iqbal, but later by Gandhiji and other political leaders of India like Nehru, Abul Kalam Azad. Another source of influence for him was Mustafa Kemal Pasha of Turkey. Abdullah joined hands with Iqbal to found the Muslim Conference, the goal of which was to replace the King's rule and set up a responsible government. This saw him in prison for more than 15 years, under various arrests. But his Muslim Conference was able to snatch a decision in favour of its demand for a people's assembly, and it won landslide victory in elections to the assembly.

The Jammu-Kashmir Muslim Conference, under the Sheikh's leadership, decided to admit non-Muslims also into it, and so its name was changed as 'Jammu-Kashmir National Conference'. Nehru and the other Indian leaders supported Abdullah's demand for a popular rule for Jammu and Kashmir. In October 1947 an interim government was formed, Abdullah as its head. Shortly he became the Prime Minister, though the King continued as someone like a governor. Abdullah was a member of the Indian team to the UN (1948), and a member of the Constituent Assembly which drafted the Constitution for India (1949) and then the Prime Minister of Kashmir. But he was ousted, arrested and imprisoned on the charge of conspiracy to free Kashmir from India. He was freed in 1958, but seeing that he had turned more anti-Indian by this time, he was jailed again. He was freed after six years to mediate between India and Pakistan on the Kashmir dispute, but Nehru's death in 1964 made things more uncertain.

The following years saw Sheikh Abdullah becoming in and out of favour with the government of India several times. But peace dawned between New Delhi and Abdullah again and a pact was signed according to which the state became a regular member of the Indian Union, and brought under all the provisions of the Constitution, and he became Chief Minister of Jammu and Kashmir. Elections were held in the state and he became Chief Minister again in 1977. He died in 1982, leaving the leadership to his son, Dr. Farooq Abdullah.

2

Political Career

The Backdrop

During British rule in India and Maharaja's rule in Kashmir, Kashmiri Muslims had little or no English education, They were engaged in various occupations other than those of the Imperial Service of the State. Their professions were the Kashmir Crafts, and the majority of the population lived in the villages, where they worked as sharecroppers to the landlords. The standard of living of an ordinary peasant was very low, but his physique was, as it is now, excellent. We could find excellent cultivators, best craftsmen, artisans, first rate shawl weavers etc. among the Kashmiri Muslims. Besides, Kashmiri Muslims offered the best Hanjis (boatmen) and *Khamamans.*

Ninety-six out of every hundred in the State lived on land in 8,740 villages where they were oppressed by want and disease. The average yearly income of a peasant barely reached eleven rupees, and therefore Kashmiris were seeing the bitterest type of poverty and strife. So backward were the Kashmiris in general, and the Muslims in particular in Western education and civilization that even the upper classes of Kashmiris were deemed unfit to be employed in the administrative services of the State, or recruited in the military, where Dogras enjoyed the monopoly of being the only community fit for this service. Of the community itself, since there were no prospects, very few Muslim gentlemen were matriculates. Even the parents of children thought it "useless" to educate their sons, to whom, as the parents felt sure, education would do no good in the long run since even the educated had no option but to make their parental professions the vocations of their utmost like.

Thus, the policy and technique of the Government had closed the honourable and responsible careers to the talent and intellectual cleverness of certain " brilliant" youngmen of Kashmir. Kashmiris were looked down by those in office and power. Even the Gracculus in the early days of Roman Empire was not subjected to so much discrimination and insults as the Kashmiri was before Sher-e-Kashmir launched his hard fight for the emancipation of the Kashmiris He could not see his people worth only the palanquin bearers of Government officials and their subordinates. Kashmiris were dwarfed by centuries of servitude and oppression, poverty, degradation and superstition. He could not really see his brothers in distress.

Rise of the Sheikh

Sheikh Mohammed Abdullah, the burly leader of Kashmir was born in 1905 at Soura, some miles towards North-East of Srinagar. His father was a shawl merchant. His trade had bestowed him with a middle class living which later made it possible for Abdullah to acquire higher education. His father died before his birth and his mother also died when Abdullah was still a boy. He was, thus, left to the protection of his elder brothers who brought him up and somehow spent a good sum of money on his education.

He could easily talk much about the administration of his State from his experiences at the school. The school teachers of his time were mostly the well-read Kashmiri Pandits, who, because of no other prospects in the State, had to become petty school teachers. Some of his teachers told him of their classmates who were placed differently in life because of there being the Punjabis. Sometimes he was perplexed to find unfit officials in the offices while brilliant youngmen were idly numbering their days of the month to see when the day came when these clerks and teachers would be getting their meagre salaries with which these people could barely make both ends meet. Did he ask his mind at that time, 'Why should this be so. Did his experience make a reply, "Don't you know they are the Dogras?" And his school days also passed like this in disgust and experience.

In 1930 he passed out of Aligarh Muslim University with M. Sc. and came to Kashmir with the hope of getting a nice job. He was now a different man. The varsity life had brought about many changes in him. Western science had interested him. He wanted to live nicely on a good salary. The old-fashioned living of the Kashmiri household had no charm for him now. He hated life of desperations, since he thought it a right of every human being to make life worth living and live it for livings sake. He was that time among the very few Kashmiri Muslims who had achieved this academic qualification. Many Kashmiris approached his brothers for his marriage. His brothers sought his consent. But he was able to convince them with his notion that settlement was more important than marriage and therefore marriage must come after settlement.

Search for a Career

He was really in need of a job then for he had thought that he had taxed the generocities of his brothers too much. He wanted to earn for himself and for them also. Likewise he tried his best for a job. He sent in applications in response to the advertisements, which appeared from time to time in the Jammu and Kashmir Gazette. He could not get a job, but what was his surprise was to find that men inferior to him and of no credit were given jobs simply on the basis that either they were the Dogras or their relatives were gazetted officers in the State. He interviewed many officials and talked truth to them, but they could only smile at his logic and the dashness with which he could dare to talk so bluntly with these, so-called, 'Bara shahebs' and 'Chota—Shahebs'. Their attitudes made him desperate, and all his attempts turned futile due to the State's policy of discrimination. In fact had he been given a job, the history of Kashmir would have been written differently.

His persistent efforts to procure a job, however, resulted in something. He could get a job and that was of an ordinary school teacher, the profession he bitterly hated because of its monotony. There was no other option for him but to be a teacher. He tried to carry on for some time, but its experience, he found, was nothing more than disgust.

Void for Leadership

Those days, Muslims of Kashmir had no political leader. Their politics was their religion and their leaders were the *Moulvis, Pirs* and *Mullas* who were generally well versed in their religious literatures. These people used to address the masses on some religious days in mosques or *Ziarats,* and the subject of these lectures always was religion and morality. These *Moulvis, Pirs* and *Mullas* were highly esteemed by the people who took them as the deputies of *Allah.* Besides this they had to do nothing with politics or the Government of the State.

Those days were also the happiest days of communal concord in Kashmir. Muslims were found in Hindu households as servants, friends, partners etc. A Muslim did not hesitate to take food prepared by Hindu households. Hindus and Muslims lived like brothers. They trusted each other to the full. This brotherhood had become proverbial too.

Political offences were absolutely unknown in Kashmir. Hindu-Muslim relations were of the most cordial character, and even the Ruler used to take pride in these two features of the Kashmiris. The inhabitants of the Happy Valley lived in a happy atmosphere devoid of bitterness, suspicion and mistrust But the policy of the Government had closed all doors for qualified Muslim gentlemen like Sheikh Abdullah.

It was in those days that people in Kashmir had developed a knack to talk about "The Lahore Congress" The Congress session was held in 1929, and the noteworthy thing about the session was that large numbers of people from the Frontier Province had attended it under the leadership of Khan Abdul Ghaffar Khan, who was also present there. This had been seen for the first time in Lahore. This had also given birth to some apprehensions in the minds of those who were in favour of Muslim League. Indian politics or what was happening in India had interested everyone in Kashmir, but Kashmir was a far off place from the Indian scene.

Rise of Sheikh

The first time Sheikh Ahdullah appeared on the public stage was in September 1930 when he collected some of his friends, won the support of religious leaders and sent a representation to the Government complaining against under representation of Muslims in the Government services The deputation met some of the Government officials and demanded a proportion of appointments to qualified Muslims in State services. But the Government turned a deaf ear to his demands.

Some of the fanatic Punjabi Muslims who were then in Kashmir as visitors carried the news to Punjab, thereby giving a subject of criticism to the Punjab papers. Thus Kashmir Government became subject of criticism of the Muslims of Punjab. Sheikh's movement, however, was more localised in nature, at that time.

These days were the days of Civil Disobedience in India. The common salt had become the subject of national struggle. People were talking about Gandhiji's ' Eleven Points' Gandhiji was arrested on May 5, 1930, and the movement was still in force. Sheikh Abdullah's movement however had nothing to do with what was happening in India at that time.

Even before Sheikh Abdullah's coming to the public stage, certain newspapers of Punjab had been conducting a hostile propaganda against the administration of the State. The All-India Kashmir-Muslim Conference held a session at Lahore in December 1930. A great deal of acrimonious criticism was passed against the State by persons who were almost vague about the situation in Kashmir. The Youngmen's Muslim Association of Jammu, which was the only organisation of its kind then, had deputed a member to the Lahore Conference. The result was that at the instance of the Punjabi Muslims, the Youngmen's Muslim Association of Jammu launched an agitation against the State. The Maharaja was in Europe and the State Cabinet was functioning in his absence. Slogan of Inqilab was creating a lot of trouble for the ' State, It was proscribed. Jammu, first of all saw the communal disturbances, which soon spread over Kashmir where the masses participated.

A serious riot broke out in Srinagar, The Ahrar Party was organising the agitation. It sent regular Jathas into the State territory, from Punjab in contravention of the law. At one time 7,000 arrests were made by the State. Later, an organised rioting broke out in various important towns of the Kashmir Valley. Sheikh Abdullah took his part not with a view to killing the Hindus, but with the intention of overrunning the State administration which had disgusted him He addressed masses at different places and raised them against the State. Politics in India at that moment had reached a critical stage owing to the holding of the Round Table Conference in London. Agitation was becoming intense. British troops had to be called in, and Sheikh Abdullah was jailed in 1931 for over six months. Thereafter Sheikh Abdullah began to be called, 'Sher-e-Kashmir'.

In 1932 Sheikh Abdullah came out of the jail when the agitation was brought under control He now found a different atmosphere about him. The State had stretched forth its hand of cooperation, and had given assurances to do its best to bring the Muslim community to the forefront. The famous constitutional conference called the Glancy Commission consisting of twelve non-official members and two official members was called by the Ruler to evolve a scheme which would enforce reforms in the State. Even the Ruler in one of his messages said:

> "I repeat that if any section of my subjects desire to submit any reasonable request they will receive my sympathetic consideration".

Abdullah was a popular name in Kashmir now. He found enough of cooperation and support from the Muslim masses. He soon organised for the first time the Muslim Conference, which immediately became the spearhead of the masses of Kashmir, more than three-quarters of whom were Muslims. But the main feature of the Conference then was to coerce the State to give more jobs to the educated Muslims. The Conference was to some extent successful in getting more appointments to the Muslims. Qualified Muslims were appointed as gazetted officers, stipends and scholarships were granted to promising youngmen for higher education and technical training in India and abroad, Abdullah, thus became an alarming figure for the State authorities, besides being the guide of educated Muslims. This naturally made him a favourite of the Middle Class homes, and his personality soon influenced the conservatives also. But his so-called politics then was not broad-based. It was limited to his circle only.

It was the time when the whole of India was shaken into new awakening by Gandhiji's call of Civil Disobedience. 128,000 persons had courted arrests in 1933 in the Bombay Presidency and 124,000 were jailed in Bengal. Later the Delhi Pact was talked everywhere. 'Red Shirts' were agitating against the Government. "Fakhr-e-Pathan", the pride of the Pathans, was becoming a great figure in Indian politics. The Congress was having a tough fight with the British Government and it had its own psychological influence on the Kashmiris.

Sheikh Abdullah soon discovered that 'jobs for the qualified' was not the thing that could solve the bigger problems of fighting the immemorial poverty of the poor. The Congress was becoming more and more the representative of the rural masses, and it had its curious effects on those of the Kashmiris, who felt for the poor masses, the peasants of Kashmir.

The vast study and practical observation of Indian politics diverted Sheikh Abdullah's attention towards the common cause that he and the Congress were fighting for, that of the end of ruthless rule. In six years time he observed the Indian scene from a distance and applied his own reason to examine Congress idealism. During this period he moved about the villages, talked to the peasants, heard their complaints and cries and thereby conducted a research into poverty. The poor hearts were calling his help to end the deep-rooted suffering of the people. The pathetic scenes of poverty created compassion in his heart, and his heart went to the poor. In the end he felt what was needed was not appointments but a popular Government for the masses, by the masses, to the masses and the masses meant poor Hindus and Muslims alike. Thereafter the Conference became an expression of the suffering of the people. And the Muslim Conference automatically became national in its outlook though it was still Muslim in name.

Thereafter Sheikh Abdullah realised that communal peace and the cooperation of all the communities was most essential for the cause, he had undertaken. In his appeal to men of all communities for Cooperation, Sheikh Abdullah said in 1935:

> "My fight is for the emancipation of my country. Let us all rise above petty communal bickerings and work jointly for the welfare of the masses. I appeal to my Hindu berethren not to entertain imaginary fears and doubts. Let us assure them that their rights shall not be jeopardised if they join hands with the Muslims".

He then allied his party with the progressive Hindus of the State and in 1938 formally converted the Muslim Conference into the All Jammu and Kashmir National Conference, which has since then weathered many storms and passed through many battles and grown from strength to strength, by virtue of its democratic ideal and the ever-expanding mass following.

From that day the All Jammu and Kashmir National Conference began to press for responsible Government under the aegis of the Maharaja and the economic amelioration of the peoples of the State, forty lakhs of human beings living "between the snow-adorned barrier ranges of the Himalayas, and earth-coloured and sun—scorched plains of Jammu and Kashmir, Ladakh and the Frontier Regions in Poonch and the Chinani Ilaqas, Muslims, Hindus, Sikhs, Buddhists, Christians, Jains and Harijans who inhabit the thirty-nine towns and nearly nine thousand villages. Consequently the All Jammu and Kashmir National Conference and All India States Peoples Conference, (A.I.S.P.C.), became identical in their ideals, and so the Sheikh gained the support of Congress also.

The first constitutional reform enforced by the Maharaja's Government was in 1932 when the Legislative Assembly was constituted. It consisted of seventy-five members out of which forty two were nominated and only thirty-three were elected. The President was also an official. For the first time the Kashmiris were invited to vote and send their elected members to the Assembly. The Conference cooperated and sent representatives to the Assembly. But it was only in 1938 that the real fight for responsible Government was actually started.

Sheikh Abdullah addressed the masses and from the platform declared the achievement of 'People's Government' as the aim of the National Conference. Meanwhile Muslim League was winning the support of communal Muslims, who came to be known as *Bakras* by Abdullah's followers who, now, called themselves as *Shers.*

Sheikh Abdullah constantly attended the sessions of A.I.S.P.C., which was a tributary of the Indian National Congress. He thus came into close contact with Pandit Nehru, the President of the Conference. Promotion of the establishment of fall responsible Government in all the Indian States, was the demand of the Congress and as of the A.I.S.P.C. It was also the demand of the National Conference and so Sheikh Abdullah's politics merged into the politics of the Congress, and the Jammu and Kashmir National Conference naturally became an informal tributary of the Congress itself. This was a headache for Jinnah. He employed his meddling tactics but he could not succeed in Kashmir because Abdullah's leadership was unquestioned.

In July 1941 Pandit Nehru and Khan Abdul Ghaffar Khan were invited by Sheikh Abdullah to tour into the valley and study the social and economic condition of the peasantry of Kashmir. The programme of the National Conference was sketched by him before a huge gathering attended by many distinguished visitors also. On July 12, 1943 His Highness the Maharaja set up a Commission to explore the possibility of reforms in political, economic and administrative spheres.

Only two members were given to the National Conference, while the feudal landlords, pensioners, Jagirdars predominated over the Commission through their representations. The Working Committee of the National Conference met at Mujahid Manzil on the 13th and 19th and deliberated on the issue of the Commission. Those days *Kashmir's Maharaja* had become the beloved of freedom loving Indians. At the time of Cripps' proposals the Maharaja, like an ordinary Indian patriot, had declared:

> "...in any case it is the duty of the Princes to show themselves patriots and that they desire that their countrymen should feel themselves the equals of nationals anywhere in the world. Freedom must be our watchword - freedom from crippling restrictions and strangling control, freedom from the subordination of India's interests to the interests of other parts of the Commonwealth".

Freedom wave had spread over India. The National Conference participated in the Commission and prepared New Kashmir, meant to be a memorandum to be submitted to the constitutional Committee. Messrs. G. M. Sadiq and M. A. Beg were deputed as the representatives of the National Conference.

It was unfortunate that the Commission revealed lack of reality. The result was that the members could not function with right earnest, due to the policy of the State. The memorandum was not submitted to the Commission. The Working Committee, on the other hand, resolved to submit the memorandum to His Highness and also to publish and circulate it in the country. Thus NEW KASHMIR became the future "draft Constitution of the State and a draft plan for the economic prosperity of the country as a whole". By 1944 when the world was passing to a New World, the Jammu and Kashmir National Conference formulated concretely NEW KASHMIR, a Model State in which democracy would replace autocracy, and the economic structure of the society was to be completely reshaped, which served the non-Muslim population as faithfully as the Muslim population, where freedom had replaced exploitation and happiness has taken the charge of sorrow. In NEW KASHMIR freedom was not confused with privilege. It was the draft for the economic emancipation of the people. And thus the political history of Kashmir became synonymous with the life story of Sheikh Abdullah.

Sheikh was frank in admiring Soveit systems of Government machinery. From communalism Sheikh changed to nationalism and now he had progressed towards socialism. Admiring the Soveit systems, Sheikh somewhere said: "In our times, Soveit Russia has demonstrated before our eyes, not merely theoretically but in her actual day to day life and development that real freedom takes birth rom economic emancipation. The inspiring picture of the regeneration of all the different nationalities and people of the USSR, and their welding together into the united mighty Soveit State that is throwing back its barbarous invaders with deathless heroism, is an unanswerable argument for the building of democracy on the cornerstone of economic equality."

Under the premiership of Sir. B. N. Rau, His Highness introduced the first Popular Ministry in the State in October 1944.

Mirza Mohammed Afzal Beg was chosen from the National Conference and made the Public Works Minister; the second popular Minister Wazir Ganga Ram was made the Home Minister. This was the inauguration of the Constitutional changes in the State. Beg tendered his resignation from the State Council on March 18, 1946 following the decision taken by the Working Committee at its meeting held on March 17, 1946 under the presidentship of Sheikh Mohammed Abdullah. The genesis of the dissociation was briefly indicated in the following pieces by Sheikh Abdullah:

> "Certain constitutional changes were introduced in 1944 which were glaringly inadequate and fell for short of the demand of the situation. Yet we agreed to work them in order to expedite and facilitate further change and, in particular, because we hoped that this would lead to contacts with the Ruler and cooperation in bringing about essential changes. But our efforts ended in failure and the constitutional changes were reduced to a futile shadow. The intolerable privations and grievances of the people of Jammu and Kashmir found no relief or remedy. A microscopic minority of variously graded Jagirdars was, and is, allowed to exercise indefensible rights over large sections of the people, who live in appalling poverty. In Jammu Province, especially in Chinani and Poonch, the Jagirdari system presents a pathetic spectacle of degrading poverty and heartless exploitation. In recent years Kashmir Province has been, as is still being, parcelled out in Jagirs which are granted to a favourite minority. Thus when land reform is considered everywhere an essential preliminary to progress, in this State a semi - feudal land system is actually being extended with all its attendant evils. As one goes up the higher valleys of the State, one is enchanted by the loneliness of mountain and valley and, at the same time, struck dumb by the degradation of human beings there. The army of the State is drawn almost entirely from a selected class of persons of Jammu

Province. The people of Kashmir Province, whether Hindu or Muslim and even though they may live in Jammu Province, are completely debarred from entering the army. The Kashmiris may join, and have in fact joined and distinguished themselves in the Indian army, but they are not eligible for the State army. It is a humiliation which is felt deeply and which underlines the policy of the State in emphasising the inferiority of the great majority of the people."

"The State has vast and rich natural resources but these have failed to relieve poverty and utter want, Indeed no effort is apparently made to develop these resources for the common good, and Kashmir continues, in a changing world, state and unchanged and steeped in misery. This can only be due to the failure of human agency and the autocratic system of administration. It can only be remedied by the representatives of the people undertaking the task of planning and development for the rapid betterment of the masses. No State can succeed in raising the standard of people's life without educating and training them to pursue creative and productive activities."

"Prime Ministers had been coming and going in rapid succession though Kashmir remained the same. It seemed almost that some malign fate held our fair country in its vicious grip and prevented us from coming out of the quagmire in which it was sinking. War came and convulsed the world, but Kashmir remained the same backwater where time seemed to be still and the clocks did not function, except sometimes when they went backwards. The events of 1942 and 1943 shook up whole of India to its innermost depths and affected the people of Kashmir powerfully. As elsewhere in India political consciousness rose to new heights and a sense of intolerable frustration seized the people. They could not remain where they were, they could no longer continue enduring their

> poverty and misery, which had increased under the strain of war conditions. And yet they could not do any thing to change what they could not tolerate for the door of change was barred and bolted."

> "The present Prime Minister (R. B. R. C. Kak) came to occupy the seat of authority and a new and disastrous policy of alienating the people was inaugurated. The position of the Popular Minister Mirza Mohammed Afzal was made intolerable and he found himself compelled to resign".

In the spring of the year 1946 the Cabinet Mission came out to India to study India's political problem and remove the constitutional deadlock that had created serious complications between the Indian leaders and the British Government. Prime Minister Attlee's announcement for "speedy" transfer of power affected the Indian States as it did affect the rest of India, Sheikh Abdullah, being entirely disgusted with the policy of suppression of the State authorities submitted " Quit Kashmir" Memorandum to the Cabinet Mission. The memorandum opened with the words:

> "Today the national demand of the people of Kashmir is not merely the establishment of responsible Government, but their right to absolute freedom from the autocratic rule of the Dogra House. The immensity of the wrong done to our people by the sale deed of 1846 (which brought Kashmir under Maharaja Gulab Singh) can only be judged by looking into the actual living conditions of the people of Kashmir. It is the depth of our torment that has given strength to our protest".

Too much has been said in favour and disfavour of "Quit Kashmir" slogan raised by Sheikh Abdullah. Some people say that it was the greatest crime on the part of a political leader to ask the Prince to "Quit," while, on the other hand, some people say that "Quit Kashmir" was the wisest path chosen by Abdullah and that it was because of this that he became an all India figure, "Quit Kashmir," however, is still a controversial subject.

Justifying "Quit Kashmir" as being a demand for "responsible Government under the aegis of His Highness" and that it only meant "Quit Autocracy," Sheikh said:

> "The announcement (by Prime Minister Attlee) affected the Indian States as well as the rest of India, and the people of the States felt that just as the people of India as a whole would decide about their future internally and internationally so also they must have the right to determine their own future within the States and in relation to the large framework of a free India. This was not only a logical, reasonable and long standing demand, but also it seemed to be the inevitable consequence of what British Government had stated. All-India States' Peoples' Conference gave clear expression to this demand and looked forward to sharing, on behalf of the people of the States, in fashioning the future in cooperation with others."
>
> "It was clear that the old treaties with the States had to go. They represented something that had no relation to the modern world or to the India of today. They could not be reconciled with the inevitable changes in India and in the States. If this was clear to begin with, it became an accepted fact by the statement issued by the Cabinet Delegation of May 16, 1946. That statement declared that paramountcy would end when the new Constitution 'of free India came into being. It was an inevitable consequence that the old treaties and sanads and other engagements would go the way of paramountcy, and, the British Government being out of the picture a new relationship would have to be negotiated between what is now known as British India and the States. The demand for abrogation of the Amritsar Treaty (of 1846) was, in effect disposed of by this clear decision of the Cabinet Delegation. The Constitution set up in the State of Jammu and Kashmir cannot derive from the old source of relationship which was expiring and was bound

to end soon. The set up could only rest on the active will of the people of the State conferring on the Head of the State the title and authority drawn from the true and abiding source of sovereignty that is the people."

"The "Quit Kashmir" cry symbolised and gave concrete shape to this demand for the termination of a system of Government which was in process of dissolution all over India. That cry had nothing personal about it".

Consequently on his return from Delhi Sheikh Abdullah, President of the All Jammu and Kashmir National Conference and Vice-President of the All-India States Peoples Conference delivered a series of speeches in Srinagar about "Quit Kashmir". He directed his followers that all speeches, lectures and meetings should be postponed for a period of one month which he intended to spend in Delhi for consultation with Pandit Nehru and others.

Sheikh Abdullah left Srinagar for New Delhi to discuss States' problems with Indian leaders. The same day, he was arrested at Garhi, about 100 miles from Srinagar on his way to Rawalpindi *en route* to New Delhi. Sheikh was brought to Badami Bagh cantonment, and the same day the Valley of Kashmir was handed over to the military. There was "blood, sweat and tears" in Kashmir. Weaponless Kashmiris-men, women and children offered themselves for arrests and received Dogra bullets in honest contempt. Kashmir Valley was in dangerous excitement. Men and women were done to death by the Military, women were dishonoured, human beings were made to crawl or hop on one leg along roads and sweep them with their turbans, places of worship were desecrate, and an attempt was made to terrorise whole people by methods of frigtfulness.

Wazir Sarup Chand, Superintendent of Kashmir Police on behalf of the State filed a complaint against Sheikh Abdullah in the court of the Sessions Judge Srinagar for the prosecution of Sheikh Abdullah under section 124 (A) of the Ranbir Penal Code, seditious speeches delivered by him on the 13th, 14th, and 16th of May 1946.

On June 3 Sheikh Abdullah's trial began at Badami Bagh Cantonment. The case had to be adjourned till June 11 since the Sheikh wanted to consult lawyers in connection with his defence. On June 11 the case was still adjouirned till July on the statement by Sheikh Abdullah's defence counsel Baldev Sahey that Abdullah's chief legal advisor Pandit Nahru's detention on the way by the State authorities had caused much inconvenience to the defence.

Pandit Nehru's entry into the State had been banned by the State authorities. He was detained at Domel. At his insistence to proceed to Srinagar, Pandit Nehru was injured by a military bayonet. In Srinagar about 1,700 arrests were made. The leaders of the National Conference were arrested and kept in various jails, and an all round attempt was made to crush the popular movement. Pandit Nehru was called back to Delhi to resume far-more important constitutional talks. Kashmir Day was observed throughout India. At Badami Bagh hearing of the case was resumed on July 22.

Shanti Dhown, Barrister from Allahabad also joined defence. Barrister Asaf Ali (India's Ambassador in USA later, was the Chief Defence Counsel.

Meanwhile an attempt was made by the State authorities to fabricate 'Abdullah's clique with league. In this connection "Pioneer" of Lucknow in its issue of June 14, gave a disclosure of Abdullah's secret correspondence with Jinnah. The paper gave the following astounding news under a double column heading:

> 'We are both working for ultimate Muslim Ascedancy in Kashmir' What Abdullah told Jinnah: A disclosure'

The State authorities, in order to maim Abdullah's cause won many Indian newspapers to their side by giving them huge sums of money from the so-called 'Secret Fund'. An, attempt was also made to win over Pandit Nehru when a deputation consisting of Pt. Shive Narain Fotedar, Col. Sansar Singh and Pt. Shive Nath Nanda was sent to New Delhi. Pandit Nehru, much to their disappointment advised Kashmiri people for bigger moves. Later the deputation waited on Sardar Patel and tried to win him with the argument that Abdullah was a first rate communal and that his plan of Kashmir was for a communal state, and that the National Conference was not a national body but an organisation of the goondas.

Thus, State authorities had tried their best to exploit the minorities, but they had failed. Later, the State authorities tried to win over the handful of Leaguers. This policy, continued to the end of Kak regime, and it was the aftermath of this policy that Kashmir was put to the treachery of the freebooters and the Kashmiris had to see the bloody spectre.

On August 3, 1946 Sheikh Abdullah submitted his historical statement in presence of Pandit Jawaharlal Nehru, Asaf Ali, Baldev Sahey and Dewan Chaman Lal. Sheikh Abdullah was jailed under Sec. 124 A, Ranbir Penal Code. He spent 16 months in jail during which period Indian politics underwent gigantic changes.

Immediately after Sheikh Abdullah's trial the Congress Working Committee, in a resolution gave a gentle hint to the State authorities that it would be good of them to invite a delegation of the Congress leaders to carry on friendly talks for a settlement. But the State did not heed to it. The Maharaja openly declared that he wanted no dictation in his internal affairs.

Meanwhile Ghulam Mohi-ud-Din, commonly know as the J.P. of Kashmir, started underground work and kept alive the agitation of the Kashmiris to the time when Sheikh Abdullah was finally released. The State formed an Assembly and brought to prominence those who opposed the National Conference. This was an attempt to bring League elements to the forefront.

All along this period Begum Abdullah took a leading part in organising food committees, relief centres etc. It took her some time to adapt herself to the situation, but now she was Sheikh Abdullah's most ardent political follower.

Jayaprakash Narayan came to Kashmir to study the situation, and on his return bitterly criticised Kak's reign of terror. His impression about the State was that the Maharaja had been influenced by some persons which made him to act in a manner which was not expected of an impartial Head of the State.

Later, the (then) Congress President Acharya J.B. Kripalani came to Kashmir and addressed the Kashmiris for a tough and disciplined move. He told the authorities that Kashmiris were fighting for a Peoples' Government under the aegis of the Maharaja on the pattern of Government in England. On May 25, 1947, he met the Maharaja at Jammu and advised him to release the political prisoners who were not accused of violence. The Maharaja donated Rs. 25,000 to Mrs. Sucheta Kripalani for utilising for charitable purposes. The Maharaja had promised to release the prisoners, but the prisoners were not released because that was not the wish of the Premier.

The next important event in Kashmir in 1947 was Gandhiji's first visit. Gandhiji came to the valley as a people's guest. He put aside the invitations of the State. He stayed at 'Khurshid Bagh', Kishori Lal Sethi's residence, as guest of the National Conference The Kashmir Premier called on him twice secretly. It was reported that the Premier had tried his best to avoid Gandhi-Maharaja meeting, but he failed. Gandhiji went to Gupkar Palace and had profound talks with the Maharaja. The rest of his time Gandhiji spent with Begum Abdullah. He held some prayers at Srinagar and then he left and on his way to Noakhali crossed Jammu. It was some days before August 15, 1947.

August 15 came and India was divided into two dominions. Then came Sardar Patel's assurance to the Princes, and States one after the other joined the Indian Union. Kashmir decided nothing. But it was commonly talked even by authoritative sources that Kak was planning for an Independent Kashmir.

Before the transfer of power their Excellencies the Viceroy and Viscountess Mountbatten had paid a private visit to Kashmir in the third week of June. It was commonly rumoured that Kak wanted to make Kashmir an independent dominion of the British Commonwealth so that Britishers could come to Kashmir and live in the Happy Valley, Side by side League Press was creating a lot of propaganda for the State. No one could say with surety what Kak wanted to do to Kashmir, but there was really something "mysterious" about his doings.

The freedom for India did not fare well with Kak. He was asked to relinquish office on the 11th of August 1947, and the news about his retirement beamed forth happiness from the suppressed hearts. In fact nobody expected it, but it had come about. He had been the Prime Minister of the State since July 30, 1945. Next came Boundary Commission Award which gave Kashmir contiguous boundries with India and Pakistan.

Meanwhile, Pakistan created a lot of trouble for Kashmir in the strangulation of supplies. Kashmir faced a great economic crisis. Everybody was eager to know what Kashmir would decide. Along with this the popular leader of Kashmir Sheikh Mohammed Abdullah was released unconditionally.

Events in Kashmir were moving with great strides, and Ruler of Kashmir had to make a very serious decision. People were waiting for their leader. In his first public address after his release, he openly denounced Two Nation Theory and reiterated his faith in Congress idealism. He put 'Responsible Government as the first demand of the people and warned the Ruler that any decision taken by him against the wishes of the people would be resisted by the people since the will of the people was supreme in a democratic state. He addressed his millions of followers again and cleared their minds from the vague notions of Pakistan. He defined freedom as being unity between Hindus, Muslims and Sikhs and pledged to maintain it till end.

Meanwhile, the State signed Standstill Agreement with Pakistan. The State had also approached India for such an agreement, and the talks were going on in this connection.

Sheikh Abdullah went to Delhi to meet Pandit Nehru, and other members of the Indian Cabinet. On his return he found Kashmir in distress. Violent forces were let loose by Pakistan to disrupt the State with a view to coercing the Ruler to join Pakistan. Afridis were marching towards Srinagar. Kashmir was in great peril.

Sheikh again took the lead, organised National Militia, took charge of the defence of the city and exhibited a calibre worthy of his name. He controlled the panic of the Kashmiris under whose feet death was playing seek and hides. He roused the weaponless Kashmiris to face the fearful odds. Not to speak of youngsters even the adults left the warmth of their homes and came forward to die in saving Kashmir.

Meanwhile, the Maharaja had approached Indian Union for help. His appeal had the people's support, and Kashmir was saved from the inevitable destruction. On October 31, His Highness invited Sheikh Abdullah to form the Interim Government and take charge of the Head of the Administration with power to deal with the emergency. Sheikh Abdullah was sworn in, in the Prime Minister's room by the Hon'ble Chief Justice amidst great scenes of rejoicing from the huge crowds assembled in the premises of the State Secretariat.

The first popular Premier of Kashmir, then, addressed from the balcony, for about an hour the crowds that had swollen to thousands and were waiting there with searching looks and impatient ears.

That was, indeed, the day of the Kashmiris for their struggle of seventeen years had become fruitful that day when the Sheikh was called to the Durbar. It was also Sheikh Abdullah's day of greatest triumph. And thus the popular leader Abdullah agitated against autocracy for seventeen years, such a long period of persistent struggle, victory and defeat, admiration and persecution, and finally became the Head of the Kashmir Government.

3

The Invasion on Kashmir

The First Attack

On the twenty-third of October 1947 life was disappearing from the city of Srinagar. Armed gangs of tribesmen fully equipped with modern weapons supplied to them by the Pakistan Government entered the Muzaffarabad district on the 22nd October and very soon overran the entire area. The first target of raiders was the Nalouchi Gurdawara at Muzaffarabad where the gallant Sikhs numbering 1,400, faced the booters manfully. The Sikhs, in order to save their land and the honour of the temples fought to the last, but at last had to give way. By noon more raiders joined them and showered the rain of bullets over the weaponless men, women and children of Muzaffarabad.

The raiders had used Mansehra-Muzaffarabad road and reached the State territory in motor trucks supplied to them by the N.W.F. Government Muzaffarabad was completely looted Hundreds of motor trucks loaded with the looted property were sent back. Men and children were shown the worst type of deaths, old women were killed at the spot, and young girls were raped and abducted without any pity or shadow of the sin. At about five in the evening the small town of Muzaffarabad was set ablaze. During the night the raiders halted there, but they were constantly shooting in the air to give a hint to the handful of State forces that they should honourably vacate.

During the night they lit a huge fire and sat around it singing in chorus "*Zindabad Pakistan, Zindabad Pakistan* !" Some young ladies and girls had been sent to the tribal areas during the day, and some they had kept along with them as a humour of the night! At intervals a gun was fired and the roar of the gun was followed by a huge congregation of human voices, "*Khan Abdul Qayum Zindabad* !" The gangsters were making merry that night. Another of their slogans which, though they raised louder, could not rise above the invincible mountains on the Domel side was; "We shall cut Sher-e-Kashmir's head and enjoy Id in Sowara (Sheikh's residence)."

During the night some people, who had hid themselves in the day, crossed the bridge and ran towards Ghari. People from Domel had already left for Srinagar on foot and in bullock carts. In the way some motor lorries had picked up the refugees and brought them to Srinagar. On the 23rd the sun rose up and saw Muzaffarabad in ruin.

On the morning of 23rd, the raiders made their way towards Ghari and Chenari where the first thing that they did was to set fire to various public and private buildings. More State forces under the command of Brigadier Rajendra Singh were dispatched to stem the inroads of the unscrupulous and treacherous people.

Meanwhile the fifth-column had started its activities in the city. Attempts were made to degrade the morale of the people. Motor trucks filled to the top with refugees were rushing into Srinagar, and the whole people now were panicky.

The Panic

Panic was created by " traitors" in the city who were in alliance with those actually creating the disturbances. Attempts were made to sabotage the Government with a view to dividing its attention to the real centre of trouble thereby giving a free field to the booters to loot Srinagar. The situation on the front was still more tense. It was reported by the State Army commands that ahead was a regular army fully armed with up-to-date weapons and that it was not a raid but a war. Officers and fighting men of Pakistan army were seen by telescopes leading the gangs of tribesmen. All this was reported to His Highness by Brigadier Rajendra Singh.

Darkness in Srinagar

In the city of Srinagar the dark doom of death awaited 200,000 of human beings-delicate women, innocent children, new born babes and imbecile adults who had seen of no destructions of war or invasion but had only the memory stringed in their ears of the horrible stories of the invasion of Nadir Shah and the continued raids of Ahmad Shah Abdali, who had also one time oppressed the Kashmiris so much that the Sikh monarch Ranjit Singh himself had to proceed to Kashmir to rescue the Kashmiris from the brutal tyranny. The helpless Kashmiris could run to no place since there was no petrol due to the strangulation of supplies by the Pakistan Government. The hope of regaining life was fleeing from them. They could well anticipate the fate of their homes, wives and children as the memory of the happenings in the Punjab was still fresh in their minds. They had no means to defend themselves since they were not allowed to keep any arms. More horrible news were coming from Ghari and Chenari. Even the common sense had failed to function. Kashmiris were faced with a serious situation. They could not run, they could not defend themselves, and the only thing they had thought to do was to poison their women and daughters and to welcome the death that was sent to them by God!

By the evening of 23rd Ghari, Chenari and their adjoining areas were besieged by the invaders. Whole of the property, Government and private was looted and sent back in motor trucks. The inhabitants of these places, which included hundreds of villagers also, were at first deprived of their gold and silver and then shot dead. Beautiful Kashmiri Muslim girls were selected and picked up by their cheeks and placed in the trucks for despatch to the tribal areas and to Pakistan, the holy land! Those of the girls and young women who were not fit were deprived of their earrings and shot dead. Rice, wheat, maize from the granaries of the villagers was filled in bags and sent to Pakistan. Thereafter the villages were set ablaze.

It was at this stage that their director's *Pakistani friends* directed them to discriminate between a Sher (Abdullah's follower) and Bakra (the so called Leaguer) This was more deadlier for every one in the village being a *Sher,* Kashmiri peasants in hundreds were shot dead. But glory be to the Kashmiris, Abdullah's followers did not disown him even at the point of their death. The crusaders were prepared to set free a man who could only say *"Sher-e-Kashmir Murdabad"* but the valiant Kashmiris preferred the worst types of deaths to such a suggestion only because their hearts revolted against being traitors. Hundreds of the workers of the National Conference made themselves martyrs and kept high the honour of our motherland Those of the Pakistanis who were leading the invaders tempted these Kashmiris for *this* and *that* privilege in Pakistan and suggested to them that they should disown Abdullah and the National Conference, and for the safety of their lives and the protection of their property they should forthwith join the *crusade,* which was, according to their intentions, marching towards Srinagar to set up Kingdom of Islam in Kashmir.

How superb was that heroism which at that hour of peril when through the barrel of the gun death be gioping, inspired patriotism in the hearts of the Kashmiris who challenged Pakistan? They told them:

> *"The hal-wala Jhanda* (National Conference flag) has taken birth in our heart and has been nourished by our blood. It is the emblem of those who have dedicated their lives to break the shackles of servitude. It is the message of our freedom. Go back, leave our country to us, and tell Jinnah and Abdul Qayum that the Kashmiris will not be slaves of Pakistan 'but a free people worthy of freedom"?

Reason and truth are meaningless for a fascist, and therefore Kashmiris could not escape death. But their death had become a great heritage.

The State forces fought excellently that day but could not check the influx of the invaders, who were receiving regular reinforcements from behind, and so passed the 23rd of October. On 24th they made further advance and spread over Uri. This day a communication was received that the invaders were fattening themselves and that they were using machine guns, armoured cars and other modern techniques to overrun the handful of State forces. There was thus left no assured means of defending the city. During the night most of the Punjabis were given petrol and lift upto Jammu, About 200 lorries packed to the full had left Srinagar for Jammu. Government officials, leaving their jobs behind, had also left. The rich had thus managed to save themselves and the poor Kashmiris were left to the free looters. Perhaps Srinagar was seeing the last signs of life. They were left to curse our own fate, which even did not seem to function at that hour.

Now conjecture who should dare to come forward at that darkest hour when the Monster of destruction-loot, murder, arson, abduction-had rung the bugle of its approach and death was waiting at the door of Kashmiris, to inspire Kashmiri blood and to fill the hearts of the people by his magnetic force ? They had been left to meet their end. There was no Government to save them, there were no possibilities to evacuate them, there was nothing but death on all sides groping on them!

Then came Sher-e-Kashmir their beloved leader, and guide to captain then against the odds. He spoke to his people from the stage, he asked them to prove Kashmiris by worth. He smiled and the crowds plucked courage, he waved his limbs and the crowds were inspired, and thereby he created a confident atmosphere in the minds of those who had given up all hopes of life. He prompted up his followers for facing the odds to defend Kashmir, he assured the minorities that communal concord would be maintained at all costs, and that if there was nothing but to die, Muslims would lie down before their brothers, Hindus and Sikhs, were killed. Thereby he faced the delicate situation like a true leader.

Wild rumours and utter panic held Srinagar in breath. "Kabailis would raze the city to the ground, they would spare no living thing, no, not thc young girls, not the mistresses of the households; not the babies at the breasts. *As for Abdullah, death is too light a punishment; the Kabalis are fighting for Pakistan, they would sack Nationals they would roast Abdullah and his colleagues.* They would be friends with him only who raised his cry for Pakistan "that was what a fifth columnist told near the Red Square where the National

Conference leaders were seen organising the Peace Brigades and the Home Guards for the defence of the city. Meanwhile secret threatenings were given by the fifth-columnists that Kabailis on their entry into Srinagar would respect no protection; that the multitudes of "Nationals" would be brought together and starved to death in the sight of their countrymen, their friends and their kinsmen; that only way left for saving life was to fight for Pakistan in Kashmir. These were no idle threats. Parties of men were seen in all directions of the city spreading these wild rumours. A very serious situation was created by the fifth columnists to derrange communal peace in the city. At night when parties of Sikh evacuvees reached Amira-kadal Chowk, a great communal clash was averted by the tact and resourcefulness of the leaders of the National Conference, who came out of their houses, all of a sudden, and brought the situation under control and nullified the mischievous efforts of the fifth-columnists. This was an attempt to disrupt the city so to give an open field to the booters.

The National Conference High Command had to tackle a difficult situation, indeed, that night. For the whole night Sheikh Abdullah and his colleagues kept vigils and studied the, situation. Instant after instant refugees in huge numbers were pouring in Srinagar, and the foe was marching towards the city with unabated pace. During the night hundreds of non-Kashmiris fled towards Jammu in cars and motors, lorries and the Kashmiris incapable of bearing arms were left behind, as if Kashmir was meant for the Kashmiris only. It was indeed a piteous sight!

Sheikh in the Arena

For some time Sheikh marked it. The Government had failed and nothing was thought for the protection of the Kashmiris. Sheikh was in a fix. He waited for some time more, but then the call of Kashmir disturbed his balance. He found his body full of vigour, and he sent out his call to his countrymen. By dawn every worker of the National Conference was near Palladium which was now made the Operational Quarters, and the Conference took charge of the defence of the city. An order was immediately put forth that no Kashmiri should utter the word surrender or death, but should come forward to shed his blood for the defence of Kashmir, his place of birth. At Sheikh's call thousands of Kashmiris gathered together and offered their lives for the service of their motherland.

On this day the significant figure in the humming crowds was the underground leader Ghulam Mohiuddin, called *"Bulbul-e-Kashmir"*. He had come out this morning after being underground for sixteen months. A very handsome Kashmiri, *"Bulbul-e-Kashmir"* had everything interesting about him. His pace was quick but his thought was deep. He was seen merging from various directions, as if on this day he was everywhere !

National Conference workers were pouring in minute after minute and the crowds near Palladium Chowk were swelling into thousands. These volunteers were organised and posted to various positions in the city. Searches were conducted, guns, bullets, daggers and other ammunition were recovered from the outgoing non-Kashmiris.

By this time noon was advancing; and the confusion of the city was becoming frightful. By noon also many of the volunteers were seen carrying guns and hurrying to different parts of the city. This was for the first time that a National Conference volunteer had taken up a gun. These volunteers were directed to stop Kashmiris from leaving their homes.

Bakhshi Ghulam Mohammed took charge of internal security and transport, while the Peace Brigades were kept under the charge of Ghulam Mohiuddin. Everything was organised within two hours More guns were supplied to the volunteers and a handful of armed men were kept ready for internal defence.

By four in the evening Sheikh Abdullah addressed the swelling crowds and told them that it was in the interests of all the communities in the State to unite as one body in repelling the attacks of mischievous elements from outside. Mutual distrust and suspicion, he added, among the people of the State, would only lead to clashes which must deviate attention from the task of repelling the invaders. He wanted the people to take a lesson from the happenings in Eastern and Western Punjab where Hindus, Muslims and Sikhs suffered untold miseries. He called for a special responsibility on the part of the majorities in the matter. He advised them to assure full protection to the minorities so that the majority community could set up an example of communal peace, which was most essentially needed at that hour. It was here that he made a mention of what had passed between the Maharaja and Jinnah. Jinnah, he said, had asked the Maharaja to join Pakistan and had assured him of no interference in his internal matters, which showed that Jinnah did not support Kashmiris' fight for freedom that they had been fighting for the last seventeen years without any slackening, whatsoever. Regarding the attitude of the Government of India, Sheikh Abdullah openly declared that the Government were not, at all, prepared to accept the accession of Kashmir unless the Maharaja had ceded over sovereignty to the people, whose will was supreme in the democratic India. He proved how India Government were keen about helping the Kashmiris on their way to progress and prosperity. Here the crowds along with their slogans, raised the slogans 'Pandit Nehru Zindabad! 'Mahatma Gandhi Zindabad! 'Azad Hindustan Zindabad! and called *'Fie* and *Shame*!' to Pakistan.

By evening that day the whole city of Srinagar was handed over to the 'Home Guards.' Halqa Committees were formed in the mohollas, and a member from each household was called for duty. The volunteers were directed by the High Command to do their utmost to raise the morale of people. The State Rice Granary, the State Treasury, and other such institutions were guarded by the Home Guards, Conditions in Srinagar were, thus, considerably improved.

Meanwhile a handful of gallant Dogras had stopped the foe near Uri, but the situation at the front was very serious. Brigadier Rajendra Singh fought so gallantly, and every Dogra soldier fought like his general, but a handful of people had to face a big army, they could not go ahead. Sometime after even the general was killed, and at the front there were left a few Gurkha soldiers who fought to the last man and held the foe there.

At this stage, His Highness' Government sent to the Indian Union Government a request for assistance and signified their desire to accede to the Indian Union. The Indian Union accepted the accession of the State provisionally subject to the condition that with the restoration of law and order in the State and expulsion of the invaders, the question of State's accession would be finally settled by ascertaining the will of the people.

After stiff resistance even the Gurkha soldiers having harassed the foe for two complete days, fell down one after another. Their souls left their bodies with a lament and a yearning that Srinagar was in great danger. The spirits that accompanied their souls to heaven cursed Jinnah and Pakistan for this wanton destruction of flesh and material!

For the first time in history a dawn-to-dusk aerial service was conducted between Delhi and Srinagar to despatch thousands of Indian troops from the 27th of October onwards. So tense was the situation in Srinagar that nobody could be sure whether the raid would come first or the aid. But the aid reached first.

For the internal defence of the city Peace Brigades had started work in Srinagar. Groups of volunteers patrolled the lanes and the streets at night to guard against the activities of fifth columnists. They, thus, infused among the public a new spirit of resistance. The Peace Brigades were welcome everywhere since their presence was a guarantee that the city will not give way to panic.

The armed section of the Brigade, called the National Militia, was deputed by Ghulam Mohiuddin to help the Police and the Military in maintaining order. Some of them were despatched to the front where these brave Kashmiris proved themselves as worthy soldiers in a worthy cause.

Sher-e-Kashmir, having entrusted the work to the National Conference leaders flew to Delhi to tell India what a misfortune had come upon Kashmir! In his call to India to defend Kashmir, the leader said:

> "Our beloved and beautiful home land, Kashmir, is in a dire peril. In this extremity it is the duty of every Kashmiri, whether Muslim or Hindu or Sikh to defend it to the utmost. Those who are responsible for its defence have failed us and the responsibility, therefore falls on the people of Kashmir. They are determined to fight the invaders and raiders who have come to despoil the country and to compel our people to

function in accordance with the will of others. That is a new kind of slavery which we will resist to the utmost. I am going back to Kashmir to lead this resistance of the people to the invaders.

"The Kashmir National Conference has stood for Responsible Government in the State under the aegis of His Highness the Maharaja. We have fought for our freedom, suffered for it, and we had hoped that in the new order we would achieve our objective. It was our firm conviction that before any other step could be taken the question of Responsible Government must be settled. Even the question of accession to India or Pakistan or any settlement about the future must, we have stated, follow these vital constitutional changes within the State.

"Economically, Kashmir depends for its market much more on India than on Pakistan".

"Politically, it was felt that India was a much more progressive State than Pakistan, and Kashmir would have far greater scope for free development according to its own genius if she was allied to India.

"However, no decision was made or could be made because most of the leaders of the National Conference were in prison and could not meet.

"When I came out of prison four weeks ago I wanted some time to consider the situation and consult my colleagues. During my incarceration vital changes had taken place in India and a new situation had risen. Much had happened that had brought disaster and misery to millions of people. It became necessary for us, therefore, to take stock of the situation most carefully and decide in a way that would be advantageous to Kashmir and in accordance with the wishes of the majority of the people of Kashmir. I advised my people that the question of accession should, therefore, not be decided immediately and

> that the first step should be a constitutional change on the basis of Responsible Government. After that the future relations of Kashmir with India and Pakistan might be determined.
>
> "But events have moved fast soon after my release I heard of preparations along western boundaries of Kashmir for some kind of an invasion or raid. Armed people infiltrated."

A positive proof of the fact that the struggle in Kashmir had been instigated by the agents of the Muslim League and was being strongly helped by the Pakistan Government was discovered from possession of certain Muslims who under the 'pretext' of safety desired to go temporarily to Pakistan. As early as 1945 and 1946, a conspiracy seemed to have been hatched for the establishment of a Muslim State by the Muslim League in Jammu and Kashmir. A number of these detailed plans for providing residences for the Muslim League leaders and for other activists in the State when it would come under the domination of the Muslim League had been discovered. These plans were authentic, bore proper seals and names and details in them clearly showed that a plot was hatched against His Highness and his Government by the Muslim League agents in London, and these plans were subsequently sent to India and were found in possession of certain Muslim Government servants of the State.

One of these was a design of a residence named *'Masha-Allah'*, apparently for Jinnah. It consisted of 6 sheets. There was a coloured prospective design and a chart of C. S. J. calculations as well. The plan had been drawn by Haji Roshan Din of Bhopal according to specifications given by Norman F. Kingham of Wellesy Cheshire (England). This evidence conclusively proved that the designs of the Muslim League against Kashmir were hatched as early as in 1945 and the act of aggression of October 1947 was the culminating point of those designs.

A Kashmiri leader, who was an eye witness to all the incidents recorded. thus:

> "Armed people infiltrated into the State territory and in many places there were armed conflicts. I came to

Delhi to preside over the Standing Committee of the States Peoples' Conference, The very day I returned to Srinagar, news came that a large party of armed and well-equipped raiders travelling on motor lorries had entered Kashmir via Abbottabad Road near Muzaffarabad."

"These raiders created havoc and looted Muzaffarabad and other places (Destruction of Muzaffarabad already mentioned). They marched towards Srinagar. It was obvious that this raid had been carefully prepared and every kind of help had been given to it in the shape of arms, equipment and motor transport. It was obvious also that this invasion was meant to coerce and compel the people of Kashmir to act in a particular way, namely to accede to Pakistan."

That it was Pakistan's planned invasion of Kashmir was proved by the statements of some of other eyewitnesses who watched the preparations made in the Frontier and Western Punjab, and later took part in the invasion. Abdul Haq S/o Mr. Abdul Aziz Khan, once Inspector of Schools at Peshawar, and son-in-law of Raja Feroz Khan, another Inspector of the Frontier Police stated:

"I left Pindi for Kashmir on November 3, along with another 100 men of my illaqa. Before leaving Pindi there was intense propaganda by a certain Maulvi (Maulvi Yusaf Shah of Srinagar, apparently) that Hindus and Dogras were inflicting atrocities on the Muslims of the State. Maulvi Shabir Hussain of Deo Band also appealed on the wireless and gave *'Fatva'* that it was the duty of every Muslim to go to Kashmir We were given free lift in Public Transport which were hired by the Government Officials. The convoy of which I was a member halted at Rawla Camp at Pindi. There were at this camp about 600 to 700 Pathans and Punjabis. The Military and Additional Police were in plain clothes. Arms were distributed to us. At Kohala each of us was carrying 96 rounds of ammunition. At Uri there was also a big camp of 4 to 5 thousand Pathans, Afridis, Mahsuds and

> Mohamands as well as the Additional Police and Military in plain clothes At Baramulla, according to my estimation, the strength was 10,000. There was regular service between Baramulla, Pindi and Abbottabad. There were also wireless sets and they were in communication with their High Commands and their parties operating in Kashmir Valley... On November 6, I visited Mathial along with few others and there we were told by villagers that the Pathans committed rape and killed, and looted valuables and that they w e not maltreated by Sikhs, but men from Pakistan territory. I was shocked to learn that, as the inhabitants of that Village were all Muslims with tears in their eyes. They begged us to spare them. This broke my heart. I returned to Baramulla and gave my villagers the above information. So everyone of us felt greatly ashamed of our conduct and intention. We wanted to go back, but we were refused conveyance for our return journey, and told that Srinagar would be conquered that night;. They forced us and marched us towards Srinagar in 30 vehicles. On 7th morning we were ordered to occupy Zainakot village. When we visited the village, there also people repeated the same story of the atrocities committed by the Muslims, especially the Pathans".

From the statements given by various prisoners, were gathered the following informations about the preparations of Pakistan for an invasion on Kashmir:

> Certain Pirs headed by Pir of Manki were in-charge of inciting the Muslims.
>
> A great *Lashkar* was created by Abdul Qayum Khan to invade Kashmir. Tribesmen were recruited in the *Lashkar* and sent in vehicles to Abbottabad, where the organisers furnished them with directives.
>
> The invaders had anti-air-craft guns, tommy guns, bren guns, sten guns, and wireless sets supplied by the Military Headquarters at Rawalpindi. Karachi,

Peshawar, Rawalpindi and Abbottabad were, thus, connected by these sets.

The 'Jehad' against the Kashmiris had the blessings of Sir George Cunningham, Abdul Qayum Khan, K. B. Sheikh Mahboobali, K. B. Kuli Khan, Pir of Manki and Abdul Rab Nishtar.

Everyday communications were sent to Karachi, Peshawar and Abbottabad to acquaint Jinnah, Abdul Qayum and Rab Nishtar with the situation.

Patients were sent for treatment to Abbottabad and Mansehra Hospitals.

On October 17, the Frontier Government ordered all lorries in Kashmir to be present in Hazara. 400 lorries were, then, ready to carry the *Lashkar* to Muzzaffarabad.

Important military officials of the *Lashkar* included Mr. Dunean, the Assistant Commissioner at Tank, Rana Farzand Ali Khan, Superintendent Additional Police and the Nawab of Tank and Khusdil Khan of Hisarpur.

Some of the officials of Pakistan Army, who were taken as prisoners were ready to make their statements before Jinnah and Cunningham and it was their wish that their statements be sent to Pandit Jawaharlal Nehru so that he could tell Jinnah not to make Muslims fight against Muslims because there was no fight between Muslims and Hindus ever in Kashmir.

Some boxes belonging to the D.I.G. Additional Police, Kohat were recovered from Mirdad Khan F. C. of Police Station Rawalpindi, and Sher Afzal Khan of Hazara. These boxes contained most dangerous ammunitions.

Every Kashmiri was shocked by this raid and the ruin in the trail of this raid. Every Kashmiri resented this compulsion on his will. The question of accession to India or Pakistan became a secondary issue and the first duty of every Kashmiri was to defend his motherland against the intruders. They refused to accede to Pakistan in this Way.

Sheikh Abdullah declared:

> "I came to Delhi for a few hours to consult my colleagues here, and to explain the present critical position in Kashmir to the members of the Government of India. I asked them, on behalf of the people, for help in resisting this brutal raid. The Maharaja's Government had also made this request to the Government of India. I am now going back to my people in Kashmir to stand shoulder to shoulder with them in defending our heritage and to share with them the perils and sorrows that may be in store.
>
> "I know the spirit of my people, and I am sure that we shall triumph in the end. I appeal to all lovers of freedom in India or Pakistan to stand by the people of Kashmir in this hour of trial, and to denounce the raiders, who have come to bring sorrow and disaster to our country".

Even before the military invasion, Pakistan Government were carrying an economic invasion on Kashmir. About a lac of Muslim refugees were afforded safe passage through the State territory from Pathankot to Sialkot. In return for that, some 180 Kashmiris, who were being conveyed from Rawalpindi to Kohala, on the way to Kashmir at the request of the Maharaja, were killed in the way. The State's supplies, of essential commodities had been held up at Rawalpindi. The Lahore Currency Office had refused to make remittances.

The Imperial Bank Lahore was disabled from trying to meet its obligations to the State. Motor vehicles registered in the State had been held up in Rawalpindi, and the railway traffic between Sialkot and Jammu had been discontinued. People with firearms were infiltrated into Poonch and other parts. The Pakistan Radio had conducted a war of words against the State. Thus the Pakistan Government were fulfilling the terms of Standstill Agreement.

With the arrival of Indian Troops on the morning of 27th October, the situation took a sudden turn. The confidence of people was restored back, and they became more determined to face the situation heroically.

The National Conference mobilised its full strength for the defence of the city and the adjoining districts. Batches of volunteers were deputed to different places to preserve peace and to allay panic in the valley. Indian troops were directly sent to the front from the Aerodrome, and the National Conference took the entire responsibility upon itself, and helped the troops to reach the front in motor lorries and cars which were placed at the disposal of the Conference by their owners.

Meanwhile the situation at the front had worsened. The handful of Dogra soldiers and Gurkhas had faced armoured cars, cannons, hand bombs, bullets, machine guns like true soldiers upto the time their last man fell. The soldiers had stood firm at the front even after their General Brigadier Rajendra Singh was killed. But it was really too much for them to face the invasion of a big army equipped with most deadliest of the weapons ever used to shed human blood ! The foe tried his best to overrun these handful of Dogra soldiers, but they failed in marching an inch ahead. The brave soldiers stopped the foe there, till Indian Troops reached the front. The soldiers had thus left a record of their bravery, which was unparalleled in history.

Without making any positions or examining the situation, Indian Troops had to take the command in hand. They were unacquainted with the geography and strategical situation of these areas, but they fought against the odds like true soldiers of India.

Meanwhile the 'Lashkar of Pakistan' had captured Baramulla, and committed the worst acts of terrorism and tyranny on innocent people. A small army of the most fiercest kinds of Pathans was put in charge of loot in Baramulla, while 30 vehicles loaded with Afridis, Pakistan Army soldiers, and Masuds were despatched to Srinagar.

The Pathans entered the houses of the inhabitants. Wherever the door did not open of its own accord, a cannon was fired to crack it. Inside the house they first addressed the males with the words "*Zar Bideh*" (Give us gold). If a man shed tears and said, "I have nothing', he was shot dead at the spot. Those who offered currency notes, ornaments and the keys were spared and placed aside. Male children were killed at the spot, and female children above the age of ten were sent to the Headquarters.

Babies were snatched from the laps of their mothers and killed with the bayonet of "Pakistani" rifles. The currency notes, thus collected, were handed over to a man who, according to an eyewitness, was an official of the Government of Pakistan and belonged to Ludhiana.

Next the Pathans turned towards women, and with the remarks *"Tum Acha Hai"* (You are good) picked up the good looking young ladies. Those of the ladies selected by them were not touched, but those that were considered unfit were deprived of their ornaments, rings etc. If a lady had some difficulty in taking out her ring, her finger was cut by the dagger so to let out the ring easily. The selected girls—white complexioned-were raped at the spot and then sent to the camp. These women were sent back to Pakistan in the afternoon in motor trucks. Boxes filled with ornaments and gold were also sent back. The number of these abducted girls is reported to be about 900.

The Pathans did not spare the Sikhs, They picked them up with the words *'Da Kafir'!* Daggers were thrust into the eyes of human skull, and it served as a fun for the Pathans to see the blood streams rush out. Skulls were seen on the road, and men, women and children were massacred like ants. Thus the Pathans completed their assigned work of loot and murder.

In the afternoon a General of Pakistan Army entertained the Lashkar to a huge feast for the preparation of which 1,000 male sheep, and 500 kharwars (96 seer each) of the finest of Kashmiri rice were used.

Another party of the Lashkar consisting of Punjabi Muslims, then, moved about in the city and forced people to become Muslim. Those who cited *Kalma* and took beef were spared, while those who hesitated were made targets of guns. Most of the people from the minority communities, were thus subjected to forced conversion.

Afridis and Kabailis constituted the most barbarous types of men. This party reached Baramulla back from Srinagar with the news that resistance was stiff ahead. This party marauded Baramulla and adjoining areas in the afternoon and dispensed same treatment to Hindus and Muslims, Sikhs being completely exterminated by the Pathans. They violated and abducted women, mostly the Kashmiri Muslim since they "hated to touch cowards" belonging to other community. Perhaps they hate to see children for that is why they massacred them at the very sight. They looted everything and everyone. They even dishonoured the holy *Quran*. They were so mad with passions that they could not discriminate between God and devil. They converted mosques into brothels for their own gratification.

Women, who went under their control were said to have stopped their respiratory systems so to take out breath from their hearts, and they had died this death since they were left with no other means to end themselves.

Thereafter fire was set to the Government buildings, and this fire very soon spread over whole of Baramulla and smouldered everything to ashes.

Those of the Kashmiris who had preferred conversion to death had, meanwhile, assembled at a place, the so-called refugee camp. At about 6.30 p.m. some thirty armed Pathans came to them and picked the women from the terror-stricken assembly. These women, their men thought, were gone for ever; but in the morning they were brought back again. The refugees were given maize flour and asked to prepare food for themselves. The next morning sun rose up again, and saw Pattan and Baramulla nothing more than a heap of smoking ruins. The whole area was freely looted by filthy hands of the soldiers of Pakistan.

Sheikh at the Helm

The situation in the capital had taken a different turn. The Maharaja had invited Sheikh Abdullah to form the Interim Government to deal with the emergency, as had been the understanding between His Highness and the Government of India.

Sheikh Abdullah was sworn in as the Head of Administration on the 31st of October amid scenes of great rejoicing from the people of Kashmir. The leader of the Kashmiris had undertaken the whole burden upon his shoulders, and this was received everywhere with warm welcome. People throughout the State were eager for his messages, and directives.

He sent them the following message:

> "To all our countrymen, in every part of the State, I send greetings on this great and solemn occasion. We are now free, and are determined that this freedom shall endure and grow richer in content and be shared by all the people. In the face of the present grave emergency, and while the full picture of freedom is not before them, I invite all friends to down their differences and discussions of detail, and forge still stronger the sanctions of a whole people's will, which must prevail sooner than many of us expect. The power has not come to me, but even to the humblest of my countrymen, and will be used for all of them so that all exploitation of man by man and injustice and nepotism shall cease.
>
> "To the members of the National Conference, who have toiled and suffered these 17 years, I offer thanks and continued comradeship in the great tasks that lie ahead in building up the New Kashmir of our dreams. I also congratulate the Maharaja Bahadur on his patriotic choice, made not a day too soon, of sharing all power with the people rather than accept the overlordship of another and keep all power to himself. To all those who may have differed from us: I say - "We are brothers of the same motherland. Come, let us be friends not enemies. We must not be enemies. Let us forget the past and forgive each other, and resolve all differences peacefully like brothers. There is no other way. All these years we fought for freedom which is ours today, and not for accession which shall be determined by the free choice of the people of this country". But freedom never comes without bringing us its own responsibilities, its trails, and trials. We shall, every one of us, face them manfully as behoves free men; and I call upon all my countrymen to help us at this moment of difficulty and do all they can to resist and hurl back the invader who, by his wanton

aggression, and ruthless acts of arson, murder and loot, has branded himself as a marauder and an enemy of mankind and our homeland.

"To all lovers of freedom in India and Pakistan, I send my greetings also. We want their good wishes and help now to enable us to consolidate our freedom, and drive out from our homeland the wanton aggressor who by his invasion has created this grave national emergency for us and precipitated the issue of accession by the Maharaja Bahadur so that timely help could come to the State from the Government of India. On behalf of all my colleagues and countrymen, I offer my thanks to them for this help and congratulate them on the generous and democratic attitude they have shown, which I wish to make known to all the world and particularly to the people and Government of Pakistan. The stipulation for the final acceptance of the Instrument of Accession is, that when the aggressor is driven out, peace again prevails, and people of our country are really free, they will be given an opportunity to register their choice in the matter of accession or independence, freely and without duress from anybody in or outside the State. Freedom before accession has been both our watchword and policy, and we still stand by it. What form this referendum will take and under what conditions it will be held, can be decided later. For, the course of action adopted by the invader is aimed at coercing us, which cannot be accepted since it is dishonourable. This we must and will resist to the last man and to the last ounce of our energy. I, therefore, request Mr. Jinnah to accept the democratic principle of the sovereignty of people of our State, including, as it does, 78 per cent Muslims, whose free and unhampered choice must count in the matter of final accession. I request him to use his influence and power to withdraw the invader. *I am ready to came to Karachi to meet him, should he so desire.*

"To the public servants I say, 'I expect each one of you to do your duty by the people, and you have nothing to fear so long you do it honestly, fearlessly and with loyalty to the country. We must keep the civil administration going even under the stress of these difficult days.

"In conclusion I wish it to be known to all people, both within and without the State, that we are determined to save our homeland from the destruction and devastation the marauder is trailing behind him, and shall bend all our energies towards that end.

"To all those of our countrymen, who are behind the enemy lines today and suffer extreme humiliation and misery, and to them also that have lost their kith and kin, and whose property has been looted and destroyed, I bring a word of cheer and give a solemn assurance that every inch of our country will be cleared of the marauder, and as soon as conditions permit, all of them will be rehabilitated.

"Come then to the glorious task of hurling back the marauder, who shall not pass, and to the building up of New Kashmir; and let us all unite in the face of common danger and drown all differences".

This historical occasion had its due effect on the heart of every Kashmiri. With the assumption of office by Sheikh Abdullah, the morale of the people improved. The Peace Brigades consisting of 10,000 young Kashmiris got fervent and did excellent work in Srinagar and the districts. Halqa Committees were now fully organised. They kept watch in their respective Mohallas, moved about the lanes and kept vigils against the activities of fifth columnists throughout the night. The National Militia, the armed section of the Brigade, was deputed (or training on military lines.

Having failed to resist the offensive, the cowardly raiders, instead of coming face to face with the Army, had put on Kashmiri clothes and gone into the villages where by firing a few shots they would create panic to enable themselves to loot the poor peasants.

This was coward game played by the invaders since it would be hard to discriminate between an invader and a Kashmiri. The National Militia did excellent work in this field. They fought against the enemy, killing ten of them for of their own because they felt that they *had* to save their motherland. Our soldiers arrested many Afridis at different places and brought these ugly persons to 'Red Chowk'. These people were shown to the public who said that the Afridis should be roasted in an extremely heated oil - really the Afridis had taken out all compassion from the hearts of the Kashmiris then !

Action by Indian Army

On the 31st of October, the same day Sheikh Abdullah took charge of Administration, the butchering rioters were machine-gunned from air. They suffered heavy casualties and their strength was thus considerably broken. On the 2nd of November they were dispossessed of much of their equipment by successful rear action from air. Their trucks were rendered useless, and their lines penetrated. On the 3rd heavy casualties were infected on the raiders by combined action from air and land, and much of their equipment was destroyed. A large number of raiders was taken prisoners at this stage of the siege.

By now Indian Army officers of Jak Division (Division sent from India to Jammu and Kashmir) had received enough of reinforcement by air. Mopping-up operations were consequently started on both sides of Jhelum Valley Road, where some of the raiders had penetrated with a view to creating panic and causing confusion.

Indian Troops were also sent to help the State troops in Jammu Province, where the trouble had started earlier affecting Poonch and Mirpur and the bordering villages. Thus the raiders met with stiff resistance everywhere. Certain high officers of the Pakistan Army were seen among the raiders in both the Provinces leading the offensives.

On the 4th of November, the National Conference leaders, and workers and men of the National Guards had to tackle a very difficult situation when multitudes of refugees from the villages dropped incessantly into Srinagar. The raiders had spread themselves throughout the Western part of the city, in Bandipore and had come even up to Ganderbal. The poor peasants were being pitilessly looted and villages, one after the other, were razed to the ground. The National Militia squards were immediately sent to the villages to fight the invaders.

This technique of the invaders .aused great anxiety in the heart of everyone since it was a deliberate plan to besiege Srinagar on all sides. Along the main front raiders had come to the North-West and South-West of the city. This created a very delicate situation, and brought back panic among the people since the foe was at a door distance only.

The intensity of the situation was soon averted when, all of a sudden, a portion of the land convoy of armoured cars and light artillery from the Indian Union, having entered the State through the Pathankot route, reached Srinagar and passed through Amirakadal on their way to the front. Near the Lal Chowk, swelling crowds cheered the soldiers with their slogans "Hindustan Zindabad!" The soldiers in return smiled, and from their smiles and frisk countenances —through which they were emitting challenges to the fascism of Pakistan-people plucked courage and recaptured hope. More reinforcements by land and air were pouring in. Attachments from National Militia were sent to take positions in the Parade Ground, Ganderbal, and Harwan. Several other places on the outskirts of Srinagar were patrolled by police officers and the National Home Guards. In this way the city was guarded on all the sides.

By evening the same day raiders were pushed back further from Srinagar, and Sangrama was recovered. Air-strafing was conducted in the Badgam area, where it caused total annihilation of the raiders, who had infiltrated the area in large numbers. Along the main front mopping-up operations had been continued and heavy losses were inflicted on the raiders along the road between Kohala and Baramulla. Troops were stationed at all strategic points connecting the city with the front.

The National Militia did excellent work in Ganderbal, Bhima, Tulamula, Lar, and Nunar, which they cleared of the raiders.

Property looted in Tulamula and Ludawan was recovered by the Guards, and the raiders were pushed back beyond Safapora.

The Defence Minister and the Home Minister of the Government of India flew to Srinagar this day on a short visit, and after making an aerial survey of the front, met Sheikh Muhammed Abdullah, the Head of the Administration at the aerodrome. During the night of the 5/6 November, gun and rifle shots were heard in the city The firing was part of the operations against the raiders, who had spread to the North-West and South-West of the city. These activities were intensified after 9 p.m. and were continued till dawn, when air operations were restored. Battalions of invaders had infiltrated on the sides of the Sumbal-Safapora and Gulmarg-Badgam area also Mopping-up operations were continued in these areas.

In Jammu Province Mirpur and Kotli were surrounded by furious armed mobs, Rawalkot and Bagh in Poonch were besieged, and in Gilgit enemy had attacked Janglot.

Intensive air operations were carried out in the farther out skirts of Srinagar throughout the day of November 6, and the night. Our National Guards had shown great acts of gallantry in resisting the attempts of the raiders to overrun villages. Raiders, who were treacherously hiding themselves in small pockets in a desperate bid to escape chastisement, were discovered by the Home Guards and taken as prisoners.

The 8th of November turned the corner. In the afternoon Baramulla was recovered, and it marked a decisive phase in the operations of the ground and air forces against the raiders. Thousands of raiders were killed, while others took to their heels towards Uri, leaving every thing behind, even the cooked meals. The dead bodies included many soldiers and officers of Baluch Regiment of Pakistan Army, besides many persons from Frontier Additional Police. Arms and ammunition and other military equipment were seized from the raiders, thousands of gallons of petrol, and 200 bags of rice and atta were also recovered.

Meanwhile groups of raiders, who had infiltrated into small pockets towards Gulmarg-Badgam and Sopore-Sumbal sides, had caused great havoc there. Villages were looted, and then set ablaze.

These groups were captured or wiped out. After their main base at Baramulla was destroyed, the remnants were routed. The raiders were chased out beyond Uri, and the pockets from Baramulla onwards were gradually being cleared of them.

Kashmir got back Baramulla, not that old beautiful town but a heap of scattered ruins. The same time Sheikh Abdullah sent a message of comfort to the people of the place assuring them of his sympathy, and congratulating them on their bold stand against the raiders. The Head of the Administration promised general relief to those who were bereaved or had suffered otherwise at the hands of the raiders. Many of the Government officials, Wazir-Wazarat and others, who were in league with Pakistan and had supported their cause, were arrested at the spot and sent up to the National Conference Headquarters at the Red Square. This work was done by the National Guards. In the late afternoon His Highness sent his congratulations to Sheikh Abdullah and the people of Kashmir on this signal victory and expressed the hope that the recovery of Baramulla would be followed by further successes.

And so with the recovery of Baramulla ended the great anxiety of people who had been thrown in a different atmosphere during two weeks of panic and suspense. The victory of Baramulla was celebrated throughout in a spirit of sober satisfaction. Shops were opened in Baramulla town and civil administration had been restored in the district. Adequate medical relief for the sufferers was despatched from Srinagar.

The operations against the raiders were intensified still further, and they were being flung back at a rapid rate. The staff of the Mohara Power House was set to work on November 10. More arms and ammunition were seized from the raiders. The isolated groups were surrendering successively.

Return of Peace

By evening that day Sheikh Abdullah had received numerous telegrams from all over India, expressing solicitude for the welfare of Kashmiris and offering them help. Sardar Baldev Singh, Defence Member of the Government of India came to Srinagar, once again, by air on a short visit to study the situation at the front.

With the siege of Baramulla would ever be remembered the name of Shahid Sherwani (Sherwani, the martyr) He was a worker of the National Conference and an ardent follower of Sheikh Abdullah. He fought to the end for a noble cause of a noble people. Up to the end he helped refugees and gave his own life for their safety. But the Pakistanis did not spare him. As his punishment for being a national, he was shown most cruel type of death. He was made to stand erect.

A light iron rod was hammered in to crack his brow, his nose was then cut, but still he cried, *'Sher-e-Kashmir Zindabad!'*,, and then to take out the last breath from him, 14 bullets were made to pass his chest simultaneously, Such a cruel death through his own brothers — Muslims.

Sheikh Abdullah sent the following message to the people of India for their sympathy and the succour sent:

> "Today when we have retaken the town of Baramulla, and the enemy is in a disorderly retreat, I take the opportunity to render my thanks on behalf of my people to our allies in India. A few days ago, the fate of Kashmir was hanging by a thread, and we owe it to the succour that we have received from fellow countrymen in India that we feel confident that we are again the masters of our own land. The Government of Indian Union lost no time in providing us with military aid. We are grateful to them. But the sympathy that the man in the street in India has shown to us, and the appreciation with which our cause has been viewed throughout the length and breadth of Indian Dominion, has been of such great value to us that even though isolated, we have felt ourselves to be the part of a whole people fighting for freedom. I have received thousands of telegrams all over India offering help and good cheer. I have cherished these messages of friendship in the days of crisis, that have fortunately passed. I have nothing more to say at present except that (we in Kashmir will prove worthy of friendship shown to us by the people and Government of India).

Greater than all the credit goes to the officers and soldiers of Indian Army, who, though unacquainted with the place and unaccustomed to the climate of Kashmir, fought so gallantly and harassed the foe at every place, and hurled back the marauding enemy from Kashmir to the borders, where they are still pursuing them. Sheikh Abdullah sent the following letter of thanks to General Kulwant Singh, Officer Commanding Indian Troops in Kashmir, on the recapture of Baramulla.

> "Let me congratulate you on the signal success which you have achieved by capturing Baramulla. I am sure with the intelligence and courage which you are exhibiting in the task to turning out the invader, we shall soon be masters of the situation.
>
> "Will you kindly convey my thanks to Wing Commander Mehr Singh, whose aerial support has been of great help in routing the enemy ? I am also grateful to Brigadier Sen for the wonderful work he has done.
>
> "I shall certainly take an opportunity of thanking all your officers individually soon. And for the valour which the ordinary soldier under your command has shown, the people of Kashmir have nothing but unstinted praise".

Nehru's Visit to Kashmir

On the morning of November 11th Srinagar woke into new life. The whole city hummed with hilarity and activity on hearing the news about Pandit Nehru's arrival to Srinagar. People moved about friskily, and the city resounded with the slogans of the National Home Guards, Peace Brigade Volunteers and the little children, who imitated them. Minute after minute people from all parts of the city poured into Red Square, where Pandit Nehru had to unfurl the flag.

Men folks went out of their homes, women folk went up to the house tops to catch sight of the plane that would bring home the noblest son of Kashmir. They cast their searching looks over the Pir Panjal ranges, which had to be crossed by Panditji's aeroplane. Every second grew more momentous, millions of eyes were looking upwards and searching the far, spreading heavens, and cursing the duration of time that delayed the arrival of our Hero. It was really very interesting to see women, and young, girls, and men too shouting in ecstasy from their house tops. So felicitous was the time that people even forgot their breakfasts and morning meals also.

In the mosques prayers were held in his honour, and thanks were offered by the *Mullas* and *Pirs* to God, Who had saved Kashmir. In the temples *Kirtan* and *Arti* were sung, and the folded hands and concentrated minds said with the inner depths of their hearts," God give long life to our Jawahar and lend Thy glory and grace to him".

Kashmir itself—its mountains, rivers, birds-was eagerly welcoming her son back to home, for it was a clear sunshine that day, not a fragment of cloud was there on the sky. The mountains had made themselves distinct, as if they too were very eager to see him. The birds, multitudes of these, were seen hovering over head, and it seemed that Kashmir had cast off her veil to see her darling son magnificently come to here folds again.

The Home Guards and the National Guards, as they pressed through the streets singing their common war notes. (The native soldier is marching forward. He shall not retreat, come what may), were received with good cheer everywhere. Flowers were showered over their heads, and the delicate hearts of their mothers and sisters, whose honour they had saved in the darkest hour of Kashmir's history, were giving them blessings in silence, and asking God to glow their careers with success.

On they marched with rejoicing and rhythm, and inspired the hearts of those who, being men all right, were only looking at them. At every crossing more batches joined them with the welcome note, *'Jawahar-e-Kashmir Zindabad! Fakhr-e-Kashmir Zindabad'*.

(Long live the Jewel of Kashmir, long live the Pride of Kashmir) Another group consisting of about 600 strong Kashmiris came from below third Bridge, and crossed Habakadal. Their marching song was:

> Today we have invoked the spirit of the invincible Himalayas. We challenge Pakistanis to go back because New Kashmir is our own land. The bugles 'of war have been rung, and Kashmiris have buckled themselves. We shall not be slaves to any man, may he be a Kabaili or an Afghani.

This part of the National Militia was armed, and many of them had come from the front, where they had exhibited great acts of gallantry and won the admiration of the officers of the Indian Army.

The Srinagar citizens were stirring in all directions of the city. From the aerodrome to Red Square, the streets were occupied by National Home Guards, City Constables and Police officials in their gaudy uniforms to keep the crowds in order. Hari Singh High Street had dressed its front in scarlet and crimson, and rich carpet-work of Kashmir was exhibited on shawls that made the welcome gates. The other side of Amirakadal was more splendidly clothed in cloth of gold and scarlet. All the windows on either side of the road were thronged with ladies crowding to see Jawahar pass. The autumnal sun of Kashmir shone more brightly and glowed everything with its sacred light. Since the daybreak the whole town was in a sweet fever of excitement.

Glorious as the spectacle was, it reminded men of a doleful tale of wrong, for the fresh memory of what Pakistan was doing pierced through the hearts like a yearning in pain. The eyes were impatiently watching for the object. Motor cars and military trucks were coming and going, but his car did not come! Then, all of a sudden crowds looked towards something which now drew nearer. There came a motor lorry having 'the Tricolour' flag in front of it. At once the crowds, multitudes of men, became uncontrollable. They pushed each other, shouted to each other *Nicha Baithu* (Sit down). It then became difficult for the Guards to control them. From all directions people cried loud, 'Hindustan Zindabad', and saluted the Tricolour with the solemn words of 'Jai Hind'. But in the bus there was not the observed of all observers, but simply the Tricolour in front of it. The Great Hero of this glittering homage was still at the aerodrome. The flag had only brought the message that splendour's plaything of the hour, the pride of Kashmir,

Pandit Jawaharlal Nehru, Prime Minister of India, had reached the aerodrome with Mr. Rafi Ahmad Kidwai, Communications Member, and his darling daughter Mrs. Indira Gandhi. They were received at the aerodrome by Sheikh Mohammed Abdullah and General Kulwant Singh, and introduced by Sheikh Mohammed Abdullah with the Emergency Officers and the Ministers of the State.

Gulam Mohiuddin was moving up and down in a jeep to keep the Guards in perfect disciplir . He was giving them his directives regarding their positions. Instant after instant more Guards were pouring in. These were posted at different places lining the road through which Panditji had to pass.

At length the guests accompanied by Sheikh Abdullah drove to the 'Red Square' Amirakadal where, by now, tens of thousands of people had assembled from all directions to have Panditji's Darshana. Ahead was a jeep in which was Bakhshi Gulam Muhammed raising the National slogans in exult and ecstasy. He was standing erect and waving his right arm with great gusto to inspire the people.

In an open space was seen approaching another car bearing two flags, one the Tricolour, and the other the red flag of the National Conference. In it sat the two great Kashmiris—Jawahar and Abdullah-receiving the homage from the people and dispensing a warm smile to them. Both of them were very happy, brothers at last breathing the incense of unity, which they had won after great peril and huge sacrifices.

There Jawahar stood most beautiful-loveliest-most favoured of Kashmir's sons, who had saved his own land from a wanton destruction.

Nehru-the sentinel of India-he had discovered India from the throes of revolution, and splitted ancient order and tradition into national earthquakes. He has consolidated the Union even when the opposing forces were set wrestling to and fro. He has become the one symbol of peoples struggle, and stopped people from falling victims to serfdom again. He has sent on open challenge to those who, though working behind the scenes, are fomenting Fascism in India; and he has left the devil to God's forgiveness.

He looked more radiant to day, now that this time he had come to Kashmir as a free citizen of Free India.

A guard of honour was presented to Panditji by the National Home Guards. Thereafter Panditji unfurled the National Conference flag amid echoing cheers and felicitations from all sides.

Movie Cameramen, newspaper correspondents, photographers from all over the world were crowding round Panditji. Crowds standing on both sides of the road had formed a huge congregation, but there was utter silence all around, since the ears were impatient to hear Panditji's words.

In a short address Sheikh welcomed Panditji, on behalf of the 40 lakhs people of the State, and thanked him, the Government of India and its people for their sympathies and the succour sent for the rescue of Kashmir. Sheikh expressed the hope that Panditji would continue to help Kashmir as he had been doing ever since.

Panditji then stood up to reply the address. He was garlanded at the mike and cheered from all directions. First of all he expressed great satisfaction over the expulsion of the raiders from Baramulla, and paid tribute to the courage of Kashmiris, who refused to give way to panic.

Thereafter he reviewed, in detail, the situation with which Government of India were confronted and paid his tribute to the Members of the Cabinet, who had lost not a second to send succour to Kashmir. He pointed out the complicacies that the situation had caused for India Government by the protestations of the Pakistan Government that they had no hand in the trouble. Congratulating the people of Kashmir on the communal peace they had maintained in the days of crisis, Pandit Nehru said:

> "The spectacle of communal amity in Kashmir, in most anxious circumstances has rejuvenated my bleeding heart".

He told the crowds that the movement of events during the last fortnight had been so swift that Government of India had to take the decision of helping Kashmir in a great hurry, and the arrangement for despatching troops, who were scattered all over India, had to be made at a very short notice.

Above all, Panditji praised the courage displayed by the State Forces led by Brigadier Rajendra Singh, who held up the enemy away from Srinagar for a considerable long time. He assured the people of Kashmir that the Government of India would not rest until every inch of the State territory was cleared of the enemy.

Thereafter Panditji referred to Sheikh expression of gratitude for the offers of help received by him from all parts of India, and remarked that he too had received telegrams from Kashmiris all over the world requesting him to arrange for their transport to India so that they might be able to play their part in the defence of Kashmir concluding his address, Panditji gave a forthright assurance, on behalf of the Government of India, that immediate arrangements would be made for the supply of sugar, cloth and other necessaries of life to the State.

In the end, to mark this memorable occasion, the Premier of India, extended his hand of friendship, on behalf of the Government and people of India, to *Sher-e-Kashmir,* which was warmly received by Sheikh amidst hearty cheers from the audience. Thus was Kashmir allied with India on a solemn day.

Later Sheikh asked the crowds to clear the road. In a moment the road was lined by crowding people, and Panditji and party drove to the Gupkar Palaces, where they had to have lunch with His Highness. In the way Panditji gently raised his right hand and greeted the crowds on his right and left.

In the afternoon, Pandit Nehru accompanied by Sheikh Abdullah and other leaders of the National Conference, proceeded to the State Secretariat, where he met the Emergency officers and spoke to them.

In the evening, Panditji presented colours to the Home Guards, and addressed the Indian Troops at Rambag. This was followed by a dinner at the Guest House at which some high officials of the State and the Government of India were present.

On the morning of the 12th of November, Pandit Nehru accompanied by Sheikh Abdullah and Major General Kulwant Singh and others visited the wreck and ruin of Baramulla. Here Panditji addressed a huge gathering of the local population. Later in the day he flew to Jammu along with Sheikh Abdullah and his daughter Mrs. Indira Gandhi, his Secretary, Mr. Ayyangar and Dr. Bhatnagar. He was received at the aerodrome at Jammu by His Highness and a number of State officers.

Pandit Nehru then proceeded to the Satwari House, where representatives of the Jammu public had assembled to meet him. Pandit Nehru addressed them for about a quarter of an hour, and assured them of India's full help and support in the defence of the State. The Head of Administration, Sheikh Abdullah, also addressed those present. He told them that Jammu and Kashmir was one State, and that he would do his best to serve both impartially to the satisfaction of all concerned. After having his lunch with His Highness at Ramnagar Palaces, Pandit Nehru left for New Delhi at about 2-30 p.m. by air carrying the message of Victory to the whole Indian Nation.

End of the Nightmare

And so having sighted "Destruction, Devastation, and Death", bearing the wounds which still sore in their hearts, the evergreen wounds given by Pakistan, Jinnah, Abdul Quyum etc., who made the flourishing Happy Valley only a heap of smoking rubble, and left forty lakhs of human beings in the clutches of destitute and want, thereby destroying the home of those very Muslims for whose deliverance they pretended they were coming, the people of Jammu and Kashmir celebrated their V-Day, and alliance to India throughout the length and breadth of the State.

4

Sheikh's Removal

(Based on an Insider's Account)

Sheikh Abdullah's arrest on August 9, 1953, had been preceded by a whole lot of contributory events. They included a triangular correspondence (during January-March 1953) between him, Pt. Nehru and the Praja Parishad leader and founder of Jana Sangh Dr. Shyama Prasad Mukherjee; agitation and a press campaign against him; opposition within the party hierarchy: and the erosion of his popularity in Kashmir because of some of his (Sheikh's) policies, specially in respect of food and civil liberties. Besieged by these developments, the Sheikh became more defiant—he openly criticised the Central Government and suspected his colleagues of plotting against him.

Anti-Sheikh Agitation

The Delhi Accord had provided a fresh impetus to the Parishad-led anti-Sheikh agitations at the outset of the momentous year, 1953. In the wake of these agitations came the "Nehru-Mukherjee correspondence" and the "Abdullah-Mukherjee correspondence". The Praja Parishad, supported by communal elements all over India, demanded full merger of Kashmir with India and opposed the nomenclature such as Sadr-e-Riyasat and

"Prime Minister" in Kashmir. In these titles the Parishad saw the nucleus of a separate independent status for the State. The Parishad, which was merged into Jana Sangh by Dr. Mukherjee demanded complete implementation of the Delhi Agreement. His stand was fully reflected in Dr. Mukherjee's letters. In his letters to Nehru, Mukherjee suggested, in brief, the finalisation of the accession by the Constituent Assembly, without reference to the United Nations resolution on plebiscite; and opposed the election of the Sadr-e-Riyasat of Kashmir and the use of the State Flag. In his reply, Mr. Nehru clarified that the Sadr-e-Riyasat was not a "President". He said the Constituent Assembly was authorised to ratify the accession, but India was committed to the UN resolution. He condemned the Praja Parishad's agitations as a product of communal narrowmindedness and a threat to the nation-state.

In his letter to Sheikh Abdullah. Dr. Mukherjee defended the stands taken by the Maharaja and the Rashtriya Swayam Sewak Sangh (RSS) and opposed the naming of the Governor and the Chief Minister of the State as "Sadr-e-Riyasat" and "Prime Minister", respectively. Sheikh Abdullah's reply was: Kashmir had enjoyed a special position since 1949; there was no deviation from secularism and democracy; and there was no truth in the allegation that because they were Muslims, the people of Kashmir gravitated towards Pakistan.

The correspondence over, Mukherjee decided to send a delegation to Kashmir on a fact-finding mission in defiance of the permit system in force in Kashmir, then. Nobody could enter Kashmir without a permit, a condition promulgated by the Union Defence Ministry after the 1947 tribal invasion. Under the Defence of India Rule, Kashmir had been declared a "war zone". The delegation, therefore, was not permitted to enter the State. Dr. Mukherjee then himself gate-crashed into Jammu. He was taken into custody at Madhopur Bridge and transported to Srinagar, where he was kept in a private house near Nishat Garden. The Government of India had no objection to his detention as he had defied the Defence of India Rule. A heart patient. Dr. Mukherjee had an attack while in detention. He was admitted to a hospital, where the well-known heart specialist. Dr. Ali Mohammed Jan, and other able doctors looked after him. Dr. Mukherjee sent telegrams to his brother Justice Mukherjee and other relations expressing satisfaction with the treatment, he was receiving in the hospital. But, he died on June, 23 after a severe attack. His body was flown to Calcutta in an IAF plane, seen off at the airport by Sheikh Abdullah and his Cabinet members and accompanied by Pandit Prem Nath Dogra and others. Sheikh .bdullah sent condolence messages to Dr. Mukherjee's relatives. Dr. Mukherjee's death added a new dimension to the anti-Sheikh campaign not only in the State but all over the country. The West Bengal Chief Minister, Dr. BC Roy sent a telegram to Sheikh demanding to know why he had not been informed of Dr. Mukherjee's illness when he (Dr. Roy) had been his family physician for years.

It is said the Sheikh did not reply to this telegram. However, in his autobiography Sheikh refuted the charge that he did not reply to the telegram. Sheikh Abdullah has written that he invited Dr. Roy to come to Kashmir and conduct an enquiry, but he (Dr. Roy) declined the invitation. Also, the Kashmir Government had already issued a kind of a white paper in the form of a booklet giving details of Dr. Mukherjee's death. Sheikh Abdullah himself was taken aback when the Minister for Jails.

Pandit Sham Lal Saraf, broke the news of Dr. Mukherjee's death to him at dawn. All this time the Sheikh was being told that Dr. Mukherjee was in good health. Dr. Mukherjee had died at night, but the Sheikh was informed of his death in the morning. Facing attacks from all sides. Sheikh Abdullah began suspecting that this information had been purposely held back from him for some hours.

In his autobiography. Sheikh Abdullah has said that the death could have been a part of a bigger conspiracy. He writes: "But later reports started coming to the effect that during his last days, Dr. Mukherjee was planning to withdraw the agitation". The Sheikh has also written that he was against the detention of Dr. Mukherjee in Kashmir; he wanted him to be expelled, but it was a matter for Home Minister Bakhshi Ghulam Mohammed to decide. He had his own ideas and objectives and "I didn't consider it proper to interfere"? The Sheikh had already begun suspecting that Bakhshi was conspiring against him with the Delhi leadership.

During the episode of the arrest and death of Dr. Mukherjee, Prime Minister Nehru was in London attending the coronation of Queen Elizabeth and the Commonwealth Prime Ministers' Conference. On his return, he tried to reason with his agitated colleagues in Parliament, but in vain. The Members were deeply agitated and were not in a mood to listen to anything, which explained the position of the Sheikh.

Immense Stress

It was a period of immense stress and strain for Sheikh Abdullah. The lion of Kashmir felt he was being pushed to the wall by hostile forces within and outside the State. Temperamental and haughty as he was, Sheikh reacted by telling the Sub-committee of the Working Committee to stop thinking about questions like the jurisdiction of the Supreme Court in Kashmir; it should rather examine other alternatives.

Sadiq dismissed Sheikh Abdullah's alternatives as absurd and said he would rather favour a plebiscite under a new neutral authority. But since that was not practicable, he suggested that the ceasefire line be treated as the actual line of division (of Kashmir) and the accession to India be finalised.

The Sheikh felt the Centre was influenced by chauvinistic slogans which sought to take away the autonomy of Kashmir. With the exception of Nehru, top leaders at the Centre suspected not only the Sheikh, but also Kashmiris in general. In Kashmir, there was a feeling that the Sheikh was not trusted by the Centre because he was a Muslim. Some of Sheikh's colleagues added fuel to the fire by suggesting that his secular politics were alienating him from the people.

The international intriguers, too, were not far behind. American and British agents launched a disinformation campaign in the State to prevent finalisation of the accession. These agents worked on two fronts: they (i) egged on the Hindu communalists to agitate against Sheikh Abdullah; and (ii) tried to make the Kashmiris believe that as an independent State, their State could become the Switzerland of Asia. This campaign contributed to the widening of the gulf between the State and the Centre.

Sheikh-Bakhshi Tussle

Bakhshi Ghulam Mohammed opposed Sheikh's new stance and the latter began accusing him of aspiring to take his place and indulging in conspiracies and corruption. Bakhshi had a group supporting him. It included Maulana Masudi, G.M. Sadiq and D.P. Dhar. They explained to Sheikh Abdullah that he had their support in his opposition to the Centre's wrong policies but not if he changed his original stance on the question of accession to India. He told that he was not abandoning his secular principles, but he complained that the Centre was encouraging Bakhshi. But Bakhshi Ghulam Mohammed declared his full loyalty to Sheikh Abdullah when Sadiq dropped a very faint hint that a change in Kashmir's leadership was called for. He said the atmosphere was so explosive that matters that were not favoured by Sheikh Abdullah should not be discussed—more so because the latter was the Prime Minister.

Central Leadership Angered

In the midst of this tension and confusion came the Central Education Minister, Maulana Azad, to Kashmir with an invitation to the Sheikh to visit Delhi for talks. The Sheikh rejected the invitation. "What is the purpose of going to Delhi now?" he asked. He said D.P. Dhar could go to Delhi to know their views. This angered the Central leadership and activated the propaganda machinery of the Praja Parishad, which accused the Sheikh of purposely delaying the implementation of the Delhi Agreement. The Praja Parishad threatened to spread the current anti-Sheikh agitations to the rest of the country. It sent a memorandum to President Rajendra Prasad demanding full application of the Indian Constitution to Jammu and Kashmir. Praja Parishad workers took out a procession and courted arrest in Delhi.

These agitations made Sheikh Abdullah more and more sullen. The Constitution-making had come to a standstill even as the Sheikh faced attacks from the communal forces. The secular and leftist parties, too, became suspicious of the Sheikh's motives, although ideologically they were close to the National Conference. These parties suspected that Sheikh Abdullah was backsliding on the Delhi Agreement under the influence of foreign imperialist forces. Thus, within the party the Sheikh had become a suspect in the eyes of his own (progressive) colleagues. The Sheikh retaliated by abolishing the post of the Chief Parliamentary Secretary and shunting Mir Qasim. Sheikh had turned to the wishes and aspirations of the common Kashmiri and became their spokesman. This further widened the gulf between him and the Centre.

The Dismissal

In the meantime, Sheikh asked his Health Minister, Pandit Sham Lal Saraf, to resign because of corruption charges against him. Pandit Saraf refused to resign and along with two other Ministers— Bakhshi Ghulam Mohammed and Girdharilal Dogra— told the Sadr-e-Riyasat that the Cabinet had been divided into two factions and since the Sheikh had lost majority support in the Cabinet, he should be dismissed.

Dr. Karan Singh advised the Sheikh to dissolve his Cabinet and form it again, and this was how he could drop Pandit Saraf from the Cabinet. Sheikh Abdullah refused. He was dismissed as Prime Minister for 'having lost confidence of the Cabinet". But the justification given for the removal of Sheikh Abdullah was without legal support: the Prime Minister (or, for that matter, a Chief Minister) does not survive on the support of his Cabinet, but on the confidence of the Legislative Assembly. No Chief Minister in any of the Indian States has ever been removed from his post because his Cabinet lost confidence in him.

Bakhshi at the Helm

Sheikh Abdullah's place was given to Bakhshi Ghulam Mohammed, who made it clear to Dr. Karan Singh that he could not undertake to run the government if the Sheikh and Mirza Afzal Beg were left free to propagate their views. That expedited the arrest of the two on August 9, 1953, although Dr. Karan Singh, as he writes in his autobiography, was reluctant to take this step. M.O. Mathai, Nehru's Personal Assistant till 1959, also writes in "My Days with Nehru"'that Pt. Nehru was not in favour of Sheikh Abdullah's arrest. The news of the arrest spread like wild fire in Kashmir giving rise to widespread agitations and protest marches.

Some people were killed in police firing. In one case, the police would not hand over the bodies to their next of kin.

Srinagar was in total chaos. Bakhshi's own house, despite the police guard, was under attack. He was nervous and wanted to step down as Prime Minister in favour of G.M. Sadiq. The latter declined, but assured full support to him in overcoming the current situation. G.M. Sadiq urged Mir Qasim to join the Cabinet. He refused. He took him to Bakhshi, who said: Qasim, you are a strange comrade. Ideologically you were with us. I had no alternative to arresting the Sheikh. He then explained why the arrest took place.

Finally, Mir Qasim agreed to join Bakhshi's Cabinet on condition that Khawaja Ghulam Nabi (alias Nabaji) who was the second important leader in Anantnag after Mirza Afzal Beg, be included in it. But Nabaji rejected the offer outright. Initially only a two-man Cabinet was sworn in. It included Bakhshi and Girdharilal Dogra.

Later, on August 15, Mir Qasim joined them as Minister of Revenue, Food, Agriculture and Forests. Earlier, these positions had been held by Mirza Afzal Beg in Sheikh Abdullah's Cabinet. G.M. Sadiq who was the President of the Constituent Assembly joined later, in deference to the wishes of Pt. Nehru, to strengthen the hands of Bakhshi. Initially, Bakhshi was hesitant to include Sadiq because he already was the President of the Constituent Assembly and therefore could not be holding two offices of profit. But Sadiq said he would take only Re. 1 a month as a Minister.

Bakhshi was a practical, hard working man, who took quick decisions. The Sheikh had made him Deputy Prime Minister in recognition of these qualities. Bakhshi had great confidence in Mir Qasim despite his young age and entrusted him with important tasks. As a Cabinet minister, Qasim abolished the forced levy on agricultural products and introduced a voluntary procurement scheme.

The new government made education free up to the University level, increased the quantity of the rationed food, and brought down the prices. The Central Food Minister Rafi Ahmed Kidwai assured of adequate supplies and financial aid for three years. The new government launched a number of development projects, constructed roads and bridges, opened schools and health centres, and started schemes to generate employment. It also began irrigation and power projects and electrification programmes. The people were happy with its work, but would not forgive the plight of the Sheikh and therefore would not fully cooperate in development projects. One had to accept that it was during Bakhshi's rule that development programmes first began in Kashmir.

Sheikh's Leadership Intact

One day, late at night, when the valley had lapsed into absolute silence, Bakhshi, Sadiq and Qasim were discussing in Bakhshi's house the situation after about three days of Sheikh's arrest. Suddenly the telephone rang. Rafi Ahmed Kidwai was on the line. He made this Late night call from Delhi to ask Bakhshi, if he or any of the Cabinet members had made contacts with Sheikh Abdullah so far. His query was as startling as the sudden sound of the telephone bell at that time in the night.

It was clear that the arrest of Sheikh did not mean the derecognition of his leadership by the central leaders. Bakhshi was nonplussed. He found it strange specially in the prevailing atmosphere in which the common man was in a sullen mood because of the arrest and his Government was sweating it out to justify the arrest. Sadiq could at once read the message in Kidwai's enquiry. The message was simple and clear that the new State leadership must make up with Sheikh.

This was too bitter a pill for Bakhshi to swallow. Sadiq told Kidwai that Sheikh's arrest was a temporary measure taken in a state of helplessness. But meeting the Sheikh was like bearding an injured lion in his den. "Who will dare meet the Sheikh?" roared Bakhshi in desperation. "Sheikh may talk bitterly and fume at us for some time, but we will tolerate after all, he is our leader," said Sadiq.

According to the inside information, Nehru had not given a blanket permission for the arrest of Sheikh and Kidwai had used his discretion in ordering the arrest in the best national interest. Nehru would not dispose of a political personage like Sheikh by resorting to legal technicalities and subtleties. He must be talked to. Kidwai was now trying to fulfil this desire of Nehru. Perhaps that became the seed of the future Indira-Sheikh negotiations, which fructified in February 1975—after 22 years.

To give an example of Nehru's concern for the Sheikh: When Bakhshi appointed R.C. Raina as his Private Secretary, Nehru wrote a strong letter to him protesting against the appointment of a person who, in his view, did not have a good reputation and who was hostile to the Sheikh. But Nehru had been wrongly informed about the identity of the new private secretary. Bakhshi explained to Nehru that this Raina was a different person. Sadiq and Qasim appreciated Nehru's desire for negotiations with Sheikh and with that also began their differences with Bakhshi.

In Support of Sheikh

Maulana Mohammed Syed Masudi, who was a member of the Indian Constituent Assembly, had formed a group in Delhi to mobilise public support against the undemocratic action of Bakhshi Ghulam Mohammed. The group included Miss Mridula Sarabhai, Dr. Ram Manohar Lohia, Asoke Mehta and others.

Pt. Nehru sent Central Minister Dr. Subbarayan to Kashmir. He met the Cabinet members in the presence of Bakhshi and expressed his desire to meet the Sheikh, who was in Kuḍa jail at that time. Bakhshi regarded this request with disfavour. Later at a lunch given in honour of Dr. Subbarayan, Bakhshi asked Sadiq and Qasim what they thought of Dr. Subbarayan's request. They suggested that he should be allowed to see the Sheikh; there was no harm in it.

Initially Bakhshi did not agree with them; but later Dr. Subbarayan did meet the Sheikh in jail. What transpired between the two was not known. Subsequently it was learnt that, on his arrival in Srinagar, Dr. Subbaroyan had driven straight to Bakhshi's house. He had with him a bag which he left in the house while going out. The security staff of Bakhshi opened the bag and found a letter from Nehru to the Sheikh. They read the letter and put it back. Later, Dr. Subbarayan, who perhaps could sense this pilferage regretted for his mistake.

Bakhshi found himself forced into an embarrassing task of perennially explaining everywhere and to everyone why Sheikh Abdullah was arrested. These explanations which were obviously one-sided, provoked Sheikh Abdullah to demand an opportunity to tell the people his side of the story. He sent a telegram from prison to the Assembly President G.M. Sadiq on September 30 asking him to let him attend the Constituent Assembly session so that he could reply to the charges against him.

Copies of the telegram were sent to the Prime Minister and the President of India. The request was not acceded to, as it was thought this would cause an uncontrollable public reaction. But the Sheikh would not give in so easily. He now started a long correspondence with Sadiq, insisting that he should be heard in the Constituent Assembly.

The correspondence continued till 1956. Sadiq was half inclined to accede to Sheikh's request but Bakhshi overruled it on the plea that it would have an adverse effect on Constitution-making and create a law and order problem. Sadiq's replies were drafted by J.N. Zutshi, who had been arrested along with Sheikh, but was later freed after gaining the confidence of Bakhshi. Qasim did not approve of the tone of the replies and thought arguments given therein were not convincing enough. Sadiq, who discussed this correspondence with him said as the President of the Constituent Assembly, he had no power to release Sheikh Abdullah.

Rejection of Plebiscite

A month after Sheikh Abdullah's arrest came Pakistani Prime Minister Mohammed Ali Bogra to New Delhi. At his meeting with Pt. Nehru it was agreed to hold an impartial plebiscite in Kashmir without the involvement of foreign powers. However, back home, Mohammed Ali Bogra could not carry his Cabinet with him. After the assassination of Pakistan's first Prime Minister Liaquat Ali Khan, in 1951, the army under the leadership of Gen.

Ayub Khan had begun to wield real power and the so-called civilian Government, under whatever Prime Minister, was merely a benami of the Army. And the Army acted under instructions from the United States. The Nehru-Bogra agreement cracked under pressure from the United States on Pakistan to retain Admiral Nimitz as the Plebiscite Administrator. The final nail in the coffin of this agreement was driven by the Pakistani decision to join the US supported military alliances in 1954, purportedly to contain the Soviet Union and China.

India bitterly reacted to Pakistan joining these alliances because it appeared to New Delhi that Karachi (then the Federal capital of Pakistan), in spite of the UN resolutions, still believed in a military solution of the Kashmir issue, and now with the help of foreign powers. The signing of these pacts by Pakistan, thus, had the effect of sabotaging the ongoing preparations for holding a plebiscite in Kashmir in accordance with the UN resolutions. The Government of India stopped these preparations because it feared these alliances were aimed at it and not at communist Russia and China with whom Pakistan had no dispute.

The USA, while persuading Pakistan to join the military alliances, could not have been unaware of the Indian apprehensions and their negative impact on future India-Pakistan relations and above all on democracy in Pakistan. Washington perhaps thought all was fair in the pursuit of its global interests.

India was already unhappy with the idea of a plebiscite in Kashmir because, first, it made light of the Indian complaint to the UNO against the Pakistani aggression in Kashmir and, secondly, it went against the very grain of Indian secular ideology. Nehru's rethinking on the subject of plebiscite is reflected in a letter, dated July 3, 1950, he wrote to Sardar Patel. The letter read: "I agree with you that a plebiscite is unreal.

Not only that, it would be positively dangerous because my own feeling was that once the talk started, the non-Muslims in Jammu and Kashmir would start feeling uneasy and we might be faced with an exodus to India". Far back in 1950 Nehru had begun to feel distracted, like Shakespeare's tragic hero Hamlet, by India's commitment to holding a plebiscite and its far-reaching implications. To hold or not to hold a plebiscite was the tormenting question. This excruciating dilemma must have reminded Nehru of Sheikh Abdullah's counsel not to seek the UN help to get Kashmir cleared of the occupation forces of Pakistan. Sheikh

Abdullah believed there was no need to involve a third party in this dispute; the Indian army with the support of the people of Kashmir could do that job. Pakistan and the USA, in fact, helped India out of this dilemma by signing those military pacts.

In July 1955. Home Minister G.B. Pant came to Srinagar and made a historic announcement at a reception on the lush green Emporium grounds that now "plebiscite is beside the point". This was the first public statement on India's rejection of the plebiscite. Later he told a press conference: "The Government of India had made certain statements when Kashmir acceded to India, namely, that the future of the State will be decided by a plebiscite. But the circumstances then were different. The time factor was important and many things had happened since, which ruled out a plebiscite".

A few months later (March 29, 1956), Nehru, too, said that after eight and a half years the Pakistan armed forces were still (the UNO had asked Pakistan to withdraw its troops from Kashmir before the plebiscite) in occupied Kashmir. Therefore, all this talk of plebiscite had become beside the point.

Bakhshi's Peace Brigade

In the meantime, Mirza Afzal Beg had been released from jail so that he could attend the Constituent Assembly. He at once occupied himself with addressing public meetings but the attendance at these meetings was thin. Pant was still in Kashmir. One day when he, Bakhshi and Qasim were going to Pahalgam in a car, the Home Minister asked Bakhshi, why the attendance at Beg's meetings was so thin. "He is unpopular," was Bakhshi instant reply. Apparently, he could not get the meaning of Pant's query. Pant then straightaway asked Bakhshi about the activities of his Peace Brigade.

The Home Minister was certainly aware of these activities, which included breaking up of the public meetings of Bakhshi's opponents. Bakhshi tried to play down the Brigade by saying that it was a band of a very few and unarmed persons. In the whole of Anantnag their number was just 120, out of which 75 belonged to one town. Had Beg been a popular leader these 75 men could not have done anything. Pant intently listened to Bakhshi's logic and then replied: "Just one goonda can make a thousand men's life miserable, if be has the support of the area's police chief".

The insinuation was very transparent. Sadiq and Qasim had supported the action against the Sheikh only on political grounds, but Pant implied that there could be personal reasons in the removal of the Sheikh. Qasim was provoked to tell Pant to bring back the Sheikh if he (Pant) thought the new team had been unfair to him. Pant looked on and asked: "Qasim, you swear by democracy, but do you understand the meaning of it?" When he asked him to explain it, he said: "Democracy is infinite capacity to stand nonsense". Every one kept quiet, but they could read the Central Government's mind in Pant's observation.

Soviet Support

Even as the Indian leaders expressed their disillusionment with the UN resolution on plebiscite, the Kashmir question acquired another international dimension with the visit of the Soviet leaders to the State in 1956. Soviet Communist Party President Bulganin and Khrushchev included Kashmir in the itinerary of their visit to India. This was the first time that a foreign dignitary visiting India came to Kashmir. On their arrival in Srinagar, Khrushchev said his visit to India would have been incomplete without visiting "this part of India, Kashmir". With this support to Kashmir's accession to India by one superpower, the Kashmir issue got a new dimension: it got divided between the Western and Soviet blocs.

5

The Greatest Kashmiri

Great Kashmiri leader, a foremost nationalist, Sheikh Abdullah is regarded by millions of his followers and admirers throughout the world as the noblest of all Kashmiris who have ever lived, on earth. The beauty of his character and the supremacy of his achievements have been described by the press and people throughout the Rising East. He has given promise of a great millennium of Orient culture and civilization in which Sataurn reigns and the people of the world live in permanent peace and order. In a world distracted by feuds, biases, cross-purposes, and divisions of many sorts, wherein even men of goodwill cannot easily work together, he is going to discover a Way of Fellowship, which he seeks for the healing of innumerable divisions and for the solution of many baffling problems in conduct and policy of individuals, groups, organisations or nations.

Thus he proposes to be the great pioneer of the gospel of Mahatma Gandhi in India and the entire East. When the leaders of India, martyrs and soldiers, patriots known and unknown who sacrificed their everything for the emancipation of Mother India-brave people indeed-are forgotten in dust; when humanity no longer remembers the names of the dead or what these men did or say, the name and fame of Sher-e-Kashmir will go thundering down the eons since he succeeded there where other leaders failed.

Broad-based Message

Even the depressed hopes of the people elsewhere were rejuvenated by the message of Real Freedom; Sher-e-Kashmir was preaching his gospel to his followers and beating down the rotten foundations of oppression, injustice and monarchy in Indian States Today and in future he overflows over the barren tracts like a great River and enriches the soil of humanity with his physical and political buoyancy. He was the most abundant Indian leader. He emitted sparks and electrical power with every word he utters in meetings or from the platform. His eyes and his fingers which he moves while addressing the gathering spit fire. He was the New Dawn of the East that heralds the approaching day in which the Eastern Countries have not become infernos of discord, but abodes of universal brotherhood and everlasting peace. These were his miracles that have made him the greatest leader in the annals of Indian history.

The Sheikh reminded us of Mahatma Gandhi in many ways. He was an indefatigable worker, a benefactor of the poor, a guide and organiser of the back ward people, the leader of the despairing farmers, the Rousing Conscience of the dumb slaves, and in one word he should be called the Cincinnatus of the East.

The Sheikh mingled freely and easily with individuals of innumerable shades and colour, with thinkers and pseudo-thinkers, socialists and reformers representative of every shade of social, political and religious view; with publicists, statesmen, rulers diplomats educators, in his vast study during his prison stay. In future, I hope, even the socialists, communists, anarchists, will find him their friend; burglars, prostitutes, murderers, the erring individuals will discover the healing spirit of his sympathy; incorrigible youths, wayward girls, irredeemable failures will be touched and stirred to fresh efforts through the ministering warmth of his tender humanism.

He struggled hard for the cause he had made his ideal for full seventeen years during which he underwent many imprisonments. In one of his messages from behind the iron bars, he communicated:

> "So far as I am concerned these stone walls and steal bars do not exist; I do not see them. My spirit soars

> beyond this institution and mingles with the spirits of the workers of the National Conference, loyal and devoted all throughout the boundries of the Jammu and Kashmir State, and over the vast subcontinent of my India. I am proud of the blessings I enjoy of the Congress High Command and so many hundred million of Indians who are also striving for full freedom. For my own self I am serene and countless and for my Comrades I am confident that the cause in which and for which they are working, all their working hours will soon triumph, and in that blessed day the freedom lovers of the world will inaugurate the greatest liberty and democracy that the world has ever known. Tell my comrades that I am all right and there is nothing to worry about". For the greatness of Kashmir and the betterment of Kashmir, he would not shirk from any ideal or budge an inch from any ordeal that would achieve his end."

Sheikh Abdullah, no doubt, was pre-eminently an agitator, a crusader. He had lived closely to the pulsing heart of the suffering race. He had sensed the ignoble poverty of the masses, and that has made him a revolutionary, a leader, a rebel and a liberator. He avowed with faith the Congress idealism because he felt sure that it could be made to alleviate the distress of the poverty - stricken Kashmiris so that they be made rich in the good things of life. In his heart and soul was no trace of hatred for a living soul, and he has said time and again that he would serve those who opposed him just as much as those who were with him.

He saw things 'clearly', interprets his apprehensions and whatever he felt in true, he followed it. Few men in Kashmir possessed the gift of oratory that belongs to Sheikh Abdullah. "Flowers blossom upon his lips, and you can hear the ripples of silver springs in the music of his voice". In his seventeen years of agitation on behalf of the Kashmiris as also of the ten crores' of States peoples he addressed millions of individuals at home or abroad.

No man living or dead, has more faithfully consecrated his life to the cause of political justice and fair dealing, man to man than the Sheikh. Likewise he had been severely punished for it. He fought the good fight and kept its name for all ages in history. He will be revered by the children of the races. His was a tough fight for the emancipation of the Kashmiris, Different political and controversial theories might accuse him for different shades in his career; but no matter from the just verdict of mankind, world will agree that Abdullah was honest, kind, sincere, loyal, devoted, true, lovable and loving, always doing what he could in rain or shine, in prison or at home, to make Kashmir a better and a brighter place for the people who inhabit it, and for those who will come afterwards.

If once he sponsored an agitation against the Pandits, it was because he found they were standing against his cause; if at another time he raised up a slogan that the Prince should Quit, it was because the autocratic Prince and his machine of bureaucratic Government had suppressed his moment and maimed his cause and overshadowed the future, the hope of which he had given to his people.

The Sheikh fought his enemies with love, pity and compassion. They fought him with blood and bludgeon, persecution and prison, and when he was out of the prison bars he attacked their citadel with his eloquence and persuasions. But again they returned the attack with injunctions and indictments. But he was victorious in the end. He, as a man, as a leader of men, as lover of liberty and as a determined spirit, had already left his impress on the future. There awaited him a page in the history beside those who sacrificed their self for the common cause of the common people.

Above all was his daring attitude. Alone among all Kashmiris who were deprived of their legitimate freedom and were forced to bend before authority, Abdullah was never afraid. From the beginning of his political and public career he had to make decisions daily which practically made if certain that his life would be given to the service of his fellowmen.

He came out on the platform to declare certain truths about freedom and government, but they were so obnoxious to those in authority, that very soon he began to be known as a ' traitor'. They gave him threats of the punishment of sedition, but there never was a spectre of fear stealing in and out of his life. He had to do daily exactly what men at the front do. He had to live in throes of tragic wrestle with authority-military and police, courts and judges. But he went on. Hundreds of brave men who have won and deserved distinctions in the war, who could hold bullets in honest contempt did not possess the courage which would have been needed to a conviction about social conduct, or politics, or personal goodness which was uncommon in Kashmiri masses, who were illiterate and completely devoid of political education.

Man with a Mission

He was a man with a mission, a sincere Kashmiri. Though he had followed the examples of Gandhiji they could be dissimilar also. The Sheikh had a calculating realist-volcanic fires within him, but a fairly cool head. The Sher of Kashmir was a far more complicated personality, hit all over, emotional, excitable, romantically inclined, prone to sudden fury and blinding.

He was not altogether normal, there was something about him of the dreamer and the mystic. Yet this strange creature was also a man of action, laying his plans, biding his time and striking with relentless force when the hour came. Where the greatness of Kashmir was concerned he sticked at nothing. Neither treaties nor promises held him back. His followers chanted in chorus, he was sung in Kashmiri folk songs.

The Jammu and Kashmir National Conference was thick with the "unwholsome" fumes of incense The Sheikh was a preacher as well as a chief. The core of his gospel was the greatness of the Indian nation as a whole. His ideology was that curious medley of wisdom and folly, statesmanship and nationalism which had made place in every human heart. He was a highly educated Kashmiri. The Indians, members of one nation, he told that the master-builders to whom the precious fabric of Orient civilization was due, and the Kashmiris were the best specimen of this incomparable type. According to him the easy-going liberalism of the nineteenth century undermined the authority of the state. He believed in stern administration, but the base of that administration, according to him, should be the goodwill of the common man. The duty of the citizen in the *Awami-Raj*' (People's Government) his individual claims and tastes, but to dedicate himself body and soul to the service of the nation, to loose himself in the life of the whole. His greatest interest was to see Kashmir and whole of India prosperous and happy. He loved Kashmir, the land of his birth more than he loved his own life.

In his first address from the Government chair he had declared before the world, "Others woes are my own, if someone's child has died, believe it my own child has died; if someone's wife is killed, believe it my own wife is killed if someone's house has been burnt, believe it my own house has been burnt. 'When the Pakistan Government with a view to disrupting the State " from within" filtrated Tribal gangs within the State boundaries and disturbed normal life in Kashmir', the Sheikh read to the Home Guards and National Conference volunteers:

- "Every child of the soil has avowed it with faith and determined spirit that he shall not give an inch to these barbarous booters who have come here to trample over the Kashmiris. We have prepared ourselves for death if it means that, but we shall not be the slaves of Pakistan. We have already given our lives for the service of our land, and how does it matter if we die for our Kashmir!".

He gave his life in open defiance of public opinion, and he was spared nothing. At one time he had the support of the communal Muslims but they afterwards forsook him because he did not become a victim of the communal fever that was sweeped over the whole of the Punjab by the Muslim Press. The communal organisations at home or abroad conspired against him; his own community even thought him mad, and failed to stand by him. This brought about 'Sher-Bakra' conflict in Kashmir,

The league had taken over the Bakra element. The Sheikh, on the other hand, longed for good politicians who would agree with him and support his convictions. That was the stage in his life when his own politics was diverted towards nationalism as preached by Gandhiji. He studied Indian politics and his mental horizon broadened itself. He was now, confronted with the problems of India which were akin to the Indian States also. Communalism, he thought, would multiply these problems, and in nationalism he saw the cherished dream of a thriving nation, the Indian Nation, It was at that time that in one of his public speeches, he declared, 'Idea of one India is worth dying for'. That was, evidently, before July 1941 when Pandit Jawaharlal Nehru and Abdul Ghaffar Khan (the Frontier Gandhi) were invited by Sheikh Mohammed Abdullah to tour into the interior of the Happy Valley and study the conditions of the Kashmiris.

Whether the world calls him a leader or a statesman, Sheikh Abdullah sustained a conscious and continuous effort to relieve the misery of the Kashmiris. How far he succeeded in his mission was to be assessed in due course of time, and decided by future that would judge him better; but so far as his personality went, he wept over the sorrows of his people, and in their service he ignored his self also. He poured out his own self for others. The regenerating idea of a great nation, the Indian nation, of which the Kashmiris formed an integral part was the dominant thought and inspiration of his whole life. The Sheikh sweeped over the spirit of liberty over the entire East like a flame at which all the monarchies were trembling.

Really a wonderful man, to raise his cry of ' One Nation' in India's darkest hour when a biased government was set up in the name of Islam and India's poor masses were exploited under the mad fit of communalism, as preached by Jinnah and his lieutenants Never had the hope of India as a nation sunk nearer to extinction, as when Pakistan is encouraging man slaughter and senseless savagery. Never had the great political hopes, ideals, dreams became a shattered heap.

The sights of the motherless children, childless mothers, husbandless wives the refugees—pierced him to his heart. He could not really see all that. If that meant freedom, we should better remain slaves, he said. It was because of this that he may, at times, opposed Jinnah's politics also otherwise the Sheikh was the friend of all. Kashmiris, mostly the Muslims, were poor. They did not own the land that they tilled, they did not know why they paid the taxes, cycles of unemployment had brought about colossal strife. "The peasants mostly were sunk in unimaginable poverty. Their mud huts contained hardly a trace of visible property save a few pots and water jars. Every household was in debt, and the money lenders charged rates of interest raging to 48 per cent. If a peasant owned his holding, it was rarely big enough to feed his family throughout the year and he made up the deficiency by trekking as a seasonal labourer across the mountains to the plains, where he did the work which was quite unfit for human hands. People looked down upon him, he was called ' Hatto'. He could only clothe his body by rags. He had no land, he worked a sharecropper and paid to the owner by way of rent one half of all his produce. His wooden plough dated from the dark ages and his cattle, if he had any, were of such miserable breeds that they were hardly worth the trouble of milking.

Worse than all this, much of the land was held under feudal tenure by great landlords known as Jagirdars who drew their tribute from the cultivator as a reward for some services rendered to the Maharaja or his ancestors. Peasant's children did not receive education, their undernourishment was obvious at a glance and the bodily destruction was due to the lack of medical care. In some cases sheer penury had compelled the people to make prostitutes of their wives and daughters for the sake of feeding their bellies. Of this community, then, was born the lion of Kashmir to overthrow the shackles of slavery and to resurrect the people of Jammu and Kashmir State so that its call would cut through the massive mountains and send down messages of ' One India', 'One Nation, ' One Government' throughout the entire subcontinent of India, where, from the graves and cremation grounds the spirits of the millions of those men, women and children whose lives were paid as price of freedom in that darkest time of India's history when the British with a view to engulf India in the throes of perpetual warfare divided our land of birth, would rise and cherish with us the exult and ecstasy of ' United India ' and Complete Independence. It was then that the greatness of Abdullah would be sung by the poets and chronicled in golden letters by the historians of the world, who had predicted that Kashmir would lead the East.

Leader of the Subcontinent

Sometime, the happenings in many parts of India caused despair in the heart of every Indian patriot. We have seen in

European history that the religious discords between important sections of the people did not lead to any disastrous failure of patriotism The Catholics and the Huguenots fought each other to the death, but even then the patriotism of the French masses strengthened the definitive unity of the French nation. In England, Catholics and Protestants joined hand in hand and rose against the Spanish Armada, and surprised the agents of Philip II. In more recent times, in Germany Catholics and Protestants have united in all national wars. Religious feud is an affair of the home. Even in Europe, the country distorted by incessant wars, patriotism has stood firm against the evil forces of political disruption.

Gandhiji's great desire was that patriotism and the sense of nationality be securely founded lest people were put to the strain of religious disunion He had time and again stressed upon the Indian leaders the imperative need of welding and hammering the nation into political unity so that this political unification was made so strong that it could bear the strain and stress of religious strife which has, now, been made more positive and active by the British by dividing India on communal basis.

Ninety years of India's great struggle for freedom (1857-1947) contain records of British tactics, which they employed in weakening the national unity of India, of which they were mortally afraid. We have seen how the Imperial Government were encouraging periodical religious outburst so to disrupt the programmes of the Indian National Congress, which above all fought so hard for the national unity of India and independence. It was the policy of the British to disunite the Hindus and Muslims-two major, communities of India in the political and social spheres. They made them claim communal electorates, communal quotas in the administrative services, legislative safeguards, and thus the British administration promoted and kept alive communal disunion between the strivers of liberty. The seeds of the present communal warfare were sown by the British because they did not want to see India a thriving nation.

Gandhiji was decidedly right in saying that strong nationalism was more important than the freedom itself. He had foreseen the ruin of the nation in communalism He did not support nationalism as being political criticism of British administration. He wanted it to be a nationalistic movement. Even before Gandhiji in about 1885, the British Indian Association of Bengal, the Indian Association of Bombay and the Sarvajanik Sabha of Pune were crying about nationalism, but they were more liberal in their outlooks. The Indian National Congress itself in the beginning aimed far less at nationalist organisation. The original idea of Mr. Hume, according to some, was of a national gathering of Indian public men to discuss social matters and to cultivate friendly relations with each other, but Lord Dufferin had made it a gathering, where Indian politicians would meet and point out to the Government where the administration was defective and how it could be improved.

When Gandhiji came to its forefront the active promotion of nationalism became the base plank of its platform. Before that, despite all its good features, the Congress was a middle class movement. Gandhiji had taken the Indian platform. Britishers were apprehensive of their future in India. They were dazed by the probability of the transfer of power from their hands to the hands of Indians, whose sole representative, then, was the Congress alone. Tempted by the possibility of regaining that power through some foul means, they influenced some distinguished members of the Muslim community, and won their hearts by telling them the truth that education was their greatest need. Consequently a Mohammedan Educational Association was formed. Later the British told them that political power was being placed more and more on Indian shoulders and in that the majority community enjoyed the better chance since in Responsible Government a rule by majority would be a rule by a permanent majority — the Hindus. Thus, by political reasoning, they convinced them of the need for a political organisation, and in 1906 was established the Muslim League.

The Sher-e-Kashmir later discovered that League was a British-made concern and that it did not aim at the amelioration of Muslim masses, while on the other hand the Congress had championed the cause of the popular national interests like those of the ryots and the villages, the conditions of labour, the promotion of Swadeshi, the Indianisation of everything from the success of which Muslims would profit equally with Hindus and take India long way ahead. Indian nationalism under the influence of Gandhiji got hold of the masses, Gandhiji was still striving to achieve the positive unity of the people of India. Nationalism, as preached by Gandhiji and followed by Sheikh Abdullah had to neutralise the dominant influence of communalism. It had to become people's way of life. So far it might have been used as a stick to beat British rule, but later it had to cement the political union of the people of India. That was Sheikh Abdullah's creed and conviction on which he had seen the prosperity of Kashmir in acceding to Indian union. Indian nationalism was to spring from the depths of Indian life.

Sheikh did not believe in 'Two Nation Theory' since that theory was absurd. He wanted nationalism to be fed and nourished by the love of the land and the people, and a man who had no love for his land and his people was not worth being a man. It was the love of the country that made it possible for Poland to resurrect itself after hundred and twenty five years of dismembered existence. Rousseau laid down love of the country as the foundation of any durable Constitution.

Sheikh Abdullah's first thing in his life was the love of his country, India of which Kashmir, his place of birth was a part. Sheikh Abdullah's nationalism was based on the love of the land. It gave us the hope of counterblasting British policy by which they had uncircled us in communal squabbles. India was not for division. Its natural frontiers had decisively separated it from its neighbours. India was the most picturesque country of the world. Hindus and Muslims and Christians and Sikhs and Parsees were bound up in cordial relations by 'Orient culture and civilization, which was common to all these. It was the natural and historical home of the Hindus and Muslims who had settled down in India for many centuries and had made India their home. History had brought the people together and united them in bonds of unity that would never break. The idea of division, therefore, was absurd. Hindus and Muslims had fundamental diversity in following their religions, but their politics was closely connected together.

Sheikh Abdullah's fight was a political fight, not a religious one, and thus there was no question why, being a Muslim, he was not a leaguer. The movement from Kashmir, the head of India that Sheikh Abdullah had started must cure Indian nationalism from the malaise from, which it had been suffering. Crores of Muslims domiciled in the dominion of India were looking up to Sheikh Abdullah. His leadership had restored back their confidence. Why did he not care for those crores of Muslims, who made him Qued-e-Azam, the Sheikh asked Jinnah. If Jinnah proclaimed to the world that Pakistan was demanded for the safeguard of Muslims, what were his arrangements for the safeguard of those several crores of Muslims who were to be stranded in India, should India be declared a Hindu State, as he wanted it to do?

Sheikh Abdullah was not only the leader of lakhs of the people of Jammu and Kashmir State, he was the leader of the crores of Muslims of India besides being the voice of ten crores of States People. He had done more for the cause of Islam than Jinnah with his British support and Pakistan had done or would do. Sheikh Abdullah was a shrewd politician. He did not see the good of Muslims in Pakistan since every Muslims was not a Zamindar or an estate holder.

Muslim masses like the Hindu masses were poor. They had to be ameliorated, and this gigantic, task, Sheikh Abdullah felt could be properly done by the national Government of India. The major part of India was agricultural. Nationalism and rural economy were, therefore, the dominating considerations before the Government. Pre-war Russia was like India. It had made strides in years because it had not confused religion with Government. It did not mean that Sheikh Abdullah was anyway, in favour of communism, but in sound nationalism he sew the remedy of ignoble wrongs, definitely.

The post-war East was in the most acute and widespread poverty, but it was endeavouring to become a great power in the face of terrible obstacles and handicaps, Japan had been ruined industrially and economically, India's way to prosperity was thickened with obstacles. Vast regions of China were in utter chaos. Huge provinces were on the verge of starvation. Millions perished annually from hunger and malnutrition. In India itself the average per capita income was meagre and tens of millions dwelt continuously in pitiable poverty. Indeed three fourths of all the people on earth were not adequately fed, clothed or housed, while at last one quarter of all human beings were actually destitute and in terrible misery. The arrogance of the white race and the discriminatory practices of the great powers had churned up a whirlpool of resentment, among the Indian leaders, and it was on the conviction that the people of the East be allcwed to live in peace that our leaders sought freedom for all the slave countries. Indians — Hindus and Muslims alike were victims of insults, discrimination, exploitation and countless injustices at the hands of white men. Freedom as sought by our leaders was freedom from all these desperations. We had never strived for the partition of India and man-slaughter in which Millions of Indians and property worth crores was burnt to dust.

The responsibility of the communal warfare which spread like wild fire throughout India vested entirely with Jinnah and not a single Muslim could be blamed for what he did by his arms and match boxes. Kashmir was not consulted when the Indian leaders consented to the partition of India. India was divided, when the voice of Kashmir was shut up behind the prison bars.

Still Kashmir was proud of Sheikh and his leadership that it could maintain communal peace even to the last. Division of India was their (the Indian leaders') affair. The Sheikh had to do absolutely nothing with it. When he was set free, he found India divided into two dominions. Before him, now was the question: which of the two dominions would be helpful to the cause he had undertaken that of ameliorating the Kashmiri masses, the peasants. He also saw that India government had not deviated from its drafted programme. The India Government had openly declared that it stood for the people and the poor, while on the other hand Pakistan had become a purely communal body in which the people would least count. Likewise he openly declared his policy in favour of India.

Through years of discipline this great leader and statesman, the Gandhi of Kashmir, had achieved rare poise and sublime sublimity. This task to which he was devoting himself, according to a Pakistani leader was an 'impossible" one, because as he felt, he could not succeed to unite India again when once it had been divided. His greatness was noted there where he had taken upon himself the hard task of freeing of his people from dire poverty, political bondage, religious strife, superstition, ignorance and debasing traditions. Millions of his countrymen in India as in Kashmir were subjected to indescribable privations. Illiteracy and superstition hold multitudes in tyranny, while dogmas and customs shackled countless millions. For years Sheikh Abdullah had borne the burdens of his people. He had opposition and persecution in unlimited measure. Whole of India looked to him for leadership and guidance, but demands on his time were unlimited, the load he carried had crushed the leadership.

Though the task was very hard, yet there was little worry or anxiety in his experience. Enmity and hostility long ago disappeared from his attitudes. His countenance shone with radiance and joy from which the desperate Indians plucked hope and courage. He was the symbol of United India in which his countrymen were free in the real sense of the word.

The pre-eminence of Sher-e-Kashmir's influence in Kashmir stood unquestioned. His name was a household word. He was the one towering figure in Kashmir. No other leader equalled him in political strength. He wielded an illimitable power over his followers who would sacrifice anything at his bidding. Sheikh Abdullah was the greatest of all Kashmiris in fact. In him we found embodied the hope of a new India in which there was no religious strife, but the peasantry was gleamed and Government was based on nationalism, not on communalism as in Pakistan.

The Great Task before Him

The Sheikh was clear about his principles and objectives and that's how he was always prepared for compromise even with his enemies. But he hated that person, that leader who would be made to slur over his principles and objectives by an external agency. According to his convictions to mislead was far worse than to offend. The task before Sheikh Abdullah that of making Kashmir really a 'Heaven on Earth', and that of leading India to its destined goal, seemed rather "impossible" to many, when they saw that communalism as preached by Jinnah was gaining grounds in India, that the trouble inevitable at the boarders of our country showed an ugly sign, that certain undermining forces were set at work by those of our enemies who did not want us to be free. But when we saw that the countries which encouraged fascism were seeing the worst of days, so, we became alive to that Great Hope of Great India, and we avowed with faith the leadership of those who proposed to take India a long way ahead so that it could lead the East in the years to come to the skies vaulted over the Indian soil.

Kashmiris said in one voice:

> "Let us, therefore come together, one and all, irrespective of caste, creed or colour, and after raising the slogan of Sheikh Abdullah - 'Hindu - Muslim Sikh-Ittihad, Zindabad' !"

Kashmiris believed that it was the inalienable right of the Indian people, as of any other people, to have freedom and to enjoy the fruits of their toil and have the necessities of life, so that they might have full opportunities of growth. They believed also that if any government deprived a people of these rights and oppressed them, the people had a further right to alter it or to abolish it. The British Government in India had not only deprived the Indian people of their freedom but had based itself on the exploitation of the masses and had thereby ruined India economically, politically, culturally, and spiritually, It was, therefore, that India had to sever the British connections and attain complete independence.

Situation before Freedom: India had been ruined economically. The revenue derived from our people was out of all proportion to our income. Our average income was seven pice (less than two pence) per day, and of the heavy taxes we paid 20 per cent were raised from the land revenue derived from the peasantry and 3 per cent from the salt tax, which fell most heavily on the poor. Village industries such as hand-spinning, had been destroyed, leaving the peasantry idle for at least for four months in a year, and dulling their intellect for want of handicrafts, and nothing had been substituted as in other countries, for the crafts thus destroyed. Customs and currency had been so manipulated as to heap further burdens on the peasantry. British manufactured goods constituted the bulk of imports. Customs duty betrayed clear partiality for British manufacturers, and revenue from them was used not to lessen the burden on the masses but for sustaining a highly extravagant administration. Still more arbitrary had been the manipulation of the exchanger ratio which had resulted in millions being drained away from the country.

Politically India's status had never been so reduced as under the British regime. No reforms had given real political power to the people. The tallest of them had to bend before a foreign authority. The rights of free expression of opinion and free association had been denied and many of the countrymen were compelled to live in exile abroad All administrative talent was killed, and the masses had to be satisfied with petty village post and clerical positions.

Culturally, the system of education had torn people from moorings and the training had made to hug the very chains that bound the people. Spiritually, compulsory disarmament had made people unmanly and the presence of an alien army, employed with deadly effect to crush the spirit of resistance had made people think that they cannot look for or put up a defence against foreign aggression, or even defend their homes and families from the attacks of thieves, robbers and miscreants.

People had, therefore, held it to be a crime against man and God to submit any longer to a rule that had caused this fourfold disaster to their country. People had also, however, recognised that the most effective way of gaining freedom was not through violence. They had prepared by withdrawing, so far as they could, voluntary dissociate from the British Government, and were prepared for disobedience, including non-payment of taxes. By this they were convinced of the end of this inhuman rule.

In a nationalist's words:

> "We have not been able to digest the pill of freedom. One of us stabbed the country in the back. He dissociated himself from forming a 'joint front' which would have proved formidable even for the ablest of British diplomats. We heard of the 'Statute of Westminister' 'the Simon Commission of 1930', 'Linlithgow offer of 1940' and last of all 'Cripps Mission of 1942' which evolved a scheme in which rights of non-accedence was given to the provinces. This laid

the basis of vivesection and dashed the hopes of United India. Thus the British taught their pawn the theory of 'Two Nations' which, after the division of India seems 'absurd' to Hindus and Muslims alike. Consequence of Pakistan is an wholesale destruction for the East Some time after even Mr. Jinnah, we shall see, will be dismayed since he would not stand the imminent internal rebellion of those who stand for 'liberty and fraternity' and the external howl of the freedom loving people of the world. To dignify a religious minority into a sort of divine nation and then to demand holy land (Pakistan) and a sovereign state indicate clearly the gradual growth of Fascism which dies hard". Moreover "the ugly happenings of the three months after the transfer of power have conclusively demonstrated that the Two Nation Theory is nothing but a dangerous doctrine conceived by Fascists and executed by gangsters. Religion can never form the basis of nationality; while, on the other hand, it has been stated in unequivocal terms from the national forum that the Indian Union would not be a sectarian or religious state. Naturally, then, when the passions have subsided, India's problems will be viewed in their proper perspectives by the people of India and the false doctrine of Two Nations in India will be discredited and discarded by all".

In a Kashmiri scholar's words:

"Today the Happy Valley is in distress, but the Kashmiris have routed their foes admirably. They have stood their ordeal heroically and superbly proved to the world that these are still the days of chivalry and patriotism. They have taken the pledge to shed their last drop of blood at the command of *Ghazi Abdullah* to save their land from anything bad. The whole Valley today is resounding with the cries."

The common slogan of the 'Home Guards', which they sing in tilting notes to rekindle inspiration even from the dead souls is:

> (We shall pour our own blood to save our land)
>
> "Let these slogans come like clarion calls to every Indian-Hindus Muslim, and Sikh alike, so that once in his time also he is roused and inspired to the performance of a desperate task, and proves to the world that Indian patriotism far more superior than that of the Romans and Greeks who have been but the followers of India in its ancient culture and civilization !"

Another Kashmiri nationalist scholar's view:

Along with it let us record our resolution of remembrance to those who have suffered for India, patriots known and unknown:

> "We the citizens of 'one India' record our proud and grateful appreciation of the sons and daughters of India who have taken part in the great struggle for independence and have suffered and sacrificed so that the mother land may be free; of our great and beloved leader, Mahatma Gandhi, who has been a constant inspiration for us, ever pointing to the path of high purpose and noble endeavour; of the hundreds of our brave youth who have laid down their lives at the altar of freedom; of the martyrs of Peshawar and the whole Frontier Province, Sholapur, Midnapur District, and Bombay, of the heroes of Netaji's National Army; of the scores of thousands who have faced and suffered barbarous lathi charges, gun bullets; of the men of the Garhwali Regiment, and all other Indians in the military and the police ranks of the British Government, who have refused, at the peril of their own lives, to fire or take other action against their own countrymen; of the indomitable peasantry of Gujarat which have faced without flinching and turning back all manner of acts of terrorism, and the brave and long-suffering peasantry of the other parts of India, which has taken full part in the struggle despite every effort to suppress it; of the worst victims

of the Punjab and Bengal, whose homes have been burnt, whose families have been wiped out of existence, whose properties made after years of endless toil have been looted; of the merchants and the other members of the commercial Community, who have helped, at great loss to themselves, in the national struggle; of the hundreds of thousands of men and women who have gone to prisons and suffered all manner of privation and sometimes assaults and beatings even inside the gaol walls; and especially of the ordinary volunteer who, like a true soldier of India, without care of fame or reward, thinking only of the great cause he served, has laboured unceasingly and peacefully through suffering and hardship.

"And we record our homage and deep admiration for the womanhood of India, who, in the hour of peril for the motherland, forsook the shelter of their homes and, with unfailing courage and endurance, stood shoulder to shoulder with their menfolk in the front line of India's national army, to share with them the sacrifices and triumphs of the struggle; and our pride at the youth of the country and the Vanar Sens, whom even their tender age could not prevent from participating in the struggle and offering marty's for the cause.

"And, further, we record our grateful appreciation of the fact that all the major and minor communities and classes in India have joined together in the great struggle and given of their best to the cause; of particularly the minority communities the Muslims, Sikhs, Parses, Christians and others, who, by their valour and loyal devotion to the cause of the common motherland, have helped and taken a vow to bear with us all the perils of building up united and indissoluble nation, certain of victory, and resolved to achieve and maintain the independence of India, and to use this new freedom to raise the shackles from, and to remove the inequalities among all classes of the people of India, and thus also to serve the larger cause of humanity. And with this splendid and inspiring example of sacrifice and suffering in India's cause before us, we repeat our Pledge of Independence, and resolve to carry on the fight till India is united again, and the soil is completely freed from the menaces of Pakistan.

"In the same breath are our spirit and enthusiasm roused by these lines which carry to the reader the call of the Motherland, direct us to the rightful course, let us all together say with one voice so loud that the alarm sweeps over the territory of Pakistan the common slogan of the Kashmiris."

"Interestingly, never in the history of the world was set up an empire on the name of 'Islam', Pakistan, the 'holy land', as we are expected to call it, whose one great motive- which is but an allusion to its dictators is to stream across Asia in successive waves of advance, and conquest, vanquishing, exterminating, overwhelming, overmastering, taking possession. I mea . the blinding vision of which the dictators of Pakistan have caught sight of ! What is more "humorous" about what we are seeing inside Pakistan, is that Mr. Jinnah even did not know what he was made to do and demand by Churchills etc.

"The case for Pakistan and the balkanisation of India, it would be worth while to note, was tossed up for the first time by British politicians-to whom we should pay a tribute for the painstaking research they have made into Indian political history, for the impartiality and justice towards all parties of thought and action to cure the political evils of India. The celebrated Indian poet Sir Mohammed Iqbal, a Kashmiri, had raised his voice for the liberty of every Muslim. We might as well say that he pleaded for regionalism, about which, Professor Coupland threw a brighter light later on. But it never meant Pakistan. India with her geographical situation, her population, and her resources was equally entitled to be a world power like America and Russia. Only the failure of democracy and the disunity among various communities could prevent India from this development. Indians claimed the social foundations of democracy which are akin to their tradition. In case democracy flourished and nationalism prevented disunity, no power on earth could have thought of obstructing India's path to Greatness.

"History, itself had decided that India shall be neither Hindu nor Muslim but Indian. Geography made for the political unity of India, and therefore a demand for the division of India was completely *"absurd"*. Division of India was, decidedly an attempt to prevent India from being a great world power.

"One great drawback, which stood in the way of nationalism in India, was, according to Sheikh Abdullah and others of his creed, the domination of social inequality in Indian society. The lack of cohesion between Hindus and Muslims was entirely due to the asceticism of caste Hindus. Gandhiji had, therefore, made untouchability the great problem of India. He had likewise prescribed the removal of untouchability as the recipe for freedom.

"Patriotic Muslim leaders like Badshah Khan (the Frontier Gandhi), Maulana Abul Kalam Azad, Asaf Ali, Sheikh Abdullah and others were impressed by the philosophy of Gandhiji that of ' one nation' and had dedicated their lives to the service of the common Motherland under the pride and prestige of tricolour national emblem of India.

"So came the Government of India Act of 1935. Congress was prepared to accept anything that would mean independence; but the Muslim League which was gradually taking the hold of Muslim masses by its creed of *"Religious protection"* denounced *"Federation"* and *"Democracy"*. Congress in order to take the British by surprise were prepared for all sorts of concessions and privileges to the Muslims, whose Voice then, as *'Dawn* wrote somewhere was Mohammed Ali Jinnah. What next surprised the nationalist Indians was the utterance of Jinnah in March 1941 at Aligarh Muslim University where he told the world, Democracy is impossible in India since there is not a single homogeneous nation and a single culturally and socially organised society". My friend, who represented a Congress-minded daily paper of India at the meeting told me that B.B.C. correspondents were, so to say, out with joy at the thesis of 'Two Nations' Theory as discovered by Jinnah at the Conference. This caused great despair in the heart of every Indian patriot.

"A few days after it was seen that Jinnah enjoyed the British journalistic support also. Moreover he had warned the Muslims of India against the 'permanent domination of a Hindu majority'. Before that in 1937 at its Lucknow Session, the Muslim League had denounced Federation which, as the memorandum of the League read, was a scheme detrimental to the interests of the people of India generally and to those of Muslims in particular'. Later in 1939 the Working Committee of the League had adumbrated its new constitutional theory that of dissociation from any compromise with the Congress.

"With the demand for Pakistan, Jinnah had won over much of support and favourable opinion in Muslim India. On his assurances and promises many educated Muslims also spoke in favour of Pakistan. The Press and the platform were commenting too much on 'Transfer of population'. 'Exchange of property' etc. Everybody talked about Pakistan in his own fashion, and every one was vague about his conceptions. Too much literature was published by the Congressites and Independents, and from the material so obtained Mr. Jinnah taught himself what he was made to demand.

"Congress, on the other hand, was firm with its conviction and followed its programmes with the same might. It wanted to give special and peculiar position to the Muslims of India in spite of the opposition that was raised by Hindu organisations. The Congress had, likewise hoped that the Muslims of India shall occupy an honourable place in the national life of India, Government and administration of the country so that both Hindus and Muslims could work for a free India with a free and independent nation, the Great Indian nation so that Indians could play an equal part with the comity of nations in bringing about an everlasting peace in the world.

"In the nationalism of Gandhiji, or say of the Congress, in the past as today, every community enjoys complete sense of security for its religious, political, cultural, social and economic rights and interests. It stands against all types of communal rule.

"Congress stands against the exploitation of the people of India and has time and again reiterated its pledge of free India. It is determinedly opposed to the vassalisation of Indians and is irrevocably opposed to any Constitution, any Government that undermines the masses. Indianism composed of various communities and the draft Constitution of the Indian National Congress plans for a national state of India.

"With a view to counterblasting the 'United India' demand of Indian National Congress, Jinnah formulated the theory of Two Nations at the Muslim League meeting of April 1940. He said, Such divergent nationalities as Hindus and Muslims could not be transformed into one nation by the artificiality of British parliamentary statutes. The two represented differences not merely of religion but of distinct social orders of peoples who neither intermarried nor interdined, who differed in philosophy, culture and literature, whose inspiration was drawn from different sources of history, whose epics and heroes were different and whose victories and defeats overlapped'.

"This caused commotion throughout India. This was also the greatest blow to the sincerity of the Congress idealism. Just the same time the Viceroy informed Jinnah that ' His Majesty's Government are not under any apprehension as to the importance of the contentment of the Muslim community to the stability and success of any constitutional developments in India'.

"The Muslim League Press, likewise, particularly the *Dawn,* now wrote columns of editorials, splashed banners, double columns, about ' Rule by Majority', ' Right of veto.' ' Communal Electorate.' ' Dyarchy ' The Congress, on the other hand, made many attempts for a mutual compromise-Gandhiji called on Jinnah many times, but these parleys resulted in nothing Jinnah wanted neither Federation, nor Provincial Self - Government, nor Responsible Government, nor Dyarchy at the Centre nor the Franchise, not even Separate Electorate. Some of India's ablest politicians and statesmen made it clear to Jinnah that Pakistan was a ' negative demand ' and that its consequences would be disastrous to Hindus and Muslims alike. They had anticipated the army of mad communal warfare which was, according to their predictions, inevitable after the division of India. One of his own lieutenants said that 'Quid-e-Azam's method was a devastating one'. But Jinnah could not be corrected. Even Maulana Azad suggested that the new Constitution should be built on the facts of Indian geography, history and life, but nothing came out of it.

"Congress which was a representative body of the Muslims also, had, after years of profound deliberation and planning pinned its faith on *Equal Democracy*. In a representative democracy there was the danger of class legislation on the part of numeral majority, which would inevitably result in Rule by Majority. But this danger was abated by an equal representation since the Government planned by the Congress was the Government of the whole people by the whole people, equally represented. The Minorities, particularly, had an equal representation with the Majority and what was most noteworthy of the 'Appeasement policy' of the Congress was that the Minorities had the priority of being heard first. Every or any section of people was represented. The Minorities were fully represented as the Majority. Congress Government even later, when Jinnah wanted it to be called a Hindu State, was not the Government of inequality and privilege, but it is what the whole world calls it, an 'equal Government'. Indian Government, apart from all other features, is based on the principle of democracy, which professes equality as its very root and foundation. In it every individual enjoys fair and equal share. It is, thus, what *Sheikh Abdullah* calls it, ' Peoples' Government.

"This argument would be somewhat confusing to that *League* friend of mine who once said that the task before *Sheikh Abdullah* is an "impossible one. He would, here, again comment, ' Even, then it is the Minority that would suffer since the democracy so constituted would give powers of Government in all cases to the numerical Majority'. But I would like to illumine the mind of my friend with an argument that tells everything about 'equal democracy' The argument is, 'it does something very different, it gives powers of the Government to a *Majority of the Majority*, who may be, and often are, but a *Minority* of the whole'.

"Congress quarters time and again invited Jinnah for a constitutional compromise for solving the Indian political problem. It had, also, with equal sincerity offered an *equal* representation in all spheres. Muslim leaders inside the Congress were fully convinced of the sincerity with which the Indian statesmen were trying to evolve a constitutional scheme. Gandhiji, Pandit Nehru and other high rank leaders called on Jinnah with a view to getting his friendly support to the cause of the common people. They failed in all their attempts. After that Maulana Abul Kalam Azad was sent to Jinnah. It was thought that the Maulana being a Muslim himself would be able to make Jinnah understand what really was truth in what the Congress proposed. Jinnah did not have any political talk with Azad perhaps because Maulana knew better about the cause of Muslims being a great statesman and a religious scholar.

"In 1942 Japan made a violent eruption in East Asia. United States of America's fleet was withdrawn to the American coast, "Prince of Wales" and "Repulse" were sunk. Singapore had surrendered, and the circumstances with which the British were confronted left them no ' assured means' of defending India from the invasion by the Japanese. And the Cripps Offer was made to India. Congress could have as well given no head to the tactics of the British diplomats. Glorious opportunity awaited the people of India. Netaji was marching towards 'Delhi' with his National Army. Calcutta was bombarded everyday. India's sons were bathing in blood for the sake of their motherland on Burma front. Indian soldiers had joined the National Army of Netaji. Even after Indian soldiers were removed from the Burma front and Yankees were posted there, the onward march of Netaji's soldiers could not be checked. Netaji was marching towards Delhi with unabated pace.

"Where would have been Jinnah or his Pakistan had Congress, then, not sacrificed everything for its faith on nationalism? Atom bomb was dropped on Hiroshima, and it could never be dropped on India. Had the Congress then changed its policy, map of India would have been certainly different today.

"Well, then we had the Interim Government headed by Pandit Nehru. Again came Jinnah's turn. The League boycotted it and Mr. Jinnah raised his voice for the haphazard fragmentation of India.

"Next there was the ' Direct Action' declaration of the League which devastated large part of Bengal, and was the cause of riots, stabbings, arson, loot in many other parts of India Only the Punjab had been safe from this bloody spectre.

"Later came the proposal for the division of India to which, much to the surprise of Hindus and Sikhs of the Punjab, Pandit Jawaharlal Nehru consented The Punjab and Bengal were divided. Pakistan was made, and what were the consequences of Pakistan are known even to the playing children — so horrible have been the happenings.

"Jinnah was made Quid-e-Azam by the Muslims of India who constituted nine crores of India's huge population of forty crores, then. Some Muslims of India, who were very eager about Pakistan, had thought that Pakistan would bestow bliss upon their lives, that all of a sudden it would transform their lives and credit them with concessions and privileges so that they along with their families would be the happiest.

"Well, then India was divided into two dominions of India and Pakistan. Jinnah and his Cabinet Ministers, it would be worth while to note, called India not India but Hindustan. But India is India even after the division since its policy remains unchanged. It professes to be, not what Jinnah wanted it to be - a Hindu State-but a national state of all the people of India since its Constitution is a democracy of the whole people. There live crores of Muslims in different parts of India. They include men of all trades, peasants, factory workers, office clerks, business men, technicians, landlords estate holders, etc. That leaves only few crores of Muslims in Pakistan. How then is Pakistan a Muslim State if greater number of Muslims live under a Government, which according to Jinnah is not a State of the Muslims but a Hindu State? No one can call Pakistan a Muslim State when a majority of Muslim population lives and proposes to live in future also outside Pakistan. It was in fact Jinnah's State."

"Let us suppose that at the instance of Jinnah, India could become Hindustan, a Hindu State just as Pakistan is a Muslim State. It inevitably means that the National Government of India shall break, Jawahar and Gandhi shall vacate, and the Hindu Mahasabha shall form the Government and come to the forefront. Hindus have been almost vacated from West Punjab. The attitude of the Pakistan Government towards the minorities in Sindh and other parts has forced them to vacate to Hindustan. More or less Pakistan is free from Hindus and Sikhs, even Christians and Anglo-Indians also. Since its establishment it has been the policy of the Pakistan Government to coerce the minorities by disbanding them from services and blocking their commercial prospects so that they are forced to leave the soil of Pakistan More of it we are reading in papers everyday.

"India Government had to face great problems of the rehabilitation of the refugees. They had done with it with great ability and statesmanship. Evacuees from Pakistan are gradually settling down in India Whole of the North Western Frontier Province has been vacated by the Hindus and Sikhs. India Government had to spend huge sums in evacuating the minorities from there. Cooked chappatis everyday were sent by air to Kohat and other places where the poor refugees were stranded and held in breath by the citizens of Pakistan whose guns and sabres were ever pointed towards the heads of the innocent women and children of these refugees.

"This was happening in Pakistan, while on the other hand Muslim refugees in East Punjab and Delhi were protected and fed by the Government of India. Gandhiji himself visited the Muslim refugee camps in Delhi. Government made arrangements for the transport and helped the refugees to reach their places. In Delhi itself stern measures were adopted to check all communal outbreak so that in less than a week Delhi was set right again.

"Did Pakistan Government do anything like that to save the minorities? I remember one of the officials of Pakistan justifying his argument that the Government itself, being new, had failed to control the religious zeal of the citizens of Pakistan who were out with joy on the achievement of Pakistan. Well sir, if that is what is happening in Pakistan, it has no right to call itself a Government? I have been taught by great writers on politics and administration that a Government which fails to maintain law and order is not worth being a Government and must at once be broken ere it brings ruin to people's life and property.

"Are there any such accusations against the India Government - let me ask my *Pakistani* friend? The responsibility of the happenings in East Punjab also vests with those who demanded the division of India, though part of it is also due to the retaliation of the Hindus and Sikhs of the Punjab whose labour and love of years was molten into dust in a seconds time. For the rest is perfect peace in all other parts of India. People Hindus and Muslim alike have resumed there duties of their life and life is returning to normal again. The credit of all this goes to India Government and those ablest of Indians who are shouldering the responsibilities purely in a spirit of rendering service to the peoples of India.

"Muslims of India hear from their friends and relations about what is happening in Pakistan. They have seen what happened to those miserable refugees who had to be moved from place to place, who have lost their precious comrades, darling children, their property and social status in the so-called transfer of population. Nobody howsoever fanatic he may be, shall like to lose the warmth of Home for his fanaticism which might make as it has done in many cases, the public road his home! Such has been the fate of many people who were nicely settled and socially reputed before the transfer of power. The horror of the sense has alarmed everyone and today almost five crores of Muslims oppose Pakistan and plead for United India. In case India is declared a Hindu State, there naturally should be no place in Hindustan for the Muslims for then Hindustan shall have to accommodate crores of Hindus. Therefore the Muslims shall have to vacate and go to Pakistan, because in a Hindu State Muslims have no right to live. Imagine now how the Muslim brothers of Jinnah would be stranded in Hindustan and what a colossal task it would be for Pakistan to accommodate so many crores of human beings. Idealism of Mahatma Gandhi shall not impress the Hindus then nor shall the sincerity of Pandit Nehru have any effect in the nation building of Hindustan. Hindu India shall become alive to fanaticism since, as Jinnah wanted it, it shall be a communal rule everywhere.

"It shall not, in any way, be a task which human agency can perform History, our culture and civilization have settled the Hindus and Muslims of India on this land.

It has been the natural process of the centuries which brought us closer and together. We have had the experiences of the transfer of population in the Punjab and we have seen what wholesale destruction it has caused, and we would have ourselves seen that this process is not repeated.

"Rehabilitation of people is not an easier task. Different sentiments work in different ways in different people. Today hark to the cursings of those hearts of the refugees whose bungalows have become the roads, who are living in refugee camps, whose newborn babies die dog's death in these unhygienic places, whose lacks are nowhere and who are wandering from place to place in search of jobs, and accommodation! Do they curse Gandhiji who brought back soul to their hearts? Do they curse Pandit Nehru who is sharing their woes in his heart of hearts ? Or do they—the countless miserables-curse Jinnah who has brought about the blight and is still looking forward to an all out destruction? Really this tale of woe is heart renting!

"Praised be the leadership of Sheikh Abdullah that he has maintained even to this day the Communal concord in whole of the Jammu and Kashmir State. His message to each and every worker of the National Conference is that he (the worker) shall maintain communal concord and stake his own life also for Hindu-Muslim-Sikh unity. This is also his message to the States' People. Unity is the very foundation of nationalism, says Sheikh Abdullah "It is the definition of freedom and the very secret of progress. If we want to see India happy, we must maintain it at all costs".

"Sheikh Abdullah's politics has strengthened Mahatma Gandhi and Pandit Nehru's creed of nationalism. In him they see the great leader of the Muslims of India and Pakistan. He shall be the voice of Muslims in India. India Government shall time and again seek his support and cooperation regarding all the problems concerning the Muslim community of India. He is the one great Muslim who can represent Muslims better than Mr. Jinnah did, and, therefore he is, in the true sense of the word, Quid-e-Azam of Muslims.

"Today everyone in Pakistan and many other Muslims outside Pakistan, because of their religious zeal, feel differently about Pakistan and look with prejudiced eyes at those Muslims who oppose or criticise the politics of Jinnah. But this fervour would be soon over when people would realise that Pakistan is a Government only and not a religious institution where everyone could.

"Government" and *"freedom"* are meaningless for individuals unless they give them better opportunities for growth and provides those means with which the people can feed themselves better than what was their due when they were slaves. A Government that fails to achieve this for its people is not spared by a peoples' rebellion like the one that finished the Czar in Russia and challenged the monarchy of France in that crusade for liberty and equality. 'Bayonets cannot enforce loyalty'. When passions are roused fate of nations is not decided by dictator's convictions. Blimps can no longer rule destinies of human beings. A voice has come from the inner depths of the Himalayas to the people of India, 'Wake up your destiny awaits you now. You have to decide your future yourself.' Popular movements cannot be crushed by misinterpretation of religion. India has been given to her people. It is they that shall decide its future. How long can Jinnah hold the freedom loving people of India in shackles of religious bondage ? One day a revolution will come before which the greatest cannons shall not stand. That is in fact the fate of Governments which are not national—peoples' Governments.

"Sheikh Abdullah of Kashmir, heretofore, believes that National Government is the thing that is wanted in India. He is not in favour of the transfer of population, which would cause collapse of the machinery of administration and leave the home of forty crores of human beings in utter chaos.

"If ever a nation had to despair of life, it was India in 1947 Every hope on which Indian nation was built lay prostrate. Riots occurred pitilessly day after day. Cities were burning and through this, with no protection, men, children, delicate women, strove to hurry, always with the dread of rioters at their heels. Mothers unable to nourish or carry their infants took out the breath from them rather than abandon them to die with the butchering swords of the rioters. ? I have heard the unknown patriot at the last moment of his life saying 'My last wishes are for my country's welfare. Please ask the leaders to end party strife and consolidate the Union.'

"Freedom of the Motherland was the one consuming passion of every Indian. No body wanted to see the horror of man slaughter. Hindus and Sikhs are also to be equally blamed for this. This was not their mistake. It was the blunder of those who demanded division of India. The dominions that have been founded will go down in history in respect of their merit, and in between the names of the martyrs will ever and rightly be held in honour.

"The India that Sheikh Abdullah saw with his youthful imagination was India of the Indians, a great nation. And Kashmir was the symbol of one United India. It is the India of all the communities—Hindus, Muslims, Sikhs alike. And this great patriot has not the least illusion about the almost desperate chance of saving India from further destruction and of Uniting India and Pakistan into one great National Government somewhat like the one that is functioning in Russia today.

"Every Muslim is not a Nawab or a Zamindar. There are millions of Muslims who, like the Hindus, are poor, illiterate, ignorant and backward, who have been dwarfed by the centuries of servitude, and whose lives call for amelioration. If Jinnah is for Pakistan, who is their leader?. Is not Sheikh Abdullah their guide, their Quid-e-Azam?

"He has his shoulders to the performance of huge duties in Kashmir, tomorrow a bigger responsibility that of championing the cause of the five crores of Muslims awaits him, and he has to perform all these duties, and lead the erring people through the darkest caverns within which they are held up today.

"The idea that India will be a Hindu State and that Muslims shall have to vacate is a "fantastic" one. India cannot remain divided for long. One day it shall be reunited again, and that day shall be the day of Sheikh Abdullah.

"India has become free but the one great end is still undermined. Together again two great Kashmiris Sheikh Abdullah and Pandit Jawaharlal Nehru have now set themselves to determine the undetermined end. They represent the symbol of unity and brotherhood and give a great promise of India. The two represent the two major communities of India. None of the British games can influence them, no Jinnahs can weaken their cause, because their cause is a holy one.

"This, naturally would be headache for Jinnah. He had hoped that his ways of undermining the Muslim masses would not be exposed and that he would be successful in defeating Mahatma Gandhi and Pandit Nehru by preaching a new theory which was nothing more than "baseless".

"Time is fast approaching when our people would realise their mistakes and correct themselves. Congress idealism will flourish again. There would be no Nawabzadas nor Jinnah's but Jawahars and Abdullahs would be the sentinels of India."

6

Builder of New Kashmir

The First Spark

The 13th of July 1931 (21 Kashmiri's lost their lives in the police firing) an incident about which historians say "the dumb driven cattle raised the standard of revolt; the people were never to be cowed down again by punitive police action". This event saw the metamorphosis of Sheikh Abdullah from a teacher (member of the reading room association) to a rebel! The 13th of July 1931 proved to be the precursor to the political awakening that led to the formation of Muslim conference in 1932.

Path to Secularism

Was he a statesman? "In 1938 the Muslim Conference after considerable internal debate, decided to redefine the basis of its politics. Primarily at the behest of the Abdullah group, which included a handful of progressive Pandits and Sikhs, the party declared its intent to end communalism by ceasing to think in terms of Muslims and Non-Muslims and invited all Hindus and Sikhs who believed in the freedom of their country from the shackles of the irresponsible rule and wanted to participate in the popular struggle" writes Sumantra Bose,' Kashmir Roots of Conflict, Paths to Peace'. Would he be considered as a political convert? When the political reasoning in the subcontinent was based upon religion and ethnicity, it was Sheikh Abdullah who led his people to fight against their coreligious tribal from Pakistan! It was he who was able to provide popular sanctity to the instrument of accession made by the Dogra ruler. It was only in Kashmir that Mahatma Gandhi was to see a ray of light when whole of the subcontinent was burning in the communal violence.

Not Communal At All

Was he a communalist then? He was accused of religious bias for bringing an end to the Jagirdari system, by giving the rights of the land to the tiller. "Although a religious man, he was not communal and initially his progressive socialism was welcomed by both Hindus and Muslims. He appealed directly to the poor people and consequently was disliked by the upper classes of both communities. The supporters of the Muslim conference who represented the interest of those Muslims favouring accession to Pakistan, his secular stance amounted to betrayal of the Muslim community. To the Hindu aristocrats, who were the inevitable victims of his sweeping land reforms his socialist politics had communist and communal overtones favouring Muslims," writes Victoria Schofield, Kashmir in the Crossfire.

True Patriot

Was he a separatist aspiring to be the Sultan of Kashmir? Why did he then join India at the first place? Perhaps he was looking for a space within the Indian federation; that would preserve the Muslim majority character of Kashmir in a secular India. He pointed this out in his speech at the first session of the Jammu and Kashmir constituent assembly on 5th of November 1951, "After centuries, we have reached the harbour of our freedom. Once again in the history of the state, our people have reached a peak of achievement through what I might call the classical genius for synthesis, born of toleration and mutual respect. The Indian Constitution has set before the country the goals of a secular democracy based upon justice, freedom and modern democracy". But his secular ideals proved to be a mirage in the backdrop of the communalisation of politics in the Jammu and

Laddakh regions "The confidence created by the National Conference in the people here (regarding accession to India) has been shaken by the Jana sangh and other communal organisations in India". (While addressing a National conference gathering on 25 July, 1953).

The Tragedy

On 9th of August 1953, Sheikh Mohammed Abdullah, the first elected Prime Minister of Jammu and Kashmir was dismissed and detained on the charge that he was about to secede from the union. What happened in 1953 is history, but how and why the situation came to such an impasse, different narratives are in circulation, but about the consequences of the incident, obviously they were far-reaching. His understanding of Kashmir was as a quasi independent entity within the Indian federal structure. And for India it was a beginning of a process to fully integrate Jammu and Kashmir in the Union of India.

Special Status

Though Sheikh had reached an agreement with New Delhi called Delhi agreement in July 1952 that confirmed the special status of Jammu and Kashmir within the Indian union under the article 370 of Indian Constitution, New Delhi had its own ideas. N. Gopalaswami Ayyangar, (who moved the article in India's Constituent Assembly in October 1949) proposed a special status for Kashmir because of its special circumstances. "The State is not in a position to merge with India. We all hope that in future the State of Jammu and Kashmir will get over the hurdles and completely merge with the union, like the rest of the states". What perplexes one further is Nehru's comment about the article 370 quoted by Balraj Puri in his book, 'Kashmir towards insurgency'.

In fact, it was Nehru himself who had expressed the hope that the article would be gradually eroded (Ghiste ghiste ghis jaegi). The space Sheikh was looking for was simply not there in New Delhi's scheme of nation building. Had it been so, the whole concept of autonomy and special status could not have been diluted over the years when Sheikh Abdullah was forcibly removed from the Kashmir's political scene.

Also adding to it was Indira Gandhi's comments in the year 1975 in the response to Sheikh Aubdullah's demand for the restoration of the special status that "clock can not be turned back". One is prepared to see the reason in the complexities of nation building and requirements of a strong centre in India especially in the backdrop of bitter partition But what profoundly affects ones' sensibilities and confidence in the state, is the manner in which this task is undertaken. The problem today is not simply what happened in the past that can be overlooked but what is happening at present. The establishment has not learnt lessons from the past. Process of nation building can not be devoid of peace making with the people. Any process that overtooks this fundamental issue casts a deep shadow on the relationship between people and the State.

The Kashmir Issue

Sheikh Muhammed Abdullah, was quite old and had been for years, the most important figure in Kashmiri politics. He had spent many years in prison and was released from his longest stretch, in detention. In his first moments of freedom, the Sheikh was quick to exhibit the outspokenness and the sense of love for Kashmir, which had been his trademarks. These qualities were the basis of his popular support and the main ingredients of his now legendary role as the Lion of Kashmir also accounted in large measure for his long incarcerations. The major between India and Pakistan over possession of Kashmir and the magnitude of this Issue in Indian politics would be greatly influenced by the role Abdullah played now.

Difficult Situation

Sheikh Abdullah had first come into the limelight internationally when there was a conflict over Kashmir between the newly independent dominions of India and Pakistan. They broke into fighting and then was taken to the UN Security Council. The withdrawal of the British and subsequent splitting of the subcontinent along Hindu-Muslim communal lines faced the Hindu Maharaja of predominantly Muslim Kashmir with the decision whether to accede to India or Pakistan or to take another course. In keeping with Kashmiri separateness, the Maharaja chose to remain aloof from both India and Pakistan. Within two months, Kashmir was invaded by Pakistan and the ruler sent Sheikh Abdullah to New Delhi for Indian help. The Maharaja's accession to India quickly thereafter, and Abdullah being made Prime Minister of largely autonomous Kashmir in India. India, in keeping with its claims to secularism, made use of Abdullah's role. The Sheikh had led his Muslim majority state into the union and that was for the blunt denial of the very basis on which Pakistan had been achieved. Pakistan's basis was the theory that South Asia's Hindus and Muslims formed "separate nations".

Nehru's Secularism at Work

There can be no doubt that Nehru's secularism appealed to Abdullah. They had long been friends and had cooperated closely during Nehru's long struggle against the British. Abdullah had never hit it off well with Muhammed Ali Jinnah, the prime mover behind the creation of Pakistan. Very early Abdullah had secularised his political organisation by admitting Hindus and Sikhs to its membership and by deleting the word "Muslim" from the title. Allegedly, Abdullah was also initially moved strongly by Kashmir's feeling of separateness. Conversations with him with his wife and some close associates revealed that he then favoured some option in which the state would go its own way. He seemed to have agreed to accession on the strength of his regard for Nehru and his fear that otherwise the state would be overrun by Pakistan.

During his early years as Prime Minister, of the State the Sheikh accepted the accession and formally agreed with Nehru that Kashmir's foreign affairs and its defence, should be in Indian hands. His friends said, he did not give up the idea of an autonomous role for Kashmir altogether, but that rather, he felt these had to be submerged out of gratitude to India for its military and economic support.

Beginning of a Sad Story

In times, as Nehru continued to build up a centralised federal structure in New Delhi, Abdullah found himself questioning New

Delhi's policies privately, and then publicly. He began speaking out on the need for a measure of autonomy in the state, and his enemies accusing him of advocating Independence. All of this amid considerable public disorder in the state, Abdullah was dismissed from the prime ministership and subsequently jailed on charges of "disruptionalism, nepotism, and establishing foreign contacts, dangerous to the prosperity of the State. He was replaced by his former deputy Bakshi Ghulam Muhammed who, although weak at the time, gave every evidence of being willing to cooperate with New Delhi.

The suspicion of foreign contacts was directed mainly at Pakistan, but also at the United States which, in the heyday of anti-American feeling in India, was portrayed as encouraging Abdullah in his scheme for an autonomous Kashmir which would then provide a base for it. That overtones of this persistence in the left wing of politics could be noted in a speech by the vocal former defence minister, Krishna Menon, who had said that Kashmir would be "an American Kashmir". Abdullah was released from prison but his outspoken talks fell him out from the authorities. He was jailed again within four months and formally charged for a conspiracy aimed at bringing Kashmir into Pakistan. He was still on trial on this charge until the day he was released again.

Why then, with this fairly consistent record of espousing policies not acceptable to New Delhi, did the Indian government sanction Abdullah's release? The answer was not simple nor was the evidence firm.

Discontent among People

Kashmir had in effect been rudderless for some time, when Nehru forced Abdullah's successor, Bakshi, to step down as part of the sweeping proposal then current to rejuvenate the Congress Party by bringing high-powered Chief Ministers into full-time party work in actuality, the inclusion of Bakshi was to an admission by Nehru that Bakshi's value in Kashmir's integration into India and in keeping the lid on continuing Kashmiri discontent with Indian rule had depreciated relatively to the mounting burden of his corruption, his venality, and his police state methods. There appeared to be some moves, however vague, to improving New

Delhi's image both in Kashmir and abroad by introducing a measure of good will into the New Delhi Kashmir relationship. This appears to have a miscalculation based on a faulty reading of the extent to which Kashmiris had accepted their lot in the Indian union. Bakshi contributed to the confusion by Nehru into accepting a Bakshi puppet who proved unequal to the job. The theft of the much-revered Muslim relic, the popular association of the Bakshi family with the crime, and the anti-Bakshi, anti-government, and internally anti-Indian disturbances served thoroughly to discredit both Bakshi and his puppet. The clamour over the relic, with its communal overtones resulted in Hindu-Muslim violence in (the then) East Pakistan and northeastern India.

On the scene, Pakistan raised the dispute over Kashmir in the UN Security Council and stepped up military pressure along the UN-supervised ceasefire line in Kashmir itself. And, in New Delhi, Jawaharlal Nehru, the architect of India's policy on Kashmir, fell ill; Lal Bahadur Shastri returned to the Cabinet in the role of a heir and began grappling with the Kashmir problem.

With Nehru's approval, Shastri effected the retirement of Bakshi's puppet and put Ghulam Muhammed Sadiq, Nehru's original choice, a prominent politician with long-standing leftist connections, in the driver's seat in Kashmir. Liberalisation measures followed, but not fast enough for the Kashmiris, who had been whetted by the ousting of the Bakshi regime and were not satisfied with Sadiq.

Sheikh, Still Popular

Sentiment began to move towards some gesture in favour of still-imprisoned Abdullah, whose followers had covered themselves with glory during the relic crisis and whose popularity, even after and perhaps because of his long imprisonment, was undented. Sadiq appeared to have seen in the release of Abdullah as an opportunity, which he might be able to play off the remnants of the Bakshi regime against the Abdullah to his own benefit. Bakshi, however, moved to support Abdullah's release, apparently in an effort to capitalise on his popularly and was serious enough to force New Delhi to turn again to his own strong arm.

Return of Sheikh

In New Delhi, Shastri concluded that Sadiq could not last long in the given circumstances and that events in Kashmir were moving towards an explosion which would expose the use of New Delhi's representatives to dominate the state. Despite strong pressure from both the right and the left for maintenance of a line on Kashmir, Shastri seemed to have decided that Abdullah might hold the key to easing the problem.

The hope of Shastri and other moderates in New Delhi was that even if the Sheikh's views had not mellowed in his remarks subsequent to his release, did suggest they have might at least sense the changing situation in India and act reasonably to calm the situation in Kashmir just as his followers had done during the relic crisis.

In persuading Nehru to agree to Abdullah's release, Shastri appeared to have believed that an explosion could just as easily take place with Abdullah in prison as without, but that his release, however risky was a possible way out. If successful, the gamble could pay off in the Kashmir situation improving. New Delhi would in most respects be no worse off than it would have been if the chance had not been taken.

Sheikh Abdullah's actions since his release suggested that he knew he had the strongest hand he had ever had in dealing with New Delhi, but he was not yet ready to play it out. His initial remarks were that his basic views had not changed. He was not to believe the Kashmir question was over, but India's public position was that the accession was final and irrevocable. Abdullah thought that Kashmir settlement must be reached by means of taking account of all parties' interests — those of the Kashmiris.

Although, much was thus to depend on Abdullah to keep his pressure on New Delhi within bounds. New Delhi had a ready hand and the courage to play the game out. Even then, the buildup of pressures on both sides might badly restrict their room for manoeuvre. Kashmir was the "sacred cow" of Indian politics. There was a furor that India was weakening its line on Kashmir. Abdullah's release had promoted such a furor, and the leading characters like Shastri, were under attack. Sheikh Abdullah seemed intent on saying only enough to secure his political base in Kashmir and to test Indian intentions without actually pushing New Delhi far enough at that time to warrant his rearrest.

He had deferred public discussion of specific matters until he met Nehru in New Delhi and had sharply silenced those who were attempting to promote a new rift between him and Nehru, his "dearest comrade and colleague". A press report had already suggested that Nehru might be having second thoughts and that he had privately criticised Shastri for the "mess". At the same time, Nehru's public remarks had been quite mild, perhaps in the form of a letter of reassurance from Abdullah.

Nehru had publicly described the Sheikh's initial remarks as "unfortunate" but had also alluded to the press exaggeration. Nonetheless, Nehru had shown himself capable of taking even unpleasant decisions regarding the Sheikh, and he was also noted in the best offer his lack of follow-through on risky projects once the clamour reached a certain level. If the gamble was to pay off he would probably have to go beyond merely the Sheikh's remarks and avoiding his reimprisonment.

He and his government would have to come forward with enough flexibility in their policies towards Kashmir to meet Abdullah's as yet unspecified minimum requirements and to persuade the Sheikh that he had good reason to stay out of the comfortable confinement he had just left. The possibility of a new approach to the Kashmir problem was to rest on the success these leaders could have in working out a new relationship between New Delhi and the Kashmir State.

Mixed Reactions

History does not forgive anybody; today we find the 'tallest leader' of Kashmir in the witness box. Shall Kashmiris punish him for going against the tide in 1947 and 1975? Or, shall they hail him for showing exemplary courage at times? Years after his death, Sheikh Muhammed Abdullah continues to dominate the political discourse in Jammu Kashmir. He is widely discussed and ridiculed as well. Some hold the 'tragic hero' in high esteem and some accuse the 'saviour' of betrayal. For some he continues to be an inspiration but for some he was a 'chicken hearted' and 'myopic' leader who 'brought misfortune to the people who loved him. As they say history does not forgive anybody; today we find the 'tallest leader' of Kashmir in the witness box. Shall Kashmiris punish him for going against the tide in 1947 and 1975? Or, shall they hail him for showing exemplary courage at times? It becomes necessary to study; nay rediscover Sheikh Muhammed Abdullah with a nascent mind to have a better understanding of Kashmir history. It is widely believed that Sher-e-Kashmir was ditched by government of India in 1953. This chapter of his life has been widely discussed by people across the globe.

It still remains grossly misunderstood. He is accused of having a truck with government of Pakistan. Some believe that Sheikh resisted New Delhi's onslaught aimed at diluting the special status of Jammu Kashmir. The exact reasons for the August 9 episode were divulged by former member of constituent assembly, Abdul Gani Goni. He was a staunch supporter of Sheikh Muhammed Abdullah. In his address to the constituent assembly he not only opposed the move for ratification of accession but also sought right to secession. He vehemently sought Sheikh Abdullah's release. However, he later joined Bakshi's bandwagon and became a minister. During 2008 June uprising, he gave the inside story of the August 9 episode in an exclusive interview with a journalist. He said: "During those days, Sheikh Muhammed Abdullah was at his best despite facing severe opposition from his colleagues including Bakshi". It was during these days that Sheikh Muhammed Abdullah roared and also behaved like a lion for the first and last time in his political career.

The Betrayal

Sher-e-Kashmir was fully aware of the activities of his colleagues. He knew his government was in danger. He was also aware of Bakshi's game. A shrewd Bakshi, however, assured him of his loyalty. While addressing a public gathering he said: "A Muslim has to believe necessarily in five fundamentals of faith. These are: Oneness of *Allah* the almighty, *Salaat,* Fasting, *Zakat* and *Hajj*. I, however, believe in six fundamentals. Besides *Salaat, Zakaat* and *Hajj* I also believe in the leadership of Sher-e-Kashmir

Sheikh Muhammed Abdullah". This speech silenced one and all including Sher-e-Kashmir. But behind the curtain he continued his preparations for the coup.

Goni, while giving details said: "By 1948 Sheikh Sahib had realised his mistake of supporting state's accession with India. He had started dreaming of an independent state and expressed it without any reservations. Jawaharlal Nehru visited Kashmir immediately after Maulana Azad got humiliated at Hazrat Bal shrine. Sheikh delivered a fiery speech against India. Azad also wanted to address the people but the Sheikh did not allow him. Nehru was accompanied by his sister and the then home minister of India Mr. Katju. Sheikh told Nehru that he wanted to change his relationship with India. He forcefully put forth his views during a meeting of the National Conference working committee. He also made a mention of an autonomous Kashmir. Nehru, his sister and Katju watched the proceedings with keen interest. The meeting lasted three days. Nehru's sister and the then Home Minister watched the developments keenly".

"A shocked Nehru, however, reacted politely. A park has been named after me in Srinagar. I was under the impression that people from India would come here to enjoy themselves and strengthen the relationship that exists now".

This incident has been narrated by Goni in his autobiography *Sada-e-Bazgusht*. "Nobody expected Nehru to arrest and dethrone Sheikh Sahib. Soon after the working committee meeting I went to Doda. In Doda I heard about the arrival of a Union Minister Shri Mahavir Tyagi in Srinagar. He was very close to Bakshi. And what happened is history".

The roar that created a stir in the entire subcontinent did no good to Sheikh Muhammed Abdullah and Kashmir. The caged lion fell from grace slowly but surely. Goni unveiled another side of Sheikh's personality. Goni was the speaker of legislative assembly in 1975. One day he was informed about Sheikh Sahib's arrival in the assembly complex. Goni narrated the incident:

> "I greeted Sheikh Sahib. He was dejected. He said, `Show me my room.' I informed him no room in the complex was meant for him. I further informed him

that only Chief Minister can have a room in the assembly complex. I was surprised by his answer. `I want to see that very room.' I was pained to see the lion of Kashmir in such a state of mind. Before leaving the assembly complex, Sheikh Sahib said, 'I have offered enough sacrifices. I cannot offer more.' I shook hands with him and watched him leave the complex amid shock and utter disbelief".

Goni revealed vital details about the constituent assembly members and their stand viz-a-viz accession of Jammu Kashmir to Indian union. "Please do not make these details public during my life time. Further some of the members are still alive. I do not want to embarrass them", he had requested.

The roaring lion had to be caged and that is exactly what happened. Nehru planned to tame the lion. On August 9, 1953 he was dethroned and arrested. The roar created a stir in the subcontinent but did no good to Sher-e-Kashmir and his Kashmir. Surprisingly Sher-e-Kashmir has not made a mention of his only roar in his *Aatish-e-Chinar*. He has not mentioned about the working committee meeting as well, for unknown reasons.

7

Sheikh's Historic Role in Kashmir

The affairs of Jammu and Kashmir can not be seen in isolation to the role of National Conference. Sheikh Mohammed Abdullah emerged on the scene in 1930s. He was an educated Kashmiri youth who took prime interest in the socio-economic conditions of the masses of the Kashmir valley.

The Backdrop

The people in the valley were poor, simple and very less exposed to the outside world. Most of the local people worked in the fields, attended to the visitors or tourist and survived on the local handicraft or fruit industry. Those who could not afford the cost of cold winters and had not much labour job available indoors used to manage some means to go for labour outside valley in the plains. Some Kashmiri pandits who were not in government or other service jobs too left the valley during winters. Some of them visited their coreligionists even in other states and collected some resources against the blessings they extended as priests. Majority in the Valley remained indoor during winter. Very few people left the Valley for business, service or touring during the summer months. A few who left the Valley for reasons other than Government service were from the rich segment and some of those who took to handicraft trade.

The Kashmiri Hindu (Pandit) remained engaged more in education or government service. Pandits could also raise some wealth and influence. So, Pandits could secure more role in decision-making and economic affairs of the J&K. No doubt the Kashmiri pandits formed the bulk of the Hindu in Kashmir Valley in 1930s. Good number of them also succeeded to actively participate in the socio-economic and administrative affairs of Kashmir Valley, including decision-making. Some Kashmiri pandits also took part in the protests against the Maharaja directly or indirectly.

Initial Activities

Majority of the population (over 90%) in Kashmir Valley was that of Muslims. Hence Sheikh Abdullah and his associates who were working particularly for the welfare of the Muslims could secure support quite early. They later shaped themselves as Muslim Conference and started raising questions on the trueness of the rule of Maharaja Hari Singh. Membership of Muslim Conference was open to Muslims only. Since majority of the Kashmiri Muslims were not that much engaged in acquiring education it was easy for Sheikh to influence them. Muslim Conference argued that very few Kashmiri Muslims were in the services of the Maharaja government and hence a larger number of the poor and unemployed were from among the Muslims. Sheikh´s Muslim Conference did gather reasonable support in the Valley.

Valley was far away from Jammu by standards of normal means of road transport in 1930s and most of the trade was through Jhelum Valley road Punjab via Muzaffarabad. The most of the rich and those from services or government found interest in visiting only Kashmir valley for her beauties.

Kashmir Valley being a Muslim majority area and being a part of the State of a Hindu Prince would have surely attracted the British. Kashmir Valley drew more notice from the British India Government and even the political leadership of Congress. The British in 1920s were irritated by the Indian people asking independence. Maharaja Hari Singh was also an irritant for the British since he too did not sponsor much anti-Indian independence movement policies or programmes in J&K.

Another thing that mattered at that time was the contents of the Government of India Act 1935 where in the British had put the choice of the Prince of a Princely State as exclusive tool to decide the future of a Princely State in times to come. Where as the Indian National Congress was in principle opposed to it. Congress also found a useful ally in persons like Sheikh Abdullah Jawaharlal Nehru drew close to Sheikh Abdullah. Sheikh Mohammed Abdullah was brought on the Indian political scene by Jawaharlal Nehru. Later Sheikh Abdullah decided to convert Muslim Conference in to a political organisation and open its membership to all including Hindus.

Some of his colleagues in Muslim Conference were opposed to the proposal and did not come along with Abdullah to National Conference. Some of his associates continued with the name Muslim Conference. This brought Sheikh Abdullah more close to Nehru and hence close to Indian National Congress as well. Nehru started giving very special treatment to Sheikh and his National Conference. Congress left it to the National Conference to play main political role in J&K.

Congress was not wound up in J&K. But under the advice of Nehru Congress played a dormant role in J&K. Sheikh Abdullah got encouraged with the special preferential status that Jawaharlal Nehru worked out for him with the Congress leadership. Rather Sheikh Abdullah appeared to rear some extra ambitions as well. Sheikh Mohammed Abdullah even proposed that the British Empire and the leadership of Congress should have a special look at the accord between the British India Govt. and Maharaja Gulab Singh as of 1846 (Amritsar Treaty). Sheikh in a way demanded that with the retreat of the British from Indian sub continent, the Democratic Government in Kashmir should also be handed over to National Conference as was being done with Indian National Congress in Indian Dominion. He was advocating that Maharaja should also quit like the British.

British Policy

The forces and circumstances which ended the Dogra rule over Jammu and Kashmir and gave rise to the "Kashmir Problem" can be directly traced to the socio-political revolution that began to take shape in British India from the early years of the 20th century. The British rulers of India foresaw quite early the birth of national awakening of a different type than the one which had manifested itself in 1857, and formulated a set policy to checkmate it. It was thus enunciated by Sir John Stratchey, one of the ablest British administrators in India in 1874, "The existence side by side of these (Hindu and Muslim) hostile creeds is one of the strong points in our political position in India. The better classes of Muslims are a source of strength to us and not of weakness. They constitute a comparatively small but an energetic minority of the population whose political interests are identical with ours".

In pursuit of this policy, the British began to use the Muslims to further their own political ends and to counteract the national upsurge which had always been essentially Hindu in inspiration. The partition of Bengal in 1905, the command performance of Agha Khan deputation in 1906 and the subsequent formation of the Muslim League at Dacca and the introduction of separate electorates in 1909 were calculated steps in the pursuit of this set policy.

This British Policy got a momentary setback during the short-lived honeymoon between Khilafat movement, which aroused Pan-Islamic consciousness and extra - territorial loyalties of the Indian Muslims under the leadership of Maulana Mohammed Ali, and the Indian National Congress under the mystical leadership of Mahatma Gandhi. But this marriage of convenience of the two incompatibles could not last long. The abolition of both Sultanate and Khilafat in Turkey by Kamal Ata Turk; enabled the British to divert against the infidel Hindus the religious frenzy aroused by the Khilafat Movement amongst the Muslims against the Christian Britishers. The bloody communal riots that followed in Malabar, Kohat, Multan, Saharanpur and many other places marked a convincing failure of the Gandhian experiment in communal harmony through appeasement of Muslims and success of the British policy.

The growth of aggressively communal Muslim separation in Indian politics that followed had its reverberations in the princely states as well. But as in British India, it needed support from British Political Department to find its feet there. Since Jammu and Kashmir State was a Muslim majority state under a Hindu Maharaja who was proving to be inconveniently independent and patriotic, the British decided to raise the Muslim bogey in his State to chastise him and bring him to his knees.

This marked the extension of religio-political awakening and sectarian political organisations of British India into Jammu and Kashmir State. A clear grasp of the religio-political awakening in Jammu and Kashmir state, which took different shape and colour in its different regions according to their socio-religious complexion, is essential for any scientific study of genesis of Kashmir problem.

Geographical barriers and socio-economic backwardness precluded the frontier area of Laddakh, Baltistan and Gilgit from being affected by the religio-political influences which began to enter the State from 1921 onward. They were shaken out of their blissful ignorance or indifference to developments in the rest of the State by Quit Kashmir movement of 1946 and shots and shells of Pakistani invaders in 1947-48.

Of the remaining three regions, Kashmir valley was the first to experience political activity. Mirpur, Muzzaffarabad, and Poonch areas followed the lead of Kashmir. The Dogra area of Jammu remained steeped in its sectional and factional politics till the revolutionary changes in the State's administrative and constitutional set up following the Pakistani invasion of Kashmir in 1947 forced its people to organise themselves politically and adjust themselves to the new order.

Broadly speaking, the political life in the Jammu and Kashmir State revolved around four organisations - The Muslim Conference, the National Conference, the Praja Parishad and Laddakh Buddhist Association.

Muslim Conference

The most important role in creating political awakening and turmoil in Jammu and Kashmir was played by Jammu and Kashmir Muslims Conference. The brain behind it was Sheikh Mohammed Abdullah, who dominated the political scene in Kashmir till his death in 1982. He has given a graphic but subjective account of the political developments in Kashmir in his volumious autobiography in Urdu - "Atish-e-Chinar". Like most other notable Kashmiris, Abdullah also was a scion of a Kashmiri Brahmin family of Srinagar whose head, Pt. Ragho Ram Kaul, was converted to Islam in 1766. Manufacture and trading in shawls was his family profession.

Sheikh Abdullah was put in a "Maktab" in 1909 where he got his first grounding in Islam. He got his early education at Srinagar and moved on to Lahore after passing FSE examination from Shri Pratap College, Srinagar. He was deeply influenced by Islamic thought during his stay at Islamia college, Lahore, from where he passed B.Sc and Aligarh Muslim University from where he passed M.Sc. in Chemistry in 1930. After returning to Srinagar he joined State High School as Science Teacher. But he was dismissed within a year for his political activities.

This proved to be a blessing in disguise for him. The British Political Department and the British Resident in Srinagar who were annoyed with Maharaja Hari Singh for his patriotic speech at the Round Table Conference at London had already begun to fan discontent among the educated Muslims in Kashmir who till then had little share in the administration of the State.

They found in Abdullah a ready made tool who could be projected as leader of the Jammu and Kashmir Muslim Conference formed in 1931 to institutionalise the agitation against the Maharaja and his government. The Muslim Press of Lahore, and Ahmadiya Jamat and Majlis Ahrar, two religio-political movements of Punjab, also gave him a helping hand in that formative period.

Quick rise of Sheikh Abdullah can be ascribed to a number of factors. He was the first Kashmiri Muslim to get a postgraduate degree in science. This gave him a special status among his people. His youthful looks, histrionic talents and command over Holy Quran, which he recited in a melodious voice in all his public speeches added to his appeal. But his greatest asset was the support of the masses. Muslim organisations and the press of Punjab which wanted to project him as leader of the Muslim majority in Kashmir.

Abdullah was an effective speaker in Kashmiri and Urdu and a good organiser. Muslim Conference soon became a mass organisation under his leadership. The communal riot at Srinagar in July 1931, proved to be a turning point in the politics of Kashmir. The Maharaja was unnerved. He appointed a commission to go into the causes of unrest and suggest remedies.

The report of Glaney commission proved a boon for Kashmiri Muslims. It gave them a number of concessions. The Maharaja also agreed to set up a legislative assembly - The Praja Sabha - and take some elected leaders into his council of ministers. This naturally gave a boost to Muslim Conference and Sheikh Abdullah.

The British got the lease of Gilgit region for sixty years beginning from 1935 in the bargain. This made British *de facto* master of the tributary state of Hunza, Nagar and Chitral also. They raised a local militia - the Gilgit Scouts - to police the area.

National Conference

Sheikh Abdullah converted Muslim Conference into National Conference in 1939. To be able to get support of the Indian Press and leadership in his struggle for power in Kashmir. Khan Abdul Gaffar Khan persuaded him to do so on the plea that with overwhelming majority of Muslims in Kashmir, political power, wherever and in whatever way it was transferred to popular hands, would come into his hands. As such, the change was more cosmetic than qualitative by opening the doors of Muslim Conference to Non-Muslims, Abdullah lost nothing but gained much; Kashmiri Pandits joined it in good number.

But his colleagues of Hindu majority Jammu region and Punjabi speaking belt from Mirpur to Muzzaffarabad refused to fall in line with him. They kept the Muslim Conference intact. It was led in Jammu by Chaudhary Ghulam Abbas. Mir Waiz Yusuf Shah kept it alive in the Kashmir valley.

The conversion of Muslim Conference into National Conference brought Sheikh Abdullah on the national stage. He began to be lionised as "Sher-e-Kashmir" or, Tiger of Kashmir. He also became an important leader of the state's peoples conference, a front organisation of the Indian or National Congress.

The second world war and arrest of all top leaders of the Congress in the wake of the quit India Movement of 1942, gave a new turn to Kashmir's politics. The communist party of India, which began to support the British after German attack on Soviet Russia and Russian entry into the Anglo-American Camp. They began to take special interest in Kashmir. Many top communist leaders of Punjab like B.P.L. Bedi, his European wife Freda Bedi and comrade Dhanwantri came to have a good hold over Sheikh Abdullah and his colleagues. Some of them like Ghulam Mohammed Sadiq, Mir Qasim and D.P. Dhar formed a group called "Friends of Soviet Union" and began to give pro-communist tilt to politics and policies of the National Conference.

The end of the second world war in 1945, victory of Labour Party in UK and beginning of the cold war between the two super powers - the USA and USSR - and their allies, gave a new turn to Indian politics as well. The Labour Government of Attlee was committed to transfer of power to Indian hands. Announcement about the visit of the Cabinet Mission to India in early 1946 to hold on the spot discussions with Indian leaders about transfer of power made this crystal clear.

Sheikh Abdullah and his communist friends saw in this situation a new opportunity to fulfil their own dreams. Abdullah wanted to get control over Kashmir valley before the British left India for good. The communists wanted to make Kashmir a communist base which could serve as a jumping ground for a push forward into the rest of India in the days to come.

The Cabinet Mission included Lord Pethic Lawrence as leader and Horace Alexander and Sir Stafford Cripps as members. As it reached Delhi in early April, 1946, it made it clear that the British would quit India after an agreement was reached with the Congress and the Muslim League about the shape of free India.

According to the tentative plan it placed before Indian leaders for consideration, India was to be a federation in which the centre would have control over specific matters, including defence, foreign affairs and communications and the residual powers were to remain with the federating units.

It also stipulated sub-federations of Sindh, Punjab and NWFP. In the west, Assam, and Bengal in the east, United Provinces, Bihar, Central Province, Orissa, Bombay and Madras Presidencies to cover the rest of India. The idea was to create two Muslim majority and one Hindu majority blocks. The princely states were advised to join the new Indian Federation retaining the same powers as the federating provinces. The decision to join the federation or stay independent was to be left to their rulers.

Jinnah and the Muslim League endorsed the view that decision about joining the federation should be left to the rulers. But the Congress favoured participation of the people of the respective states in decision-making.

Sheikh Abdullah wanted to strike before the plan was finalised and the British left. He therefore, visited Delhi, met Gandhiji and Congress President, Acharya Kripalani and sought their support for a mass movement to force the hands of the Maharaja to quit Kashmir and hand over power to the people. Both advised him against any such agitation at that juncture. But Abdullah and his communist friends had made up their mind to go ahead.

In the meantime, the Cabinet Mission decided to visit Kashmir. It reached Srinagar on April 19. Sheikh Abdullah sent it a long telegram from Lahore in which he gave "clear indication of his intention to launch a movement to wrest power from the Maharaja". The gist of the telegram was: "The people of Kashmir do not only want responsible government. They want complete independence and end of personal rule of the Maharaja. Hundred years ago, the East India Co. had sold Kashmir for 75 lakhs to Gulab Singh. We challenge the moral and political basis of this "sale deed" miscalled "treaty of Amritsar" and do not accept the right of the ruler to rule over us any longer".

Quit Kashmir Movement

In accordance with his ideology that in 1946 Sheikh Abdullah gave the call of Quit Kashmir against the Maharaja. Sheikh was so much encouraged with the support of Nehru that he did not even take Indian National Congress in confidence before giving the Quit Kashmir call (1946) on the lines of 1942 Quit India call. The Congress leaders were annoyed but Nehru still supported Sheikh Abdullah. Quit Kashmir movement of National Conference was out of personal ambitions of Sheikh Abdullah.

Nehru's out right support to Sheikh added more irritants in the bag of Hari Singh. Sardar Vallabbhai Patel appeared helpless before Nehru. The result was that some other view makers could come close to Hari Singh and suggest him even some special plans for the future after the British left India. Hari Singh even arrested Sheikh Abdullah and it was with the pressures from Jawaharlal Nehru that Sheikh was released after Sheikh assured a peaceful behaviour to Maharaja.

Muslim Conference did have some members in Jammu province like it had in Kashmir province and they offered more opposition to Sheikh Abdullah from Jammu after Sheikh Abdullah entered into direct confrontation with Maharaja Hari Singh in 1940s By this time the date of 15th August 1947 had passed. Before 15 August 1947 unfair conditions existed for accession with Indian Dominion for Hari Singh since the confirmation of Redcliff Award on Indo Pak boundaries was made by Mountbatten only on 16th August 1947. In the absence of this award J&K would have no link with India like it has now through Pathankot. May be this too provided some reasons for delayed accession with India to Hari Singh.

Sheikh Abdullah had eyes particularly on Kashmir Valley and wanted to reinterpret the March 1846 Amritsar Treaty between the British India Government and Maharaja Gulab Singh to secure sovereignty at least over Kashmir (only) to National Conference. At that time National Conference had no much political role in Jammu Province as well as in Laddakh region. Jammu Province and Laddakh were already part of Gulab Singh's Empire before March 1946 Amritsar treaty was signed.

It was Kashmir Valley only that came under him in 1846 under the Amritsar treaty. Out side Kashmir Valley Congress could play a senior role. It was Nehru's support and outright or blind alliance with Sheikh Abdullah that made Sheikh ambitious and he dreamt of extending his tentacles over whole of J&K under the quit Kashmir movement. Muslim Conference too got encouraged after Hari Singh became sore to Sheikh Abdullah and Nehru. Had Vallabbhai Patel not been there may be Nehru would have succeeded in the exit of Hari Singh from J&K in September or October/ 1947 itself (much before 1949 June). It was not all over yet. Even After 1947 October Accession of J&K with India, New Delhi handled J&K affairs only as Kashmir Affairs.

Call to Quit Kashmir

On reaching Srinagar, Sheikh Abdullah made a public call to the Maharaja to quit Kashmir and exhorted his people to do everything possible to end the Dogra rule over Kashmir- His speeches were so fiery and virulent that the government had to order his arrest. He was arrested on May, 20, 1947.

It was followed by large scale violence and arson by the followers of Abdullah in the valley. Many key bridges were burnt down and government offices were attacked. Pt. Ram Chandra Kak, a Kashmiri himself, who had been appointed Prime Minister of the state by Hari Singh in 1945, came down on the agitators with a heavy hand. The movement died down within a short time.

But a new turn to the situation was given by Pt. Nehru who decided to visit Srinagar much against the advice of Gandhi and Sardar Patel. It would have been wise on the part of the state government to allow him to enter Kashmir and see for himself the situation. But Pt. Kak thought otherwise. He blocked entry of Pt. Nehru at Kehala bridge. When Nehru persisted, he was arrested on June 22, and kept in the Dak bunglow at Domel, near Muzzaffarabad.

This arrest made Pt. Nehru, who was then tipped to be the head of the Interim Government to be formed at New Delhi, an inveterate enemy of Maharaja Hari Singh. Even though he returned to Delhi after two days on urgent summons from Gandhiji, he continued to nurse animus against Hari Singh until his death. The antipathy that began between Hari Singh and Jawaharlal with this unfortunate incident did more to create the problem of Kashmir than anything else.

Sheikh Abdullah was tried by a special court under section 144 of the Ranbir Penal Code pertaining to armed rebellion and was sentenced to three years imprisonment. He was thus put out of the picture during the crucial period preceding partition and freedom of India in August, 1947.

The Quit Kashmir movement had very adverse reaction in Jammu and Laddakh. It alerted the Hindu majority of Jammu and Buddhist majority of Laddakh and gave rise to political moves with definite pro-India orientation in these two regions.

Jammu Praja Parishad

The Hindus of Jammu had no political organisation worth the name until then. There was one Dogra Sabha. But it was primarily a sociocultural organisation. A branch of Hindu Mahasabha was started in Jammu in early thirties. But it never took root. A branch of Rashtriya Swayam Sevak Sangh (RSS) was started there in 1940. It made steady progress and soon became a force to reckon with. It extended its activities to Kashmir valley also in 1944. But it claimed to be a non-political organisation.

The most important Hindu leader in Jammu region was Prem Nath Dogra. A retired civilian and an elected member of the state Praja Sabha, he was appointed the "Sangh Chalak" of Jammu in 1942. As an enlightened and keen observer of the political scene he was quick to realise the implications of the Quit Kashmir movement for the future of Jammu. He therefore began to think seriously about forming a regional political party of Jammu. But, he could not take the initiative without a green signal from the RSS leadership at Nagpur.

Jammu, therefore, had no effective political party until Praja Parishad came into existence. The people of Jammu welcomed it enthusiastically. Praja Parishad soon became a force to reckon with in Jammu region. It was committed to full integration of the whole state with the rest of India and autonomy for Jammu Region.

Laddakh Buddhist Association

The Buddhists of Laddakh had been upset by inroads of Kashmiri Muslims who used to marry Buddhist women leading to rise of a mixed breed of Laddakhis who professed Islam, controlled trade and took active interest in conversion of Buddhist Laddakhis to Islam. They had formed a Sociocultural organisation under the name of Laddakh Buddhist Association to safeguard Buddhist identity of Laddakh. Its leaders were quick to realise the implications of the Quit Kashmir movement and impending partition of India for the future of Laddakh.

The Laddakh Buddhist Association submitted a memorandum to Maharaja Hari Singh in 1947. It recalled the history of Laddakh, the basis of Laddakh's link with Jammu and Kashmir state and asserted that the Buddhist people would not like Laddakh to join Pakistan at any cost. They suggested that before taking any decision about accession of the state, the Maharaja should restore the freedom of Laddakh. In case, he acceded to India, Laddakh would like to be linked with the Hindu majority Jammu region; in any case it would not have anything to do with Kashmir valley.

Thus, the Quit Kashmir movement had deep impact on Laddakh and Jammu. In the meanwhile, things were moving fast both in London and Delhi. Failure of the Cabinet Mission Plan was followed by appointment of Lord Mountbatten as the Governor General of India. He put forth his plan of partition and freedom of India known as the "Mountbatten Plan" on June 3, 1947. It gave option to Princely States to join truncated India or Pakistan keeping in view their geographical contiguity. This plan put Jammu and Kashmir state in a difficult situation and put its ruler on the horns of a dilemma, which shaped the future course of history.

8

Kashmir's Hero: an Impression

(Based on an Account)

What is lately being referred to as the "first family" of Jammu and Kashmir was not so until two generations ago. Sheikh Mohammed Abdullah, the grandfather of Omar Abdullah, the present Chief Minister of the State, came from a humble background, led a difficult childhood, and moved ahead in his personal and political life by sheer hard work and pragmatism.

Ajit Bhattacharji has done a commendable biography of the Sheikh which focuses on the political life of the towering leader, who led a mass movement in Kashmir in the 1930s and 1940s with a secular and progressive agenda. The Sheikh was the dominant political figure in the State for nearly half a century. His was an eventful political life: arrests, confinement, banishment, relegation to political wilderness, and rise to the prime ministership and chief ministership of the State. In all, he spent nearly 17 years in prison.

First, Maharaja Hari Singh arrested him for "waging war" against the state as he was engaged in a mass struggle against the feudal order. In 1953, when he was the Prime Minister of the State, he was arrested again on the charges of carrying out "anti-national" activities and conspiring for an independent Kashmir, which were never proved. In this case, which came to be called the "Kashmir

Conspiracy", it was alleged that Abdullah was on the verge of meeting a Pakistani spy in Tangmarg. In the earlier instance of arrest, by Hari Singh, Jawaharlal Nehru supported the Sheikh's cause and worked towards getting him released. In the latter instance, the Sheikh believed, Nehru was complicit in his arrest. He was incarcerated in the jails of Ooty (Udhagamandalam), Kodaikanal, Udhampur and Kud.

There were pacts such as the Delhi Agreement with Nehru and the Kashmir Accord with Indira Gandhi, which became reference points for negotiations on the extent of autonomy that the Sheikh had envisaged for the State at the time of accession. He remained at the administrative helm of the State from October 1947 to August 1953, first as the Head of Emergency Administration (until March 5, 1948) and later as Prime Minister.

On August 9, 1953, his government was dismissed and he was arrested. He was exiled from Kashmir in 1971 and was allowed back only in 1972. He was again the Chief Minister of the State from 1975, until his death in 1982. He was, however, at the centre of political developments whether in or out of power. Called Sher-e-Kashmir affectionately, he stayed a secularist until the end.

The Sheikh's life was intertwined with the politics of the State for nearly half a century. He returned to Kashmir in 1930, after getting an M.Sc. degree in chemistry from Aligarh Muslim University. He wanted to go to England for higher studies and applied for a scholarship to the State government. He was denied the scholarship as he was 24 years old. He considered this yet another evidence of discrimination by the Maharaja. He then settled for a school teacher's job.

The Sheikh played a pioneering role in mobilising opinion against the oppression and discrimination of the Dogra rulers in Kashmir in the earlier decades of the 20th century. Before the 1930s, the process of political mobilisation in Kashmir was driven by communal identities: Kashmiri Pandits, Hindu Dogras, Kashmiri Muslims, all had separate associations to put forward their demands. These community-based programmes laid emphasis on jobs, religious practices of individual communities, and dealing with religion-based discrimination.

There were several types of protest movements such as campaigns against the Dogra rulers by the Gilgit and Poonch principalities; protests by the shawl weavers and the landless labourers who were forced into beggary; conflict over religious places; and campaigns for increased participation of the Muslim community in the affairs of the state. All these spontaneous struggles eventually formalised into a long-drawn struggle against the oppressive rule of the Dogras. From 1930, educated Muslims started debating issues that adversely impacted their social and economic condition and sought to ameliorate it. As a result, the "Reading Room Party", a cell in Fatehkadal in Srinagar, was set up by these people with the Sheikh as the secretary.

At a meeting in Jammu in June 1931, the Sheikh made his maiden speech explaining the reasons for the backwardness of the Muslim community. The dominant rhetoric of these meetings was religious as the community felt threatened by the Hindu ruler and by the sectarian mobilisation of the Pandit community in Kashmir and the Hindus in Jammu. The attention that these protest meetings received from Muslims outside the State led to increased repression by the State administration.

National Flavour

The Sheikh's contribution in changing the direction and character of the Muslim Conference, which was renamed National Conference, is well documented. The formation of the All India Jammu and Kashmir National Conference in June 1939 under the Sheikh's leadership led to a transformation in the thrust of the political movement against the Dogra rule. The Muslim Conference was later revived by Chaudhary Ghulam Abbas. He supported the Maharaja in not aligning with the Indian Union at the time of Partition.

The political sagacity of the Sheikh is evident in the manner in which he formalised the campaigns and programmes of the party for mass mobilisation. The Naya Kashmir Manifesto, as it became known, was adopted by the National Conference in August 1945. It had an inclusive charter for social change with emphasis on equal rights for women, the right to education and the right to work, among other progressive measures.

The most radical measure was the abolition of landlordism and the distribution of land to the tiller. He argued that such a progressive agenda could be implemented only by overthrowing the feudal order. The Quit Kashmir slogan became a potent movement, which kept large sections of people from all faiths together during the prolonged struggle. The Sheikh had to struggle against supporters of the Muslim Conference in Kashmir, the Muslim League in the rest of India, and sectarian Hindu associations within and outside the State.

The affinity between the Sheikh and Nehru as well as between the National Conference and the Indian National Congress developed as the struggle against the Maharaja drew support from the latter. At the Karachi session of the All India States People's Conference in 1935, the Congress declared that it would support the freedom movement of the people of the princely states unlike the Muslim League, which supported the rulers of the these states, including the Maharaja of Kashmir. Mohammed Ali Jinnah condemned the Quit Kashmir movement, while Nehru supported it.

The Congress accepted the Sheikh as the true representative of the people of the princely state. Balraj Puri, the writer and human rights activist, points out that the Sheikh received loud applause when he declared at public meetings that Pakistan was an enemy of Kashmir as it had tried to enslave it through force, whereas India was its friend, and that the Indian Army had come to defend its freedom.

The Sheikh was treated like a hero by Nehru through the 1940s. He was considered a beacon of secular politics by Nehru and Gandhi in 1947. According to Bhattacharji, Nehru and the Sheikh reinforced each other's faith in the secular and progressive ideology. However, within five years, doubts about the Sheikh's loyalty to India were raised and Nehru increasingly gave in to the opinions of those opposed to the Sheikh's politics. As the Sheikh implemented land reforms, the landed class, both in Jammu and Kashmir, went against him.

It was easy to colour this event as communal since most of the landowning population was Hindu and the poor peasantry, who got the land, was Muslim. As anger against the distribution of land mounted, Nehru advised the Sheikh "to avoid provoking Jammu and Dogra sentiments in decisions concerning the sequestration of excess land and Hari Singh's orchards".

The Sheikh was dismayed at the anti-Muslim riots that took place in Jammu in 1947-48. He held the Maharaja responsible for the murder of hundreds of Muslims. He often pointed out that while he and his party maintained communal harmony in Kashmir, the Maharaja and his wife incited communal violence in Jammu. The Sheikh's protests against the riots annoyed the Maharaja. Sardar Vallabhbhai Patel, the Home Minister, sympathised with the Maharaja and gave a communal turn to the statements made and the measures taken by the Sheikh.

According to B.N. Mullick, the intelligence chief, Sardar Patel did not trust the Sheikh and maintained that "[Abdullah's] his antipathy to the Maharaja was not really an antipathy to the ruler as such, but to the Dogras in general and with the Dogras he identified the rest of the majority community in India".

Communal Colour

The mobilisation by Hindu hardliners against the special status of the State was spearheaded by the Praja Parishad and supported by the Jan Sangh. The agitation became a galvanising force against the Sheikh. As the Praja Parishad started its campaign against the special status of Jammu and Kashmir, Nehru described the agitation "as a subversive movement of the most reactionary communal type".

In another note to the Home Ministry in January 1953, Nehru showed that he was aware that "communal organisations like the Jan Sangh, RSS [Rashtriya Swayamsewak Sangh] and Akali Dal [would] create trouble in Delhi on the basis of the Jammu Parishad agitation". The demand for complete integration of the State with India by the Praja Parishad and the Jan Sangh was made on purely communal grounds. The Sheikh's belief in a plebiscite and, pending that, the special status of the relationship of the State with India was further strengthened by the intensity of the agitation led by the Praja Parishad, the Jan Sangh and the RSS. In his much-quoted speech at Ransinghpura, he raised the issue of the hold of communal forces on politics in the country and the difficulty of the Muslim-majority State to function effectively under the increasingly communal atmosphere. Hence he advocated even more strongly the proposal for greater autonomy for the State.

With the former Maharaja's son, Karan Singh, as the Sadar-e-Riyasat and Sardar Patel as the Home Minister at the Centre, the Sheikh became a victim of conspiracies to oust him from his position of leadership. Mullick "imported suspicion and a tinge of communalism into his interpretation of Abdullah's actions and speeches, eventually compiling the charges required to justify arresting the Prime Minister of Jammu and Kashmir".

Bhattacharji gives details of the Sheikh's arrest at midnight on August 9, 1953, in Gulmarg. He highlights the role played by Mullick and Sardar Patel in undermining the Sheikh's position with the central political leadership.

Nehru made it clear that he thought that the Sheikh was confused. He wrote to Maulana Abul Kalam Azad, "My fear is that Sheikh Sahib, in his present state of mind, is likely to do something or take some step, which might make things worse".

Subsequent correspondence between Nehru and the Sheikh indicates that Nehru had distanced himself from the Sheikh. In fact, the Sheikh was accused of delaying the implementation of the Delhi Agreement. The bias had reached such proportions that Nehru accepted the suggestion to dismiss the Sheikh's government on the pretext that he had lost the support of his Cabinet, and he was arrested on trumped-up charges. Commentators have termed this as the major rupture in the faith and trust that the Sheikh had placed in Nehru.

Political developments in India after Nehru's death, the creation of Bangladesh and the Shimla Agreement made the Sheikh change his demand for a plebiscite to one on the extent of autonomy for the State. He found it difficult to deal with Indira Gandhi, who wanted to strengthen the Congress' presence in the State.

On February 25, 1975, the Sheikh was sworn in as Chief Minister of the State, after a gap of nearly 22 years. Though from 1977 to 1980 he had some respite from Indira Gandhi's continuous attacks, he realised that the new formation at the Centre was not favourable to his ideals of autonomy. The Hindutva elements of the Jan Sangh in the newly formed Janata Party revived the "issue of closer integration with the Indian Union, while Home Minister Charan Singh even favoured abrogation of Article 370".

Bhattacharji's biography of the Sheikh emphasises his belief in secularism and his distrust of the two-nation theory. He had faith in Indian secularism, which was amply articulated in his speech to the Constituent Assembly. It was the short-sighted policies propagated and implemented by the Indian political class that alienated the Sheikh and made him at times difficult to deal with. On the whole, he stayed loyal to the democratic and secular tradition, which he espoused in his earlier years of political mobilisation.

Crucial Times

Sheikh Abdullah, fundamentally a nationalist, frequently imprisoned by Maharaja from 1931 and literate among illiterate Muslim majority made him very popular and the people as a whole visualised through him a very rosy political future. He had a master's degree in Chemistry from Aligarh Muslim University, joined Government service as a teacher but soon gave up the job to join political struggle against Maharaja.

It is said, he was introduced to Jawaharlal lal Nehru in 1930 who offered him a hand of friendship. A charismatic leader, Sheikh Abdullah, was a crowd puller and was revered, loved and admired for the inherent qualities, as a leader. Apparently, an independent Kashmir as his dream and to achieve this objective he backed wrong horses.

The caucus of opportunists around Sheikh Abdullah, an old lion now, convinced him of a political defeat and forced him to commit his life's blunder by signing the 1975 accord and accept whatever was being offered by Government of India. Unfortunately, Sheikh's political history that could have been written in golden words was archived never to be mentioned again.

Sheikh Abdullah's great achievement as Prime Minister for six years of rule was the abolition of feudal land ownership, 'Land to tiller' as it was referred to, a step to hit the Pandit landowners and Dogra Rajputs very hard, who carried on entertaining grudge, sabotaged and scuttled his every move thenceforth.

Spearheading attacks from white collar Pandits in the valley, Abdullah faced another formidable opposition from Hindu-dominated Jammu region. Disgruntled officials in Hari Singh's administration and deprived Hindu landowners formed an organisation Praja Parishad that always managed to give Abdullah a tough time. A special mention must be made of a school teacher Balraj Madhok, a Hindu fundamentalist of Jana Sangha party, vehemently opposed to Muslims all over India in general and Kashmiri Muslims in particular who did not spare a moment to unleash scathing attacks on Abdullah and Kashmiri Muslims.

Abdullah did try to convey his intended political compulsions based on friendship, mutual trust and above all sincerity but the message seemed to have filtered through, for thoughtful Nehru always looked focused in different directions. Abdullah failed to understand the international situation towards the beginning of 1940's when United Kingdom faced with acute economic slump had virtually decided to quit as they could not afford to keep their foothold in India any longer.

Sheikh Abdullah's support for Maharaja Hari Singh for latter's effort to keep both India and Pakistan away by offering to sign 'standstill agreement' could have paved the way for a sovereign independent Kashmir. Under the circumstances, Abdullah could wait to keep Maharaja engaged in domestic politics allowing him to rule as sovereign head of the state especially when political support was visible.

The subsequent development of relations between him and Nehru sent alarming bells to Pakistani leadership, who were rather emotionally attached to Kashmir. The disappointed Chaudhary Ghulam Abaas another Kashmir leader and Kashmiris who had become part of the newly created Pakistani army (notable among them was the mastermind of Pathan invasion Major Khursheed Anwar), if taken into confidence, would have joined hands and a strategy evolved would culminate into a situation that would leave Kashmir undisturbed and Pathan invasion would have been out of question.

On June 16, 1949, Sheikh Abdullah, Mirza Afzal Beg, Maulana Masoodi and Moti Ram Bagda joined the Constituent Assembly of India. Negotiations began in earnest on Article 370. N. Gopalaswamy Ayyangar tried to reconcile the differences between Patel and Abdullah. A text, agreed on October 16, was moved in the Constituent Assembly the next day, unilaterally altered by Ayyangar. "A trivial change," as he admitted in a letter to the Sheikh on October 18. Patel confirmed it to Nehru on November 3 on his return from the United States. Beg had withdrawn his amendment after the accord. Abdullah and he were in the lobby, and rushed to the House when they learnt of the change. In its original form the draft would have made the Sheikh's ouster in 1953 impossible.

Constitutional Structure Altered

The State's Constitution was overridden by New Delhi's orders. Its basic structure was altered. A Governor nominated by the Centre replaced the head of the State elected by the State legislature. Article 356 (imposition of President's Rule) was applied despite provision in the State's Constitution for Governor's rule (Section 92). This was done on November 21, 1964. On November 24, 1966, the Governor replaced the Sadar-e-Riyasat after the State's Constitution had been amended on April 10, 1965 by the 6th Amendment in violation of Section 147 of the Constitution. Article 370 was used freely not only to amend the Constitution of India but also of the State. On July 23, 1975 an Order was made debarring the State legislature from amending the State Constitution on matters in respect of the Governor, the Election Commission and even "the composition" of the Upper House, the Legislative Council.

After a long time, the bye-bye handshake of that 1975 accord, on the left, Sheikh Abdullah accepted the post of Chief Minister and it is widely believed that he was rather forced, by political opportunists and greedy people closely related to him, to accept anything that was offered smearing his name and consigning his glorious past to history.

Sheikh Abdullah had no cards to play when he concluded an Accord with Indira Gandhi and became Chief Minister on February 24, 1975. At the outset, on August 23, 1974, he had written to G. Parthasarathy: "I hope that I have made it abundantly clear to you that I can assume office only on the basis of the position as it existed on August 8, 1953". Judgement on the changes since "will be deferred until the newly elected Assembly comes into being".

This was explicitly an accord on "political cooperation between us", as Indira Gandhi wrote (December 16, 1974). On February 12, 1975, Abdullah recorded that it provided "a good basis for my cooperation at the political level". In Parliament on March 3, 1975 she called it a "new political understanding". He was made Chief Minister on February 24, backed by the Congress' majority in the Assembly and on the understanding of a fresh election soon. Sheikh Abdullah's memoirs Aatish-e-Chinar (Urdu) record her backtracking on the pledge and the Congress' perfidy. It withdrew support and staked a claim to form a government. Governor's Rule was imposed. The Sheikh's National Conference won the elections with a resounding majority on the pledge to restore Jammu and Kashmir's autonomy, which was also Farooq's pledge in 1996. The 1975 accord had collapsed.

The developments leading to the dismissal and arrest of Sheikh Abdullah in August 1953 and the signing of USA - Pak Military Pact early in 1954, were closely linked up with the cold war politics of the two power blocs. They in their turn contributed to a further intensification of the cold war in regard to Kashmir which made an objective approach and a negotiated settlement of the problem all the more difficult. Internally, these developments were closely linked up with Sheikh Abdullah's personal ambition to secure absolute power for himself in the Kashmir valley. To achieve this end, he had leaned first on the Communists, who gave him the idea of independent Kashmir but later moved towards the west, particularly the USA to the great chagrin of the Communists.

Sheikh Abdullah's main object appeared to be to put pressure on the Government of India to make definite commitment about same sort of greater autonomy for Kashmir before the Constituent Assembly ratified accession. Thus, he secured a free hand to abolish the Dogra ruling dynasty and have a separate flag and Constitution for the State. Accordingly the hereditary Dogra ruler as the head of the State was replaced by an elected president called Sadar-e-Riyasat, the red flag of the National Conference was adopted as the State flag and machinery was set up for drafting a separate Constitution for the State while the question of ratification of accession was kept pending. These moves of Sheikh Abdullah sent a wave of resentment in Jammu and Ladakh as also in the rest of India. The Praja Parishad launched a movement for the integration of the State with the rest of India like other acceding States with a common Constitution, a common President and a common flag. The popular discontent against discriminatory economic and administrative policies of Sheikh Abdullah's Government with regard to Jammu added strength to this movement which spread to every nook and corner of Jammu region.

In the meantime within the National Conference as also in Sheikh Abdullah's Cabinet a rift was developing. The pro-Communist elements which had been the staunchest protagonists of the independence for Kashmir had been alarmed by Sheikh Abdullah's tilt towards Anglo-American camp which had become very marked after his last visit to Paris towards the end of 1951. Sheikh Abdullah, it appeared, had realised that his dream of absolute power in Kashmir was more likely to come true with the help of the Anglo-American bloc which dominated the U.N.O. and the Security Council than the Communist bloc. He had therefore, begun to shift his allegiance from his Communist friends inside and outside Kashmir to the Western countries. As the Praja Parishad movement for fuller integration of the State with the rest of India gathered momentum, he began to rouse the sentiments in Kashmir in the name of Kashmiri nationalism and demonstrate his indifference and disdain for the susceptibilities of the people of Jammu and the Government of India in different ways.

The trend became particularly evident after the visit of Adlai Stevenson to Srinagar early in May 1953. This alarmed the pro-Communist Ministers of his Cabinet. They now turned against him. Bakshi Ghulam Mohammed, the right-hand man of Sheikh Abdullah, joined hands with them. These internal developments coupled with the pressure from outside resulting from Dr. Mukherjee's death made Sheikh Abdullah desperate. But before he could show his hand by dismissing the dissident Ministers and making a formal declaration of his plan about independent Kashmir, Yuvraj Karan Singh, the only son of Maharaja Hari Singh, who had been made 'Sadar-e-Riyasat' - head of State - after the abolition of the hereditary rule of the Dogra dynasty dismissed

Sheikh Abdullah and commissioned Bakshi Ghulam Mohammed to form a new Cabinet. Sheikh Abdullah was soon after arrested under Defence of Kashmir Rules. This sudden turn of events took by surprise both Pakistan and the USA which had begun to lay great hopes on Sheikh Abdullah for a solution of the Kashmir problem suiting their ends. Their chagrin was clear from the hostile comments in their press.

The Communists, inside India and outside, on the other hand, hailed the overthrow of Sheikh Abdullah as a victory for themselves and started denouncing the USA in the strongest terms. They thus successfully exploited the popular feeling roused by the Jan Sangh and Sheikh Abdullah's separatist policies for creating an anti-American hysteria in India.

The pro-Communist bias of India's neutralist foreign policy and the persistent support given by the USSR and other Communist countries to India's stand on Kashmir in the Security Council, many Americans genuinely began to feel that India was moving towards the Communist bloc and that Pakistan could be an asset, particularly because of the strategic situation of Gilgit for containing the spread of Communism in Asia if it could be persuaded to join the Baghdad Pact which was later re-Christened as Central Treaty Organisation (CENTO).

At the same time there was a visible pro-American shift in Pakistan's foreign policy particularly after the assassination of its Prime Minister, Mr. Liaqat Ali Khan in 1952. Even otherwise, the very genesis of Pakistan demanded that her foreign policy should counter to that of India. Pakistan's very existence required that India was presented to her people as their chief enemy and everything was done to strengthen Pakistan vis-a-vis India. By the end of 1953, it became evident that negotiations for a military pact between Pakistan and the USA were moving towards a successful conclusion. The signing of the pact was formally announced early in 1954. India reacted very strongly to this pact which meant substantial augmentation of military strength of Pakistan with free supplies of armaments from the USA.

Pakistan on its part strongly resented the declarations of Bakshi Ghulam Mohammed after his assumption of power that accession of Jammu and Kashmir State to India was full, final and irrevocable.

The actual ratification of accession by the Kashmir Constituent Assembly soon after further irritated her.

As a result, the area of disagreement about the Quantum of forces to be retained by either side which appeared to have been considerably narrowed by the direct talks of the two premiers became wider than ever before. Pt. Nehru insisted that in the new situation created by the abundant supply of military aid to Pakistan from the USA, "what we said at a previous stage about the quantum of force had little relevance. We can take no risks now as we were prepared to take previously and we must retain full liberty to keep such forces and military equipment in the Kashmir State as we may consider necessary in view of this new threat to us".

Meanwhile, the situation inside the State as also the attitude and approach of both the countries had undergone a lot of change. Within the State, the most significant development was the unanimous decision of the Constituent Assembly to ratify the accession and the specific declaration in the Constitution adopted by it on November 17, 1956, that "the State of Jammu and Kashmir is and shall be an integral part of the Union of India". This strengthened the hands of the Government of India which could assert with justification that the people of the State had given their democratic verdict in favour of accession to India.

While the unanimous decision of the Constituent Assembly strengthened the Indian position, the re- organisation of "Plebiscite Front and Political Conference" by pro-Abdullah elements in Kashmir valley and their open demand for a plebiscite and accession to Pakistan strengthened the hands of Pakistan politically. Military, her position had vastly improved because of the massive flow of the latest armaments of all types together with military experts from the USA. As a result, the attitude of the rulers of Pakistan became more aggressive. Apart from carrying on a diplomatic offensive against India all over the world, they began to actively organise and encourage acts of sabotage through their agents within the State.

As a reaction, India began to lean more and more upon the USSR and her satellites which gave a further pro- Communist tilt to her foreign policy. The visit to India of Marshal Bulganin, the

USSR Premier and Khruschev, the First Secretary of the Communist Party of the Soviet Union, towards the end of 1955 and their open declaration at Srinagar of December 10, 1955 "that the question of Kashmir as one of the States of the Republic of India had already been decided by the people of Kashmir" made the alignment of the USSR with India on the question of Kashmir as explicit as that of the USA with Pakistan. The cold war had now entered Kashmir itself. It began to be looked upon as one of the storm centres of the world like West Berlin where the interests of the two giants clashed directly.

The situation forced Pt. Nehru to do some rethinking about the stand he had taken regarding Kashmir. Doubts had already begun to assail him about the wisdom of the offer about plebiscite which was bound to be influenced by religious considerations whenever and however it was held. The tone of his utterances about Kashmir therefore changed. He began to voice his opposition to plebiscite openly and the Indian Home Minister, late Pt. Pant, declared that Kashmir was an integral and irrevocable part of India.

This change of attitude was reflected in the stand taken by the Chief Indian delegate, Krishna Menon, when the Security Council resumed debate on Kashmir. India for the first time explicitly charged Pakistan of direct aggression and declared that she had no obligation to discharge till the aggression was vacated. Indira's voluntary offer to consult the people, he said had been redeemed through elections to the constituent Assembly of Jammu and Kashmir whose actions were "declaratory and not creative". The legal right of India over the whole of Jammu and Kashmir State, he asserted, flowed from the lawful accession of the State by Maharaja Hari Singh which was full, final and irrevocable.

Some hope of a negotiated settlement outside the UN rose once again after the Military coup in Pakistan which brought Field Marshal Ayub Khan to the helm of affairs in Pakistan in 1959. As a soldier he had a greater consciousness of the indivisibility of the Indo-Pak defence against possible aggression from Communist China to meet which Indo-Pak amity was essential. He needed it to stabilise his own position as well. Furthermore, he was in a position in the early days of his new found power to take a decision even against the popular sentiments of the Pakistani people. He was even more keen for the settlement of the Canal Waters dispute in which India had a whip hand over Pakistan. Had Indian diplomacy shown any grasp of realities, it would have insisted upon a package deal embracing all Indo-Pak disputes such as the Canal Waters, Kashmir, evacuee property, partition debt and treatment of the Hindu minority in East Pakistan. But, a Canal Water Treaty was signed at Karachi in 1960 which gave Pakistan much more favourable terms than suggested by the World Bank Award.

With that ended, the short lived Indo-Pak detente brought about more by personal relations between Rajeshwar Dayal, the Indian High Commissioner at Karachi, and Field Marshall Ayub who happened to know each other well since pre-partition days than by a real change of heart on both sides. The old game of mutual accusation began once again. Communist Russia saw in the military regime of Ayub a greater threat to her position in Asia and, therefore, became more vociferous in her support to India over Kashmir. She began to use her veto to prevent any resolution to which India was opposed, being passed by the Security Council.

This reduced the discussions in the Security Council to just debating bouts between Krishna Menon of India and Zaffarullah Khan of Pakistan who began to exploit that world forum to malign India by repeating baseless charges against her which were given wide publicity all over the world, and that was despite the truth and justification of the Indian case. While these pointless exercises in histrionics were going on in New York, Communist China had started fishing in the troubled waters of Kashmir cutting across the cold war politics of both USA and the USSR. The entry of Communist China on the Kashmir stage as a third claimant to large chunks of its territories introduced a new factor in the Kashmir situation; it gave a new turn to the Kashmir problem.

Prime Minister Nehru made the last effort of his life to settle the Kashmir issue in May, 1964. He invited Abdullah to come to Delhi as his personal guest. This gesture made it clear that he wanted to placate Abdullah and made a new beginning in the spirit of forgive and forget.

Sheikh Abdullah has given a graphic account of his meeting with Pt. Nehru after eleven years of estrangement in his autobiography. He claims to have suggested to Pt. Nehru to invite President Ayub of Pakistan to Delhi for direct talks on Kashmir and other related issues.

According to him Pt. Nehru accepted his suggestion and requested him to visit Rawalpindi and invite Ayub on his behalf. According to Abdullah's version, Pt. Nehru was "Prepared to consider all earlier proposals as also any alternative proposals that may be brought forward during talks to arrive at just, fair and mutually acceptable conclusions".

Sheikh Abdullah received an invitation from President Ayub to visit Pakistan just at that time. It appeared to be prearranged and not just a coincidence. This cleared the way for his visit to Pakistan in the third week of May, 1964.

Before leaving for Rawalpindi Abdullah issued a press statement in which he gave his thinking about the possible solution of the problem. "The solution" he said, "should be such as does not create the feeling of defeat in any party, strengthening the foundations of secularism in India and satisfies the urge for freedom of the people of Kashmir". It pointed to a compromise solution suiting his ambitions about Kashmir through some kind of mutual arrangement between New Delhi and Rawalpindi.

Abdullah and his entourage, which included his son Farooq Abdullah, got red carpet reception at Rawalpindi. He had detailed talks with President Ayub and other leaders of Pakistan. He must have conveyed to them his own plan and thinking of Pt. Nehru. Ayub accepted the invitation of Pt. Nehru and June 15, 1964 was fixed as a tentative date of his visit to New Delhi. From Rawalpindi, Abdullah went to Muzzaffarabad, the capital of the so-called "Azad Kashmir". This Pak occupied district was of vital importance for Kashmir Valley because the roads which linked it with rail-heads of Rawalpindi and Havelian passed through it. He was therefore keen to woo its non-Kashmiri people to unite it with Kashmir of his dreams.

While Abdullah was still in Muzzaffarabad, Pt. Nehru breathed his last at New Delhi on May 27, 1964. This marked an end of an era in free-India. It also aborted the plan of direct talks between him and President of Pakistan for the settlement of Kashmir problem.

Pt. Nehru's death at that juncture was a great blow to Abdullah. He cut short his visit and rushed back to Delhi.

As discussed earlier, special relationship between Nehru and Abdullah was a major factor in Kashmir affairs. There was much in common between them. Both originally belonged to the Kaul Clan of Kashmiri Pandits, both were voluptuous and ambitious and both shared weakness for good things in life. Pt. Nehru banked on Abdullah to retain Kashmir valley in India. Apart from his attachment to Kashmir for parochial reasons, he wanted to disprove the two nations theory on the basis of which he had accepted partition of British India in 1947.

Sheikh Abdullah has paid handsome tribute to Pt. Nehru in "Atish-e-Chinar". But he has also betrayed his distrust for him in a very subtle way. According to him:

> "Pt. Nehru's love for Kashmir was more like love for a beautiful woman whom he wanted to possess and that he had come to regard him (Abdullah) as a Rakib or rival in love-for the possession of the beautiful valley".

Soon after Nehru's death Sheikh Abdullah went abroad ostensibly for pilgrimage to holy places of Islam. He availed this opportunity to establish contacts with heads of many Islamic states and also had a long meeting with Premier Chou-en-Lai of China at Algiers, capital of Algeria. The reports of his parleys as published in the foreign and Indian press and intelligence reports, received by Government of India from its own sources created grave doubts about him. He was alleged to be thinking of an Algeria like liberation movement to secure freedom for Kashmir. He was therefore ordered to return to India. On arrival at New Delhi he was arrested and put under detention. This pointed to a new thinking on the part of the new Government led by Lal Bahadur Shastri.

Lal Bahadur Shastri had a mind of his own. He had gained first hand experience of the state of the mind of Kashmiri Muslims during the planned disappearance and reappearancc of the reputed hair of prophet Mohammed (Pbuh) kept in Hazrat Bal Shrine at Srinagar, in winter of 1963 and the anti-India frenzy that it had created. This step sent right signal to Pakistan also. It made

President Ayub realise that he could not expect a soft line on Kashmir from the new government of India.

Indo-Pak War

President Ayub had his own assessment of the new leadership at New Delhi and State of military preparedness of India. According to his assessment Indian military machine had been badly mauled by the Chinese and it would take India sometime to regain its strength and self-confidence. Like many other Muslim leaders, he too had been nursing the fond notion about superiority of Muslim soldiers. He had an exaggerated estimate of the strength of Pak army and capability of Patton tanks that he had acquired from USA. He therefore, wanted to take advantage of what he considered to be Pak military superiority for achieving his objective of grabbing Kashmir by other means.

Pakistan's rulers also banked on cooling off of the relations between India and Soviet Union in the wake of Indo-China war, Anglo-US support to India and improvement in relations between Pakistan and USSR. He had visited Moscow and developed personal relations with Soviet leaders. At the same time he had continued to enjoy the confidence of USA and was getting massive military aid from her to modernise the Pak army. But before taking resort to arms he wanted to probe two things. He wanted to know the American reaction, if he used American supplied armament against India. India had been assured by USA that arms supplied to Pakistan will not to be used against her. Secondly, he wanted to have a measure of the mettle of the new Indian leadership. This was the main motivation of Pak incursion into Kutch region of Gujarat in early 1965.

Rann of Kutch was part of the princely state of Kutch which acceded to India in 1947. It is a marshy and sparsely populated region. Some island like uplands called 'Bets" serve as pasture lands. There were unconfirmed reports about reserves of oil and gas in this region. But no exploration had been done until then. India didn't expect any trouble from Pakistan in this sector. Therefore, it was virtually undefended. There were only a few police posts on some of the "Bets". Pakistan had no valid claim on this area. Maps of the state of Kutch and India as a whole prepared by the government of undivided India had clearly denoted it as a part of Kutch State.

Armed forces of Pakistan backed by Patton tanks made a surprise attack on Kutch, captured some of the Indian posts and laid claims on the whole of Rann of Kutch. Before India could take a defensive action and make a counter attack, UK and USA began to put pressure on India to accept ceasefire, which left a big chunk of Indian territory in Pak occupation.

Soon after Prime Minister Lal Bahadur Shastri and General Ayub met in London, where they had gone for Commonwealth Conference. There an agreement was signed through the mediation of British Prime Minister. The issue was referred to an International tribunal one of whose members was to be nominated by India and the other by Pakistan.

This was a clear victory for Pakistan. She had succeeded in creating a dispute by unprovoked aggression, tested its newly acquired arms, known the American reaction and internationalised the dispute with the assurance that Pakistan would get something in the bargain. It did get a chunk of about 1000 sq. miles of indisputable Indian territory in Kutch through the award of the Tribunal.

The Kutch adventure and its outcome gave new hope and confidence to Pakistan. It was evident from Ayub's address to Pakistani students in London in the course of which he bragged that Pakistan's tanks could have a stroll upto Delhi, if he had so wished. The way Lal Bahadur Shastri, new as he was to the ways of international politics and diplomacy, acted during this Pak aggression and the negotiations that followed made Ayub think that he could brow beat him and India with impunity. He therefore, decided to go ahead with the main plank of his programme to capture Kashmir.

Pakistan's plan was to launch a sudden attack on Kashmir Valley after sending thousands of armed infiltrations into the state to prepare the ground for proper reception and quick success of the invading army. The infiltration began in May, 1965. The plan was to take the city of Srinagar by surprise on August 9, 1965, when hundreds of thousands of villagers were to come there to celebrate the Martyrs Day call which had been given by pro- Pak leadership of Kashmir Valley. At the same time Pak saboteurs were to become active all along Pathankot- Jammu-Srinagar highway. A major attack was to be made on Chamb sector to get control of the bridge on the Chenab, at Akhnoor and cut off the north western part of the state from supply bases at Jammu and Pathankot. The bridge on the Chenab at Ram Ban on the highway to Srinagar from Jammu was also to be captured.

The operation in Jammu region began according to plan. But timely information by a Muslim Gujar of Uri about massive infiltration and timely action by the authorities made part of the operation in the valley a flop.

As a defensive action, the Indian defence forces made an assault on 9000 feet high Haji Peer Pass the only pass leading into the valley from the North West, which was under control of Pakistan, and occupied it. An equally daring action led to the recapture of Kargil Heights, which command Srinagar-Leh road. These Heights had been captured by Indian forces in April at the time of Kutch war but had been returned to Pakistan in June. These two actions sealed off Kashmir valley and ensured the safety of Laddakh.

Finding its plan of capturing Kashmir through armed infiltrators with the help of local people thus thwarted, Pakistan launched a full scale invasion of the state in Chamb-Jammu sector in September 1965. The object as stated above was to capture Akhnoor bridge and cut off Rajouri and Poonch from the rest of the state and clear the way for capturing the Ram Ban bridge on the Chenab to enable Pakistan to isolate troops in the encircled valley.

Indian troops in Chamb had no tanks to support them because the one span Akhnoor bridge could not take the load of heavy tanks. Therefore, the capture of the bridge and advance of the Pak forces on Jammu appeared to be a certainty. Indian air force went into action, when Pakistani tanks were hardly 10 miles away from Akhnoor. It destroyed a number of them and slowed down their advance.

Even though Pak advance towards Akhnoor and Jammu was slowed down by air action, it was obvious that it could not be halted unless there was counter attack on Lahore and Sialkot sectors by India.

Pakistan had planned its strategy on the assumption that as in 1947, India would not extend the theatre of war beyond the boundary of Jammu and Kashmir state and that with the logistic advantage that Pakistan had in Chamb sector, it would be able to capture Kashmir and that India would acquiesce in the loss of the valley after fretting and fuming for some time.

The experience of first Indo-Pak war, when Pt. Nehru did not allow Indian army to make a counter attack on Sialkot, which would have forced Pakistan to come to terms on India's conditions lay at the root of this assumption. Ayub had thought that Prime Minister Shastri would not have the courage to order an all out war with Pakistan. He was also confident that in case of such a war, his armoured divisions equipped with Patton tanks would be able to go right up to Delhi.

Prime Minister, Lal Bahadur Shastri, on the advice of the Defence Chiefs, learnt took the right decision. He had learned his lesson from the Kutch fiasco and was prepared to call the Pakistani bluff at all costs. Counter attack on Lahore and Sialkot had the desired result. Pressure on Chamb sector was relieved.

Pak forces fell back to defend Lahore and Sialkot. When a cease fire was ordered in response to resolution of UN Security Council, Pakistan was nowhere near Kashmir Valley while Lahore and Sialkot were within the range of Indian guns. Lahore had been evacuated and could have fallen into Indian hands, if the Indian government had so decided.

Thus, the Pak plan to secure by force of arms what it had not been able to get by diplomacy and negotiations failed miserably. Not only Kashmir eluded it once again but it also got a bloody nose. Capture of Haji Pir, Kargil Heights and part of Pak territory up to Sialkot and Lahore retrieved the prestige of Indian armed forces which had suffered badly during the Sino-Indian war of 1962. But India was once again worsted at the diplomatic table.

Attitude of UK and USA during and after the war, as expected, was anything but friendly. Their sympathy for Pakistan was open. But to the great chagrin and dismay of India, even USSR maintained a neutral stance. It gave no indication of sympathy and support for India.

After the war Soviet Premier, Kosygin, decided to play the role of a peace maker. He invited both Prime Minister Shastri and President Ayub to meet at Tashkent for peace settlement. Both accepted his invitation. Indian delegation included Foreign Minister Swaran Singh, Defence Minister Y. B. Chauhan and Indian Ambassador at Moscow, T. N. Kaul. Pakistan delegation included its Foreign Minister, Z. A. Bhutto.

The meeting began on January 4th, with an opening address by Kosygin in the course of which he said "India and Pakistan are our southern neighbours. We always came out not only for the strengthening of friendly relations between Soviet Union and India and Pakistan but also for the reign of peace and friendship between these countries themselves". He did not utter a word, which could be considered as sympathetic to India, which had been subjected to unprovoked aggression. Deliberations continued till January 10, when Tashkent Declaration was adopted and signed by Lal Bahadur Shastri and Ayub Khan on behalf of India and Pakistan.

Tashkent Declaration was a collection of platitudes. Its only concrete and operative part was clause-II which said "The Prime Minister of India and President of Pakistan have agreed that all armed personnel of the two countries shall be withdrawn not later than 15 February, 1966 to the positions they held prior to August 5th and both sides will observe the ceasefire terms on the ceasefire line".

This was a clear rebuff to India. It not only put the aggressor and the aggressed on par but also committed India to withdraw from Haji Pir and Kargil Heights, which belonged to India and had been illegally occupied by Pakistan and had been liberated by Indian armed forces at a heavy cost. It virtually gave legal validity to Pak occupation of the territory it had occupied in 1947-48, without prejudice to its claim on the rest of the state, which was still with India.

Lal Bahadur Shastri had assured the people and armed forces before his departure for Tashkent that he would not accept any suggestion for the return to Pakistan of Haji Pir pass and Kargil Heights. He stood firm on his word to the nation till the last day. But his aides, Swaran Singh, Y. B. Chauhan and T. N. Kaul, pressured him to accept the Pak demand for withdrawal of troops from there for fear of alienation of USSR.

It implied that it was the pressure of the Soviet Union which forced India to accept a patently unjust settlement. Had India not put all her eggs in Soviet basket and had maintained dialogues with USA also before and after going to Tashkent, it might have been saved from the predicament in which Shastri had to sign the Tashkent Declaration against his better judgement.

Prime Minister Shastri was found dead in his room at Tashkent on the morning of January 11, 1966. It was given out that he died of heart failure. But suspicion that he was poisoned to death lingered on. No detailed enquiry into his death was made. Indian physician Dr. Chugh, who had accompanied him to Tashkent was mysteriously liquidated sometime later.

Death of Shastri was the greater loss suffered by India at Tashkent. Had he returned to India alive, he might have given new orientation to India's foreign policy and ended her total dependence on Soviet Union, which had proved not only undependable but also dubious.

Soviet leaders were more concerned with global interests and global strategy of Soviet Union than with national interests of India. Independence of character and commitment to national interest above everything else that Lal Bahadur Shastri had displayed during his short tenure was not to the liking of Soviet Union and its supporters in India. They wanted a more pliable person committed to Nehruvian foreign policy to toeing the Soviet line even at the cost of vital national interest of India. That explained the interest Kosygin, who overstayed in Delhi for 4 days after the funeral of Lal Bahadur Shastri.

Pakistan was not sincere about Tashkent Declaration. This became clear from the statement made by Altaf Gauhar, Press

Secretary of President Ayub, soon after the signing of this Declaration. He was reported to have said that nothing but withdrawal of troops to August 5, position which suited Pakistan had been agreed upon and that Pakistan reserved the right to continue its efforts to secure Kashmir by force.

President Ayub confirmed this in his statement made at Hamburg in November, 1966. He said, "It (Tashkent Declaration) settled nothing. All it did was to enable the two countries to disengage their armies from each other".

From the Indian point of view, the futile Pak attempt to grab Kashmir by force had some positive results. In the first place even those parties in India like the Swatantra Party which had been advocating settlement with Pakistan about Kashmir in terms of UN resolutions conceded that Pakistan had forfeited its claim on Kashmir by taking resort to arms.

Mrs. Indira Gandhi, the new Prime Minister, also declared at New York on March 31, 1966: "It is now too late to talk of plebiscite. The second invasion of Kashmir by Pakistan last autumn has destroyed whatever marginal or academic value the old UN resolutions might have had.

Kashmir is now also vital to defence of Laddakh against China. Any plebiscite today would by definition amount to questioning the integrity of India. It will rouse the demand for accessation, against which is fought a civil war. We cannot and will not tolerate a second partition of India on religious ground. It will destroy the very basis of the Indian states".

Sheikh and Pakistan

The government of Pakistan in 1947 viewed Abdullah and his party as agents of Nehru and did not recognise his leadership of Kashmir. However there was a change in Pakistan's viewpoint with the passage of time. When he visited Pakistan in 1964, he was awarded a tumultuous welcome by the people of Pakistan.

Among the persons who received him was Chaudhary Ghulam Abbas his once colleague and later bitter political enemy, who earlier in his book "Kashmakash" had denounced Sheikh Abdullah as a turncoat and traitor. Chaudhary Ghulam Abbas embraced him and in his speech described him as one of the greatest leaders of the subcontinent and a great benefactor of the Muslims of the subcontinent. President Ayub Khan and his then Foreign minister Zulfikar Ali Bhutto discussed the Kashmir problem with him.

The government of Pakistan treated him as a state guest. Sheikh Abdullah had the rare distinction of having poems in his praise written by three major Pakistani Urdu poets namely Hafeez Jullundhri, Josh and Faiz Ahmed Faiz, who admired his lifelong struggle against injustice and for democratic rights of the common man.

9

Changing Facets of Kashmir Issue

(Based on various Accounts)

Nationalist and Secular Sheikh

It was long ago, that Sheikh Muhammed Abdullah, the greatest leader Kashmir has ever produced, was dismissed from the office of Prime Ministership of Jammu and Kashmir on August 9, 1953, and put in prison for 11 years, barring an interval of four months in 1958. A monstrous wrong demands monstrous efforts at cover-up and monstrous falsehoods to justify it to the people. A document came to light, which revealed the monstrosity of that wrong, the brazenness of the falsehoods that were retailed to justify it, and, sadly, the sheer folly of tha wholly unnecessary action.

The document showed also that the action was reversible before the wrong acquired a yet graver character. Someone suggested just that. That the suggestion was rejected revealed that it was not an impetuous action. It was calculated and executed in cold blood. The calculations were short-sighted.

The perpetrators of the deed overlooked its impact on those who mattered most – the people – because they had none too high an opinion of the people and imagined fondly that they were manageable. The people proved them wrong.

In 1953, Sheikh Abdullah was a symbol of the aspirations of the people. The wrong left a scar on the Kashmiri psyche that refused to heal even later, because, let alone separatists, even unionists resented it for long. Muzaffar Hussein Beg, Deputy Chief Minister in the People's Democratic Party (PDP)-Congress coalition in the State, said on May 2, 2003, while in office, that the Sheikh's dismissal was unconstitutional. He revealed what his party, the PDP, told N.N. Vohra, then an interlocutor on behalf of the Centre and now Governor of the State, when they met him on April 27. "We told Vohra that the Government at New Delhi has always been purchasing the leaders of the State. That can be done even today". He cited the record of arbitrary dismissals of Chief Ministers, since 1953.

B.K. Nehru, who was Governor of Jammu and Kashmir from 1992 to 1994, wrote in 1997: "From 1953 to 1975 Chief Ministers of that State had been nominees of Delhi. Their appointment to that post was legitimised by holding of farcical and totally rigged elections in which the Congress Party led by Delhi's nominee was elected by huge majorities" (*Nice Guys Finish Second*). In 1975, the Sheikh was reinstated as Chief Minister after he accepted the Centre's terms."

Mir Qasim was Chief Minister of Kashmir (1971-1975) and had supported the coup of 1953. He wrote in 1992:

- "Whenever New Delhi feels a leader in Kashmir is getting too big for his shoes, it employs Machiavellian methods to cut him to size". He proceeded to describe the technique which was still in vogue (*My Life and Times*).

The situation was not dissimilar in many significant respects – the rise of the Sangh Parivar; a powerful lobby at the Centre opposed to Jammu and Kashmir's autonomy; ambitious Kashmiri politicians angling for the Centre's support; hostility in large sections of the media; and unfounded fears of secession. If the lessons were taken to heart, one could devise a better course than was pursued since 1953.

The charges against Sheikh were consciously false. "It would be wrong to conclude that Sheikh Abdullah was as yet planning to take [*sic.*] Jammu and Kashmir into Pakistan. He was angling for a special status – just short of independence. He knew that he would have no position in Pakistan. He put Ghulam Mohiuddin Karra in prison in June 1953, when Karra openly came out in favour of Pakistan," wrote B.N. Mullik, Director of the Intelligence Bureau (I.B.), in his memoirs, *My Years with Nehru: Kashmir*. Could he have changed in a month and a half? The change came, not in the Sheikh, but in his friend, Prime Minister Jawaharlal Nehru, who personally gave the orders for his friend's dismissal to Mullik and his own secretary, M.O. Mathai, both on July 31. Mullik wrote that he "got information that Pir Maqbool Geelani had established contacts with Pakistan and that an emissary was on his way to Tanmarg (near Gulmarg) to meet the Sheikh.

Suspicions deepened when the Sheikh suddenly left for Tanmarg on the morning of 8 July". Actually, he left for Gulmarg, where he was arrested, and had announced his departure well in advance. Neither he nor the "emissary" could have escaped the I.B.'s surveillance. Mullik was in sole charge of the intelligence services.

The charge never figured in any of the secret letters that were published 40 years later. Pandit Prem Nat Bazaz, a former associate, who became a strong critic of Abdullah, wrote a devastating exposure of Mullik in *The Indian Express* (October 28 and 29, 1971): The I.B.'s surveillance of the Sheikh since 1948; its expulsion at the insistence of the State's Prime Minister; Mullik's intrigues with Deputy Prime Minister Bakshi Ghulam Mohammed and D.P. Dhar, a Minister.

This was the man who organised the prosecution in 1958, as a result of which he was confident that Sheikh and his colleagues "would be ruined for ever". It was on him, Nehru relied with equal disaster on the boundary problem with China. The Kongka Pass incident and the Forward Policy were his "gifts" which Nehru unwisely accepted.

Coup in Srinagar

Nehru's other confidante, Lieutenant-General B.M. Kaul, who also failed him in the 1962 war, was handpicked by him in 1953 to help in the execution of the coup in Srinagar. He was Brigadier then. Nehru "entrusted him with the task of passing on the word to Lt.-Gen. Atal, the Corps Commander at Udhampur and the Divisional Commander in Srinagar about the impending action... At this time, the Prime Minister, at the suggestion of Rafi Ahmed Kidwai, also sent A.P. Jain to Srinagar as his personal representative to hold a watching brief and ensure that the administrative action was not hasty but was tailored to the political needs" (Mullik). In Delhi, Kidwai was in charge. Kaul's memoirs, *The Untold Story* (1967), provided his version of the military debacle in the 1962 war and of the 1953 coup.

Nehru called him "in my private capacity" just as he had used him in 1949 when he was Defence Attache at the Embassy to propose an alliance to the United States, bypassing Ambassador Asaf Ali. He mentions not Tanmarg but Gulmarg. Bakshi and Dhar "knew well" in advance that Sheikh was going there "in a few days' time to meet certain 'friends' from across the border which was only seven miles away". He would then arrest Bakshi, Dhar and Co. and declare Kashmir independent. This charge also did not figure in Nehru's papers. It was too stupid for words.

Disgusted with both, Ajit Prasad Jain wrote his book *Kashmir* which was published in the Bombay monthly *Imprint* in June 1972. Kaul and he had exchanged words in the columns of *The Times of India on* August 22 and September 12, 1971. Jain wrote: "The General has reiterated that Abdullah was arrested without Nehru's approval. Unless he claims to be omniscient he would not know what had transpired between Nehru and me. Jawaharlal knew of the eventuality of arrest, and was prepared "not to resist it". The delicacy was delightful. Kaul and others falsely exclude Nehru from the deed, as do Nehru's drummer boys in the media and the academia. Jain admits it – but covers the sordid mess with an attractive veil."

These conflicting testimonies must be judged by established tests – inherent probabilities, the surrounding circumstances, and Nehru's own words as recorded by Mathai. They corroborated Kaul and Mullik and falsify Jain's assertion that Nehru "strongly felt that in no case should the Indian Army be involved in any action". This was not a military operation but a coup for which the police and the militia would have sufficed. Mullik pointed out that "it would be necessary for the Army authorities to sort out the unreliable elements of the militia and keep them under strict control", adding: "Moreover, he [Abdullah] could not ignore the presence cf the Indian Army". How then could he have arrested Bakshi and Co. or declared Kashmir independent? Besides the Army, he had to reckon with a hostile Head of State, Karan Singh, and Indian Administrative Service officers in the bureaucracy. How on earth could he have formed a government?

On one point all the three testimonies agreed – it was the Centre which inspired, directed and organised the whole affair. It was Nehru who personally inducted the I.B.'s Director Mullik and his Deputy, D.W. Mehra, at Amritsar. "The Prime Minister approved of Mehra's selection and asked me to send for him so that he could himself talk to him" (Mullik). Brigadier B.M. Kaul was deployed to secure the Army's help in need and Ajit Prasad Jain to ensure that "administrative action.... was tailored to the political needs". All three were Nehru's men, personally close to him.

However, Nehru was determined to let the responsibility fall squarely on the shoulders of Bakshi and others in Srinagar and keep himself out. He defended them in New Delhi, while calling the coup a local affair. Jain wrote: "I am afraid, General Kaul's story stating that the Sheikh was arrested on the authority of a junta made up of him and some Kashmiri Ministers on their own is no more than unfounded bragging. Nehru certainly wanted the responsibility for the action against the Sheikh to rest with Kashmiri leaders, but he would not resist any action, including Abdullah's arrest, which they considered unnecessary".

How and why did things come to such a pass between two friends of 20 years' standing? Nehru knew well the vision Sheikh Abdullah and his colleagues had of Kashmir. Their plan for Nya Kashmir (New Kashmir), which unfolded in 1944, envisaged an independent State even if India was not partitioned. The Draft Constitution of 50 Clauses provided for a constitutional Monarch as Head of State; a National Assembly with powers in respect of defence and foreign affairs and a separate citizenship. "The defence of the Motherland is the supreme and duty of all citizens".

A Peasants' Charter, a Workers' Charter, a National Health Charter and a Women's Charter formed part of this remarkably progressive plan. In his Foreword, Sheikh Abdullah cited "the inspiring picture of the regeneration of all the different nationalities and peoples of the USSR [Union of Soviet Socialist Republics]". (New Kashmir; the All Jammu and Kashmir National Conference, Mujahid Manzil, Srinagar.) He greatly admired the Soviet Union. He feli out with Jinnah in 1939, when the Muslim League criticised the conversion of the Muslim Conference into the National Conference.

The League should "leave the Kashmir Muslims alone", he said at Lahore on April 4, 1939 (*Tribune;* April 5, 1939). Jinnah and Abdullah had angry exchanges in 1944. Pakistan's tribal raid triggered Kashmir's accession to India, whose ideology and ethos the Sheikh shared. But he was soon discomfited by the distrust shown by Vallabhbhai Patel, who supported the ruler, and by Mullik's intrigues.

Kashmir was the only State which negotiated the terms on which it accepted the Constitution of India, from May to October 1949. Article 370 recorded a solemn compact. But while Sheikh Abdullah and his colleagues were out in the lobby, the draft was pushed through in the Constituent Assembly, with a change made unilaterally. (Nehru was in the US) N. Gopalaswamy Ayyangar admitted the unilateral change but called it "trivial". Maulana Azad was privy to this, as was Patel, whose letter to Nehru on November 3, 1949, justified the substantial change (*Sardar Patel's Correspondence*).

In an interview to Michael Davidson in *The Scotsman* of April 14, 1949, Sheikh Abdullah had proposed "an independent Kashmir... guaranteed not only by India and Pakistan" but also by the Great Powers (*ibid*). But he was totally opposed to a plebiscite. If no settlement was possible, he was happy to be in India. So much so that on January 12, 1949, Nehru had to assure him that, though he had accepted the UN Commission's plebiscite proposals on December 23, 1948 (published on January 5, 1949), "you know that this business of plebiscite is still far away and there is a possibility of the plebiscite not taking place at all. I would suggest that this should not be said in public" (Selected Works of Jawaharlal Nehru; volume 9). He hinted that "new arrangements" might be made, instead of a plebiscite.

The Constituent Assembly of Jammu and Kashmir met on October 31, 1951. Sheikh Abdullah wanted it to ratify the State's accession to India, but Nehru refused. At a press conference in New Delhi on June 21, 1952, Nehru disclosed: "When the Constituent Assembly met in Kashmir for the first time, I might inform you that it was its intention to pass a resolution forthwith confirming the State's accession to India. We asked it not to do it so as not to be embarrassed before the United Nations".

A grave complication arose. On October 21, 1951, the Bharatiya Jan Sangh was set up under the leadership of Shyama Prasad Mukherjee, former president of the Hindu Mahasabha and colleague of V.D. Savarkar. He had resigned from Nehru's Cabinet in 1950 and was looking out for an attractive plank. Its first annual session was held at Kanpur when it decided on December 31, 1952, to launch an agitation for the complete integration of Jammu and Kashmir with India. By then, its anti-Nehru, anti-Abdullah campaign was well under way. There were those in the Congress who sympathised with them.

Pressures grew on Nehru, from without and within, and within his own self. He had ruled out plebiscite in 1948 and proposed partition to Pakistan. He now began to chafe at Kashmir's special status and the Sheikh's assertions of autonomy. These three forces – in the Sangh Parivar, the Patelites in the Congress, and his own emotions – drove him hard.

There were none around him wise and strong enough to counsel patience. V.K. Krishna Menon, Rafi Ahmed Kidwai and Maulana Azad, concerned at his loss of power and themselves hardliners on Kashmir, had little understanding of Kashmir. Nehru had; yet he sinned against the light. After the coup, admirers defended him by attributing the deed to Kidwai. In truth, he was only a glorified operator, fund collector and hatchet man.

The decision was Nehru's alone. Kidwai was allowed free speech and choice of means. The ends were set by Nehru. Braggarts had a field day. In London, Mahavir Tyagi made such claims for his role that the High Commissioner Vijaya Lakshmi Pandit had to report to Nehru, who was contemptuously amused.

Sheikh's Preference for India

What of Sheikh? The change that came over him is regarded as perfidy in India. Nehru knew better. His friend had preferred India to Pakistan because of its secular ideals. Patel and Ayyangar disturbed him. The rise of the Sangh Parivar posed the question "What will happen to Kashmir after Nehru?" He did not have to wait for that tragedy for the worst to happen.

Nehru knew exactly how Kashmiris felt. He told a public rally in Calcutta on New Year's Day, 1952: "There can be no greater vindication than this of our secular policies, our Constitution, than that we have drawn the people of Kashmir towards us. But just imagine what would have happened in Kashmir if the Jan Sangh or any other communal party had been at the helm of affairs. The people of Kashmir say that they are fed up with this communalism. Why should they live in a country where the Jan Sangh and the Rashtriya Swayam Sewak Sangh are constantly beleaguering them? They will go elsewhere and they will not stay with us". Indeed, "If the people of Kashmir tell us to get out, we will do so". The dispute was before the United Nations. "We have given our word of honour that we shall abide by their decision. India's pledge is no small matter and we shall stick by it in the eyes of the world" (Selected Works of Jawaharlal Nehru; volume 17).

He added: "Now these Hindu communal parties like the Jan Sangh and Rashtriya Swayam Sewak Sangh and another party called the Praja Parishad in Jammu have launched an agitation against the Sheikh Abdullah government. They abuse him and want the old Maharaja to come back. Now you can imagine what this means. At the moment, it is Sheikh Abdullah, who is completely opposed to Pakistan. There is no doubt about it that he is the leader of the people of Kashmir, a very great leader. If tomorrow Sheikh Abdullah wanted Kashmir to join Pakistan, neither I nor all the forces of India would be able to stop it because if the leader decides, it will happen".

On April 10, 1952, came Abdullah's famous speech at Ranbirsinghpura. He said that Kashmir's accession to India would have to be of a restricted nature as the communal spirit still existed in India. While the government of India was trying to curb communalism, unlike that of Pakistan, it was none too successful. He did not equate the two. "So far as Kashmir was concerned, it wanted to preach the mission of secular democracy, both to India and Pakistan".

Yet, Nehru was upset and reproached his friend, relying unwisely on a Press Trust of India report. Far more unwise was the reversal of his 1951 stand that Kashmir's Constituent Assembly cannot finalise accession. When he met Mirza Afzal Beg, Maulana Mohammed Saeed Masoodi and D.P. Dhar on June 19, 1952, he told them that "even before they finalised their Constitution, the relationship of Kashmir to India must be fully clarified" (Selected Works of Jawaharlal Nehru; volume 18). It was "the first question to decide", he reported to President Rajendra Prasad. They reported the change to a disturbed Sheikh.

It was in this background that the Nehru-Abdullah accord, "the Delhi Agreement", was concluded on July 24, 1952. The issues were constitutional – the extension of Central institutions to Jammu and Kashmir. But the differences were political, and they lingered. The two had different perceptions of the accord – Nehru treated it as a step towards finalising the accession; the Sheikh, as a temporary reprieve while the Constituent Assembly finalised the State's Constitution. Banter could not conceal that. In his memoirs, *Aatish-e-Chinar*, the Sheikh recalled that during the talks Nehru exclaimed, "Sheikh if you do not stand with us shoulder to shoulder, we shall cast a chain of gold around your neck". The Sheikh looked at him and said smilingly, "But don't do that ever because you will thereby have to wash your hands of Kashmir".

The stark reality was that unpopular as accession itself was, Sheikh could manage the situation, despite the Maharaja's and Patel's obstruction, because Nehru had left him free to voice regional self-assertion within the Union.

Nehru's curbs and the rise of the Sangh Parivar combined to increase popular resentment. The Sheikh found the ground slipping away from under his feet. If on May 14, 1948, Indira Gandhi reported to Nehru from Srinagar that "only Sheikh is confident of winning the plebiscite", on July 14, 1953, President Rajendra Prasad wrote to Nehru that Vice-President S. Radhakrishnan, who had been there, reported "even Sheikh Abdullah thought we would lose in a plebiscite as Sheikh Abdullah himself had told him that" (Dr. Rajendra Prasad: Correspondence and Select Documents; volume 16).

In this situation came Nehru's definitive statement of policy of August 25, 1952, given confidentially to the Sheikh, dispelling all doubt in the recipient's mind. Nehru wanted to finalise the accession. The next step would be the end of Jammu and Kashmir's autonomy. Amazingly, in public he always sang a different tune – he would hold a plebiscite.

His speech in the Lok Sabha on June 26, 1952, for instance: "It just does not matter what your Constitution says. If the people of Kashmir do not want it, it will not go there". If the plebiscite went against India, he would accept the verdict "and we would change our Constitution about it".

Nehru's note of August 25, 1952, made a startling revelation about his change of mind. "Towards the end of 1948.... it became clear to me then that we would never get the conditions which were necessary for a plebiscite... so I ruled out the plebiscite for all practical purposes". Why then did he accept the plebiscite proposals of the United Nations Commission for India and Pakistan (UNCIP) in December 1948? The Note, written at Sonmarg, was a piece of real politik (Selected Works of Jawaharlal Nehru; volume 19). Kashmiris "are not what are called a virile people. They are soft and addicted to easy living"; "We are superior to Pakistan in military and industrial power"; the UN is impotent. "Doubts in the minds of leaders percolate to their followers and to the people generally... What is required is a firm and clear outlook, and no debate about basic issues".

Nehru was wrong on all three points. 1. It is the people's feelings which moved the leaders not the other way round. 2. The Sheikh represented them only as long as he voiced their views. 3. Nehru thought that the Sheikh would hold those feelings down and cooperate in accomplishing his designs. This he refused to do. Sheikh Abdullah turned a Becket to Jawaharlal Nehru's Henry II.

The "turbulent" friend had to be got rid of.

10

Sheikh's Legacy

Dr. Farooq Abdullah (Sheikh's Successor)

Dr. Farooq Abdullah (born 21 October 1937 in Soura, Jammu & Kashmir), is the son of Sheikh Abdullah. He is a doctor of medicine and has served as chief minister of Jammu and Kashmir on several occasions since 1982. He is married to Molly, a lady of British origin.

Abdullah was a novice in the political arena of Jammu and Kashmir when he was appointed president of the National Conference in August, 1981. His main qualification was that he was an honest and clean person. After his father's death in 1982, Farooq Abdullah became the Chief Minister of the state. But in 1984, the Abdullah government was dismissed by the Governor and replaced with a pro-Congress government under Ghulam Mohammad Shah. In 1986, that government was dismissed and a new National Conference–Congress government was sworn in with Farooq Abdullah as the Chief Minister. A new election was held in 1987 and the National Conference–Congress alliance won the election amid allegations of unfair means used. This period saw a rise in militancy in the state, with the return of trained militants from Pakistan and incidents that included the kidnapping of the daughter of the Union Home Minister Mufti Saeed.

Subsequently, the Farooq government was dismissed once again and the state was brought under President's rule. In 1996, he was once again sworn in as Chief Minister of the state, for the fifth time. In 2002, Farooq Abdullah was elected to Rajya Sabha from Jammu and Kashmir for a first six year term. He was subsequently re-elected in 2009. Farooq Abdullah joined the United Progressive Alliance government as a Cabinet Minister.

Current Status

He is now, Minister of New and Renewable Energy. His Ministry is responsible mainly for research and development intellectual property protection, and international cooperation, promotion and coordination in renewable energy sources such as wind power, small hydro, biogas, and solar power, etc.

Omar Abdullah (Now at the Helm)

Omar Abdullah, born 10 March 1970 in United Kingdom, is the scion of Kashmir's 'first family', the Abdullah family and son of Dr. Farooq Abdullah.

He studied at the Burn Hall School, Srinagar. He later studied at the exclusive institution, The Lawrence School, Sanawar. He is an alumnus of prestigious Sydenham College, Mumbai (where he did his B.Com.). After that he joined the University of Strathclyde, Scotland, for an MBA, although he did not complete it.

He became the 11th and the youngest Chief Minister of Jammu and Kashmir after forming a government in coalition with the Congress party, on January 5, 2009.

Earlier at Centre: Prior to this he was a member of 14th Lok Sabha representing Srinagar constituency of Jammu and Kashmir. He was a Union Minister of State for External affairs in Atal Bihari Vajpayee's NDA government, from July 23, 2001 to December 23, 2002. He resigned from NDA government in October 2002 to concentrate on party work. Prime Minister tried to convince him to continue his work. However, on 23 December 2002 his resignation was accepted by President A P J Abdul Kalam.

He is the grandson of Sheikh Abdullah, who formed Kashmir's first political party the Muslim Conference in 1932, which was later rechristened as National Conference. Omar joined politics in 1998, as a Lok Sabha member, a feat he repeated in subsequent three elections. He took on the mantle of National Conference from his father in 2002, though he lost his own seat of Ganderbalduring the 2002 state assembly elections, and so did his party. He fought once again from the very seat and won in the 2008 Elections.

He married Payal Nath, daughter of an Army officer, Major General Ram Nath from Delhi on September 1, 1994, and the couple have had two sons, Zahir and Zamir, hence. His sister Sarah Abdullah is married to Sachin Pilot son of Rajesh Pilot.

Political Career: In 1998, Omar Abdullah was elected to 12th Lok Sabha. In 1998-99, he was Member, Committee on Transport and Tourism and Member, Consultative Committee, Ministry of Tourism. He was the youngest Minister at the age of 29. In 1999, he was re-elected to 13th Lok Sabha (2nd term). On October 13, 1999. He took oath as Union Minister of State, Commerce and Industry. On July 22, 2001, he became the youngest Union Minister. Later, he was made Union Minister of State for External affairs a post he resigned from on December 23, 2002, to concentrate on party work.

On June 23, 2002, he became the President of National Conference replacing his father Farooq Abdullah; he was re-elected as party's President for a second term in 2006.

He lost his Ganderbal seat in Kashmir assembly elections which were held in September–October 2002.

In March 2006, much to the disapproval of the centre, Omar Abdullah had a one-on-one meeting with Pakistan President, Pervez Musharaf in Islamabad. This was the first meeting of its kind between a main-stream politician from Jammu & Kashmir and the Pakistani government thereby re-enforcing Omar's growing commitment to the solution of the Jammu & Kashmir cause - no matter what the stakes might be; Omar received a rousing reception by thousands of Kashmiris upon his return from there.

On July 9, 2007, Omar escaped a bid on his life when suspected militants threw two rifle grenades targeted at him. The incident happened when Omar was interacting with party workers at a party leader's house.

Once, he spoke in Lok Sabha thus:

> "I am a Muslim and I am an Indian, and I see no distinction between the two. I don't know why should I fear the nuclear deal. It is a deal between two countries which, I hope, will become two equals in the future. The enemies of Indian Muslims are not America or deals like these. The enemies are the same as the enemies of all those who are poor—poverty, hunger, lack of development and the absence of a voice...."

On July 22, 2008, Omar gave a passionate speech during the 2008 Lok Sabha vote of confidence, which was praised by almost all quarters, and even won him fans on the net. He was also seen briefly, playing himself, in director Apoorva Lakhia's film, Mission Istanbul (2008), based on international terrorism.

After the 2008 Kashmir Elections, the National Conference won the maximum number of seats, and formed a coalition government with Congress party, and Omar was sworn in as the 11th Chief Minister of Jammu and Kashmir on January 5, 2009 at the General Zoravar Singh Stadium in the University of Jammu, Jammu, raising a new hope amongst the people of Jammu and Kashmir who have been reeling under insurgency and violence since 1989. Omar Abdullah on 28 July 2009 submitted his resignation to Governor N N Vohra Omar Abdullah resigned over sex scandal allegations against him by the opposition PDP. His resignation was however rejected by the governor N. N. Vohra. Currently, he is Chief Minister of the State.

National Conference (The Party Founded by Sheikh)

The Jammu & Kashmir National Conference is a State political party in the state of Jammu and Kashmir, India. Led at the time of Indian Independence in 1947 by Sheikh Abdullah, it dominated electoral politics in the state for many decades. It has been led subsequently by the Sheikh's son Farooq Abdullah and now by his son Omar Abdullah.

History

The Pre-independence Period: In October, 1932, Sheikh Abdullah founded the All Jammu and Kashmir Muslim Conference. On June 11, 1939 it was renamed as the All Jammu and Kashmir National Conference. The National Conference was affiliated to the All India States Peoples Conference and in 1947 Sheikh Abdullah was elected its president. In 1946, the National Conference launched an intensive agitation against the state government. It was directed against the Maharaja. The slogan of the agitation was "Quit Kashmir".

The Post-independence Period: In the elections held in September, 1951, National Conference won all 75 seats of the Constituent assembly of Jammu and Kashmir. Sheikh Abdullah remained the prime minister till his arrest on August 9, 1953 on the alleged grounds of conspiracy against India. In 1953 Sheikh Abdullah was dismissed and Bakshi Ghulam Mohammad became the Prime Minister of the state. In 1965 the National Conference became the Jammu and Kashmir branch of the Indian National Congress. Sheikh Abdullah was again arrested in 1965 until 1968 due to his pro-Kashmir stances that were termed as conspiracy against the state. Sheikh Abdullah's splinter Plebiscite Front faction later appropriated the name of the original party when Abdullah returned to power in February 1975.

In 1977, National Conference led by him won the state assembly elections, and Sheikh Abdullah became the chief minister. His son, Farooq Abdullah succeeded him as the Chief Minister on his death on September 8, 1982. In June, 1983 elections, the JKNC led by Farooq Abdullah again won a comfortable majority. In July, 1984 Farooq's brother-in-law Ghulam Mohammad Shah split the party. Acting on the behest of the central government, the, (then) Governor, Jagmohan dismissed Farooq as Chief Minister and installed Ghulam Mohammad Shah in his place. His government was dismissed in March, 1986 and President's rule was imposed.

In 1987 state assembly elections, the JKNC, which formed an alliance with the Congress Party won the majority and Farooq again became the Chief Minister. But he was dismissed again in 1990 by the Union Government led by Vishwanath Pratap

Singh and President's rule was imposed in the state. In Jammu and Kashmir state assembly elections in 1996, the National Conference led by Farooq made another political comeback by winning 57 seats out of total 87.

But, in 2002 state assembly elections, it won only 28 seats. In December, 2008 state assembly elections no single party was able to get the majority. The JKNC led by Farooq's son Omar Abdullah emerged as a single largest party, winning 28 seats. After the elections, on December 30, 2008 the JKNC formed an alliance with the Congress Party, which won 17 seats. Omar Abdullah became the Chief Minister ot this coalition government on January 5, 2009. He still holds the position.

11

Significant Speeches and Statements

Speech in UN Security Council

Aggression, not Accession, is the issue.

I have heard with patience, attention and respect the statements made by the representative of Pakistan and members of the Security council, as well as the statements made on various occasions by the members of my own delegation. The Security Council will concede that I am probably the one man most concerned in the dispute because I happen to come from that land which has become the bone of contention between the two Dominions of India and Pakistan.

I have been quoted profusely on either side, and rightly so, because I have had the fortune-or, should I say, misfortune of leading my countrymen to freedom from 1931 onwards. In this task, I have suffered a great deal. I have been imprisoned not once or twice, but seven times, and the last imprisonment carried with it an aggregate sentence of nine years.

There are many troubles in Kashmir. I have heard patiently to the debate in the Security Council, but I feel that I am rather confused. After all, what is the point in dispute? The point in dispute is not that the sovereignty of the Prince is in question, as the representative of Pakistan stated yesterday. After all, I have suffered the punishment of being sentenced to nine years imprisonment for saying what the representative of Pakistan said with regard to the Treaty of Kashmir of 1846. I am glad that he said in the Security Council, where he is immune from any punishment. Therefore, I am not disputing that point and that it is not the subject of the dispute before the Security Council.

The subject of the dispute before the Security Council is not the mal-administration of the Princely State of Kashmir. In order to set right that mal-administration, I think I have suffered the most, and today, when for the first time, I heard the representative of Pakistan supporting my case, it gave me great pleasure.

After all, what is the dispute between India and Pakistan? From what I have learned from the complaint brought before the Security Council by my own delegation, the dispute revolves around the fact that Kashmir acceded legally and constitutionally to the Dominion of India. There was some trouble about the demarcation of the Kashmir administration within the State, and the tribesmen from across the border have poured into my country. They have been helped and are being helped by the Pakistan Government, with the result that there is the possibility of a greater conflagration between India and Pakistan. India sought the help of Security Council so that Pakistan might be requested to desist from helping the tribesmen, and to desist from supporting the inside revolt, should I say, against the lawful authority.

I should have understood the position of the representative of Pakistan if he had come boldly before the Security Council and maintained: "Yes, we do support the tribesmen; we do support the rebels inside the State because we feel that Kashmir belongs to Pakistan and not to India, and because we feel that the accession of Kashmir to India was fraudulent". Then we might have discussed the validity of the accession of the State of Kashmir to India. But that was not the position taken by the representative of Pakistan. He completely denied that any support was being given by the Government of Pakistan to either the tribesmen or those who are in revolt within the State against the constituted authority.

How am I to convince the Security Council that the denial is absolutely untrue? I am sitting before the Security Council at a distance of thousands of miles from my country. I have fought many battles, along with my own men, on the borders of Jammu and Kashmir. I have seen with my own eyes the support given by the Pakistan Government, not only in supplying buses but in providing arms, ammunition, direction and control of the tribesmen and I have even seen the Pakistan Army forces from across the border.

The denial has come so flatly that it becomes very difficult for me to disprove it here before the Security Council, unless the Security Council accedes to our request to send a commission to the spot and to find out first whether the allegations brought before the Security Council with regard to the aid given by the Government of Pakistan are correct or incorrect. If they are incorrect, the case falls; if they are correct, then the Security Council should take the necessary steps to advise the Government of Pakistan to desist from such support.

But then, this simple issue has been confused. On the one hand, the Pakistan Government says, "We are not a party to the trouble within the State. The trouble within the State exists because the people are fighting against the mal-administration of the Jammu and Kashmir Government". Yes, we are fighting, we have been fighting against the mal-administration of that State since 1931. We have been demanding democratisation of the Government there. But how is it that today Pakistan has become the champion of our liberty? I know very well that in 1946, when I raised the cry "Quit Kashmir," the leader of the Pakistan Government, who is the Governor-General now, Mr. Mohammed Ali Jinnah, opposed my Government, declaring that this movement was a movement of a few renegades and that Muslims as such had nothing to do with the movement.

The Muslim Conference, which has been talked about so much, opposed my movement and declared its loyalty to the Prince. The representative of Pakistan now says that Sheikh Abdullah, once the supporter of "Quit Kashmir", has joined hands with the Maharaja of Kashmir, and that in one of my public speeches I declared that I wanted the Maharaja to be the Maharaja of Jammu and Kashmir-not the Maharaja of Jammu only, but the Maharaja of entire State.

I should like to correct the misreporting of my speech. I did deliver that speech in Jammu, which is the winter capital of our country, but it was in a different context. As the members of the Security Council have already heard from the head of my delegation, some massacres did occur in the Jammu Province. After the Kashmir Province was raided by the tribesmen, and after thousands of Hindus and Sikhs were uprooted from the villages and towns in the Kashmir Province and found their way into the Jammu Province, there was some very bad retaliation. I could not go to Jammu Province to control that situation because I was busy with the raiders in Kashmir Province. However, as soon as I had some time, I flew down to Jammu Province, addressed a gathering of 60,000 Hindus and Sikhs in Jammu city, and gave them some plain advice.

I told them clearly that this policy of retaliation would bring no good to them as Hindus and Sikhs and would bring no good to their leader, because while they could retaliate in one or two districts where they formed the majority, and could even wipe out the Muslim population in these one or two districts, the State happens to have a population which is 80 per cent Muslim, and it would be impossible for them to wipe out the entire Muslim population. The result would be that the Prince, whom they wanted to support, would remain the Prince of only two districts, and not of the entire State of Jammu and Kashmir. I told them that if they wanted him to be the Prince of Jammu and Kashmir, they would have to change their behaviour. That was the speech I delivered, and that was the context in which it was made.

However, I have already stated how this trouble started. It is probable that the representative of Pakistan would admit that when India was divided into two parts, my colleagues and I were all behind prison bars. The result of this division of India was to start massacre on either side. Where Muslims in the West Punjab formed the majority, the killing of Hindus and Sikhs started and this was retaliated in East Punjab. All along our border, massacres of Hindus and Sikhs, on the one hand, and Muslims on the other hand, were a daily occurrence. But the State of Jammu and Kashmir, and its people, kept calm. The result was that thousands of refugees, both Muslims and Hindus, sought refuge in our State and we rendered every possible help to all of them.

Why was that so? It was because I and my organisation never believed in the formula that Muslims and Hindus form separate nations. We do not believe in the two-nation theory, nor in communal hatred or communalism itself. We believed that religion had no place in politics. Therefore, when we launched our movement of "Quit Kashmir", it was not only Muslims who suffered, but our Hindu and Sikh comrades as well. That created a strong bond of unity between all the communities, and the result was that while Hindus, Sikhs and Muslims were fighting each other all along the border, the people of Jammu and Kashmir State — Muslims, Hindus and Sikhs alike-remained calm.

The situation was worsening day by day and the minority in our State was feeling very nervous. As a result, tremendous pressure was brought to bear upon the State administration to release me and my colleagues. The situation outside demanded the release of workers of the National Conference, along with its leader, and we were accordingly set free.

Immediately we were liberated from prison we were faced with the important question of whether Kashmir should accede to Pakistan, accede to India, or remain independent, because under the partition scheme these three choices were open us as, indeed, they were open to every Indian State. The problem was a very difficult one, but I advised the people of my country that although the question was very important to us, it was a secondary consideration. The all important matter for us was our own liberation from the autocratic rule of the Prince for which we were fighting and had been fighting for the past seventeen years. We had not achieved that goal, and therefore I told my people that we must do so first. Then, as free men we should have to decide where our interest lay. Being a frontier State, Kashmir has borders with both Pakistan and India, and there are advantages and disadvantages for the people of Kashmir attached to each of the three alternatives to which I have referred.

Naturally, as I have indicated, we could not decide this all important issue before achieving our own liberation, and our slogan became "Freedom before accession". Some friends from Pakistan met me in Srinagar. I had a heart- to- heart discussion with them and explained my point of view. I told them in plain words that, whatever had been the attitude of Pakistan towards our freedom movement in the past, it would not influence us in our judgement. Neither the friendship of Pandit Jawaharlal Nehru and of Congress, nor their support of our freedom movement, would have any influence upon our decision if we felt that the interests of four million Kashmiris lay in our accession to Pakistan.

I requested them not to precipitate this decision upon us but to allow us time, supporting our movement for the while. I added that once we were free they should allow us an interval to consider this all important issue. I pointed out that India had accepted this point of view and was not forcing us to decide. We had, in fact, entered into a standstill agreement with both Pakistan and India, but the leader of the Indian delegation has already explained to the Security Council what Pakistan did to us.

While I was engaged in these conversations and negotiations with friends from Pakistan, I sent one of my colleagues to Lahore, where he met the Prime Minister of Pakistan, Mr. Liaqat Ali Khan, and other high dignitaries of the West Punjab Government. He placed the same point of view before them and requested that they should allow us time to consider this vital question, first helping us to achieve our liberation instead of forcing us to declare our decision one way or the other. Then, one fine morning while these negotiations were proceeding, I received news that a full-fledged attack had been carried out by the raiders on Muzaffarabad, frontier town in the Kashmir Province.

The representative of Pakistan has stated that immediately upon my release I went down to Delhi to negotiate the accession of Kashmir to India. That is not a fact. He probably does not know that while in jail I was elected President of the All India States People's Conference, and that immediately upon my release I had to take up my duties. Accordingly, I had called a meeting of the executive of that Conference in Delhi, a fact which I had conveyed to the Prime Minister of Pakistan. Indeed, I had told the Prime Minister of Pakistan that immediately upon my return from Delhi I should take the opportunity of meeting him personally to discuss my point of view with him. I did not go to Delhi to conclude any agreement on behalf of Kashmir because, although released, I was still considered a rebel.

I might inform the representative of Pakistan that although I am beyond doubt the head of the Administration of Kashmir State, I am not the Prime Minister. I am head of the Emergency Administration, and that not because the Maharaja of Kashmir wished it. In fact, I do not know whether the Maharaja wishes it even now. I hold the position because the people of my country wish me to be at the helm of affairs in Jammu and Kashmir State.

When the raiders came to our land, massacred thousands of people—mostly Hindus and Sikhs, but Muslims, too—abducted thousands of girls, Hindus, Sikhs and Muslims alike, looted our property and almost reached the gates of our summer capital, Srinagar, the result was that the civil, military and police administrations failed. The Maharaja, in the dead of night, left the capital alongwith his courtiers, and the result was absolute panic. There was no one to take over control. In that hour of crisis, the National Conference came forward with its 10,000 volunteers and took over the administration of the country. They started guarding the banks, the offices and houses of every person in the capital. This is the manner in which the administration changed hands. We were *de facto* in charge of the administration. The Maharaja, later on, gave it a legal form.

It is said that Sheikh Abdullah is a friend of Pandit Jawaharlal Nehru. Yes, I admit that. I feel honoured that such a great man claims me as his friend. And he happens to belong to my own country; he is also a Kashmiri, and blood is thicker than water. If Jawaharlal Nehru gives me that honour, I cannot help it. He is my friend. But that does not mean that, because of his friendship, I am going to betray the millions of my people who have suffered along with me for the last seventeen years and sacrifice the interests of my country. I am not a man of that calibre.

I was explaining how the dispute arose—how Pakistan wanted to force this position of slavery upon us. Pakistan had no interest in our liberation or it would not also have opposed our freedom movement. Pakistan would have supported us when thousands of my countrymen were behind bars and hundreds were shot to death. The Pakistani leaders and Pakistani papers were heaping abuse upon the people of Kashmir who were suffering these tortures.

Then suddenly, Pakistan comes before the bar of the world as the champion of the liberty of the people of Jammu and Kashmir. The world may believe this, but it is very difficult for me to believe.

When we refused the coercive tactics of Pakistan, it started full fledged aggression and encouraged the tribesmen in this activity. It is absolutely impossible for the tribesmen to enter our territory without encouragement from Pakistan, because it is necessary to pass through Pakistan territory to reach Jammu and Kashmir. Hundreds of trucks, thousands of gallons of petrol, thousands of rifles, ammunition, and all forms of help that an army requires, were supplied to them. We know this. After all, we belong to that country. What Pakistan could not achieve by the use of economic blockade it wanted to achieve by full-fledged aggression.

What do we request? We request nothing more than that the Security Council should send some members to this area to see for themselves what is happening there.

If Pakistan comes forward and says, "We question the legality of accession", I am prepared to discuss whether or not the accession of Jammu and Kashmir to India was legal. However, now they say, "We want a plebiscite, we want to obtain the free and unfettered opinion of the people of Kashmir. There should be no pressure exerted on the people and they should make the free choice as to the State to which they wish to accede".

Not only this the offer that was made by the people of Kashmir to Pakistan long, long ago, but it is the offer made by the Prime Minister of India at a time, I think, he had not the slightest need for making it, as Kashmir was in distress.

We realised that Pakistan would not allow us any time, that we had either to suffer the fate of our kith and kin of Muzaffarabad, Baramulla, Srinagar and other towns and villages, or to seek help from some outside authority.

Under these circumstances, both the Maharaja and the people of Kashmir requested the Government of India to accept our accession. The Government of India could have easily accepted the accession and could have said, "All right we accept your accession and we shall render this help". There was no necessity for the Prime Minister of India to add the proviso, when accepting the accession, that India does not want to take advantage of the difficult situation in Kashmir. We will accept this accession, without Kashmir's acceding to the Indian Dominion, we are not in a position to render any military help. But once the country is free from the raiders, marauders and looters, this accession will be subject to ratification by the people. That was the offer made by the Prime Minister of India.

That was the same offer which was made by the people of Kashmir to the Government of Pakistan, but it was refused because at that time Pakistan felt that it could, within a week, conquer the entire Jammu and Kashmir State and then place the fait accompli before the world, just as happened some time ago in Europe. The same tactics were used.

But having failed in these tactics, Pakistan now comes before the bar of the world, pleading, "We want nothing, we only want our people to be given a free hand in deciding their own fate. And in deciding their own fate, they must have a plebiscite".

They then continue and say, "No, a plebiscite cannot be fair and impartial unless and until there is a neutral administration in the State of Jammu and Kashmir". I have failed to understand this terminology with reference to a "neutral administration". After all what does "neutral administration" mean?

The representative of Pakistan has stated that Sheikh Abdullah, because he is a friend of Jawaharlal Nehru, because he has had sympathy for the Indian National Congress, because he has declared his point of view in favour of accession to India, and because he is head of the Emergency Administration, cannot remain impartial. Therefore, Sheikh Abdullah must depart.

Let us suppose that Sheikh Abdullah goes, who is to replace Sheikh Abdullah? It will be someone amongst the 4 million people of the State of Jammu and Kashmir. But can we find anyone among these 4 million people whom we can call impartial? After all, we are not logs of wood, we are not dolls. We must have an opinion one way or the other. The people of Kashmir are either in favour of Pakistan or in favour of India.

Therefore, Pakistan's position comes down to this that the 4 million people of that State should have no hand in running the administration of their own country. Someone else must come in for that purpose. Is that fair ? Is that just ? Do the members of the Security Council wish to oust the people of Kashmir from running their own administration and their own country?

Then, for argument's sake, let us suppose that the 4 million people of the State of Jammu and Kashmir agree to have nothing to do with the administration of their country; some one else must be brought into the country for this purpose. From where do the members of the Security Council propose that such a neutral individual may be secured? From India? No, from Pakistan? No, from anywhere in the world? No, frankly speaking, even if the Security Council were to request Almighty God to administer the State of Jammu and Kashmir during this interim period, I do not feel that He could act impartially. After all, one must have sympathy either for this side or that side.

If elections were to be held in the United Kingdom sometime after tomorrow with the Labour Government in power, would anyone say to Mr. Attlee: "The elections are now going on. Because you happen to belong to Labour Party, your sympathies will be in favour of the Labour vote. Therefore, you had better clear out. We must have a neutral man as Prime Minister until our elections are finished?

However, we have been told that Sheikh Abdullah must walk out because he has declared his point of view in favour of India. Therefore, he cannot be impartial. We must have some impartial man, we must have some neutral man.

As I have submitted to the members of the Security Council, Sheikh Abdullah happens to be there because the people wish it. As long as the people wish it, I shall be there. There is no power on earth which can displace me from the position which I have there. As long as the people are behind me, I will remain there.

We have declared once for all, that there shall be freedom of voting and for that purpose we have said, "Let anyone come in, we have no objection. Let the Commission of the Security Council on India come into our State and advise us how we should take a vote, how we should organise it, and how it can be completely impartial. We have no objection". My Government is ready to satisfy, to the last comma, the impartiality of the vote.

But to have an impartial vote is one thing; to have a say in the administration of the State is a different thing entirely. After all, with what are we concerned? We are concerned only with the fact that no influence shall be exercised over the voters, either in one way or in another. The people shall be free to vote according to their own interests. We are ready to accede to that.

It is then said: "You cannot have freedom of voting as long as the Indian Army remains in the State of Jammu and Kashmir". It is probably very difficult for me to draw a full picture of what is going on in that country. There is absolute chaos in certain parts of the country, fighting is going on and thousands of tribesmen are there ready to take advantage of any weakness on the part of the State of Jammu and Kashmir.

Once we ask the Indian Army, which is the only protective force in Kashmir against these marauders, to clear out, we leave the country open to chaos. After all, one who has suffered for the last seventeen years, in attempting to secure the freedom and liberation of his own country, would not like an outside army to come in and to remain in the country.

However, what is the present situation? If I ask the Indian Army to clear out, how am I going to protect the people from the looting, arson, murder and abduction with which they have been faced all these long months? What is the alternative? here need be no fear, since the Indian Army is there, that this army will interfere in the exercise of a free vote. After all, a Commission of the Security Council will be there in order to watch.

The Indian Army does not have to go into every village. It will be stationed at certain strategic points, so that in the event of danger from any border, the Army will be there to protect that border. The army is there to curb disorders anywhere in the State; that is all. The army will not be in each and every village in order to watch each and every vote.

It is then said: "Can we not have a joint control? Can we not have the armies of Pakistan and India inside the State in order to control the situation ?" This is an unusual idea. What Pakistan could not achieve through ordinary means, Pakistan wishes to achieve by entering through the back door, so that it may have its armies inside the State and then start the fight. That is not possible.

After all, we have been discussing the situation in Kashmir. I should say that we have been playing the drama of Hamlet without the Prince of Denmark. The people of Kashmir are vitally interested in this question. Four million people in Kashmir are keenly interested in this entire affair. I have sympathies with the people of Poonch and Mirpur. The representative of Pakistan will probably concede that I have suffered greatly for the people of Poonch as well as for the people of Mirpur. There is no difference on this part of international democratisation of the administration between me, my party and the people of Poonch. We are one, we want our own liberty, we want our own freedom, we do not want autocratic rule. We desire that the 4 million people in Jammu and Kashmir—Hindus, Sikhs and Muslims— shall have the right to change their destiny, to control their country, and to administer it as best as they can. On that point there is absolutely no difference.

However, it is not a question of internal liberation. The Security Council should not confine the issue. The question is not that we want internal freedom, the question is not how the Maharaja got his State, or whether or not he is sovereign. These points are not before the Security Council. Whether Kashmir has lawfully acceded to India—complaints on that score have been brought before the Security Council on behalf of Pakistan—is not the point at issue. If that were the point at issue, then we should discuss that subject. We should prove before the Security Council that Kashmir and the people of Kashmir have lawfully and constitutionally acceded to the Dominion of India and Pakistan has no right to question that accession. However, that is not the discussion before the Security Council.

Indian and Kashmiri forces are ready to deal with tribesmen, to come to an understanding with the people of Kashmir and to establish a democratic form of government inside the State. We shall do all that. We do not want Pakistan to lend us support to suppress an internal revolt or to drive out the tribesmen. We do not seek any support from Pakistan in that connection. Since Pakistan is a neighbouring country, we desire to remain on the friendliest possible terms with this sister Dominion. But we do ask that Pakistan shall have no hand, directly or indirectly, in this turmoil in Kashmir. The Government of Pakistan has said: "We have no hand in this turmoil". The only course left to the Security Council is to send out the commission and to see whether or not Pakistan has any hand in this turmoil. If Pakistan has had any hand in this turmoil, then the Government of Pakistan should be asked to desist from such activity. If Pakistan has had no hand in this turmoil, then that can be proved.

This issue has been clouded by very many other issues and interests. I suggested at informal talks that according to my understanding there are two points at issue, first, how to have this neutral, impartial administration; second, whether or not the Indian Army shall remain.

It is not at all disputed that we must have a plebiscite and that the accession must be ratified by the people of Kashmir, freely and without any pressure on this or that side. That much is conceded, there is no dispute about that. The dispute arises when it is suggested that in order to have the free vote, the administration must be changed. To that suggestion we say, "No".

I do not know what course future events will take. However, I may assure the Security Council that, if I am asked to conduct the administration of this State, it will be my duty to make the administration absolutely impartial. It will be my duty to request my brothers, who are in a different camp at this time, to come to lend me support. After all, they are my own kith and kin. We suffered together, we have no quarrel with them. I shall tell them: "Come on; it is my country; it is your country. I have been asked to administer the State. Are you prepared to lend me support? It is for me to make the administration successful; it is for me to make the administration look impartial". It is not for Pakistan to say "No, we must have an impartial administration". I refuse to accept Pakistan as a party in the affairs of the Jammu and Kashmir State. I refuse this point blank. Pakistan has no right to say that we must do this and we must do that. We have seen enough of Pakistan. The people of Kashmir have seen enough. Muzaffarabad and Baramulla and hundred of villages in Jammu and Kashmir depict the story of Pakistan to the people of Jammu and Kashmir. We want to have no more of this.

In concluding, I again request that in order to settle this issue of Kashmir, the Security Council should not confuse the point in dispute. The Security Council should not allow various other extraneous matters to be introduced. Very many extraneous matters have been introduced. The representative of Pakistan gave us the history of the Jammu and Kashmir State. He read to us some letters from Viceroys of India, asking the Maharaja of Jammu and Kashmir to behave, giving the Maharaja good advice, et cetera. However, we cannot forget that these States are the creation of British imperialism in India who has supported these states and this misrule for these 150 years? It is not going to convince me or the world for the representative of Pakistan to say: "These events have happened and these letters were written". We know how the Princes have acted, how the states were brought into existence, and how the Princes were supported.

This was all a game in the British imperialist policy. But this legacy has now fallen upon us. We are not here to discuss whether or not the Maharaja lawfully became the ruler of the State, whether or not there is moral administration in this State, whether or not the Maharaja is sovereign and whether or not Kashmir has legally acceded to India. These issues are not before the Security Council. The only issue before the Security Council is that Pakistan must observe its international obligations and must not support any outside raiders.

Pakistan should not encourage inside revolt. Pakistan has denied that it has in order to verify the statements made by the representatives of India and Pakistan, the Security Council must send a commission to the spot to see whether the complaint brought before the Security Council is valid or invalid. If the Security Council finds that the complaint brought before it by

India is valid, then Pakistan should be asked to desist or India should be permitted to use its means to carry out the decision of the Security Council.

As far as I can speak on behalf of India, India does not want the help of the armies of Pakistan. What it wants from Pakistan is that Pakistan should not supply bases to the raiders on Pakistan territory across the border from Jammu and Kashmir State. All along the border on Pakistan territory, there are huge concentrations of these tribesmen who are Pakistani nationals. We request Pakistan not to allow its territory to be used by these raiders.

Pakistan should not provide ammunition, arms, direction and control to these tribesmen. It should stop the passage of these tribesmen through its territory. Pakistan should not supply arms and ammunition to the people who are fighting within the State because all these matters fall under an international obligation. Therefore, Pakistan should desist from that practice. That is all.

We do not want any armed help from Pakistan. If Pakistan does what we have requested, the Indian Army, I am quite sure, will be capable of driving out the raiders and tribesmen. If Pakistan does not meddle in our affairs, we will be capable of solving all our own internal disputes with the Maharaja of Kashmir. However, as long as this unofficial war continues, it is very difficult for us to do any thing. Our hands are tied.

What is happening? The raiders are concentrated just across the border. They enter our State in large number—four or five thousand strong. They raid four or five villages, burn them, abduct women and loot property. When our army tries to capture them, they go across the border, and can not fire a single shot across the border, because if it does, there is the immediate danger of a greater conflagration. So our hands are tied.

We do not want to create this difficult situation without informing the Security Council and we felt honour-bound to inform it of the actual position. The Indian Army could easily have followed the raiders across the border and could have attacked the bases, which were all in Pakistan territory, but it desisted. We thought it would be better to inform the Security Council of the situation.

However, I did not have the slightest idea that when the case came before the Security Council, the representative of Pakistan would so boldly deny that Pakistan supplied all this help. Everybody knows that Pakistan is aiding these raiders and tribesmen and the people who are fighting with the State. However, Pakistan chose boldly to deny all these charges.

What is left for me to do? After all, I do not have any magic lamp so that I might bring the entire picture of Jammu and Kashmir State, along with the borders of Pakistan, before the eyes of the members of the Security Council so that they might see who is fighting and who is not fighting. Therefore, somebody must go to the spot. Then at that time it would be for us to prove that the charges we have brought before the Security Council are correct to the last word. That is the only help we want and no other help.

Speech in the Constituent Assembly

We must remember that our struggle for power has now reached its successful climax in convening of this Constituent Assembly. It is for you to translate the vision of New Kashmir into a reality, and I would remind you of its opening words, which will inspire our labours:

> "We the people of Jammu and Kashmir, Laddakh and the Frontier regions, including Poonch and Chenani Illaqas commonly known as Jammu and Kashmir State in order to perfect our union in the fullest equality and self-determination to raise ourselves and our children forever from the abyss of oppression and poverty, degradation and superstition, from medieval darkness and ignorance, into the sunlit valleys of plenty, ruled by freedom, science and honest toil, in worthy participation of the historic resurgence of the peoples of East, and the working masses of the world, and in determination to make this our country a dazzling gem on the snowy bosom of Asia, to propose and propound the following Constitution of our State.'

This was passed at the 1944 session of the National Conference in Srinagar. Today, in 1951, embodying aspirations, men and women from the four corners of the state in this Constituent Assembly have become the repository of its sovereign authority. This Assembly, invested with the authority of a constituent body, will be the fountainhead of basic laws laying the foundation of a just social order and safeguarding the democratic rights of all the citizens of the State.

You are the sovereign authority in this State of Jammu and Kashmir; what you decide has the irrevocable force of law. The basic democratic principle of sovereignty of the nation embodied ably in the American and French Constitutions, is once again given shape in our midst. I shall quote the famous words of Article 3 of the French Constitution of 1791:

> "The source of all sovereignty resides fundamentally in the nation... Sovereignty is one and indivisible, inalienable and imprescriptable. It belongs to the nation".

We should be clear about the responsibilities that this power invests us with. In front of us lie decisions of the highest national importance which we shall be called upon to take. Upon the correctness of our decisions depends not only the happiness of our land and people now, but the fate as well of generations to come.

What then are the main functions that this Assembly will be called upon to perform?

One great task before this Assembly will be to devise a Constitution for the future governance of the country. Constitution-making is a difficult and detailed matter. I shall only refer to some of the broad aspects of the Constitution, which should be the product of the labours of this Assembly.

Another issue of vital import to the nation involves the future of the Royal Dynasty. Our decision will have to be taken both with urgency and wisdom, for on that decision rests the future form and character of the State.

The Third major issue awaiting your deliberations arises out of the Land Reforms which the Government carried out with vigour and determination. Our "Land to the tiller" policy brought light into the dark homes of the peasantry; but, side by side, it has given rise to the problem of the landowners demand for compensation. The nation being the ultimate custodian of all wealth and resources, the representatives of the nation are truly the best jury for giving a just and final verdict on such claims. So in your hands lies the power of this decision.

Finally, this Assembly will after full consideration of the three alternatives that I shall state later, declare its reasoned conclusion regarding accession. This will help us to canalise our energies resolutely and with greater zeal in directions in which we have already started moving for the social and economic advancement of our country.

To take our first task, that of Constitution-making, we shall naturally be guided by the highest principles of the democratic Constitutions of the world. We shall base our work on the principles of equality, liberty and social justice which are an integral feature of all progressive Constitutions. The rule of law as understood in the democratic countries of the world should be the cornerstone of our political structure.

Equality before the law and the independence of the judiciary from the influence of the Executive are vital to us. The freedom of the individual in the matter of speech, movement and association should be guaranteed: freedom of the press and of opinion should also be features of our Constitution. I need not refer in great detail to all those rights and obligations, already embodied in New Kashmir, which are Integral parts of democracy which has been defined as "an apparatus of social organisation wherein people govern through their chosen representatives and are themselves guaranteed political and civil liberties".

You are no doubt aware of the scope of our present constitutional ties with India. We are proud to have our bonds with India, the goodwill of those people and government is available to us in unstinted and abundant measure. The Constitution of India has provided for a federal union and in the distribution of sovereign powers has treated us differently from other constituent units. With the exception of the items grouped under Defence Foreign Affairs and Communications in the instrument of Accession, we have complete freedom to frame our

Constitution in the manner we like. In order to live and prosper as good partners in a common endeavour for the advancement of our peoples, I would advise that, while safeguarding our autonomy to the fullest extent so as to enable us to have the liberty to build our country according to the best traditions and genius of our people, we may also by suitable constitutional arrangements with the Union establish our right to seek and compel Federal cooperation and assistance in this great task, as well as offer our fullest cooperation and assistance to the Union.

Whereas it would be easy for you to devise a document calculated to create a frame work of law and order, as also a survey of the duties and rights of citizens. It will need more arduous labour to take concrete decisions with regard to the manner in which we propose to bring about the rapid economic development of the State and more equitable distribution of our national income among the people to which we are pledged.

Our National Conference avows its faith in the principal that there is one thing common to men of all castes and creeds, and that is their humanity. That being so, the one ailment which is ruthlessly sapping the vitality of human beings in Jammu and Kashmir is their appalling poverty, and if, we merely safeguard their political freedom in solemn terms, it will not affect their lives materially unless it guarantees them economic and social justice.

New Kashmir contains a statement of the objectives of bur social policy. It gives broadly a picture of the kind of life that we hope to make possible for the people of Jammu and Kashmir and the manner in which the economic organisation of the country will be geared to that purpose. These ideals you will have to integrate with the political structure which you will devise.

The future political set-up which you decide upon for Jammu and Kashmir must also take into consideration the existence of various sub-national groups in our State. Although culturally diverse history has forged an uncommon unity between them; they all are pulsating with the same hopes and aspirations, sharing in each others joys and sorrows. While guaranteeing this basic unity of the State, our Constitution must not permit the concentration of power and privilege in the hands of any particular group or territorial region. It must afford the fullest possibilities to each of these groups to grow and flourish in conformity with their cultural characteristics without detriment to the integral unity of the State or the requirements of our social and economic policies.

Now let us take up an issue of basic importance which involves the fundamental character of the State itself. As an instrument of the will of a self-determining people who now become sovereign in their own right, the Constituent Assembly will now re-examine and decide upon the future of the present ruling dynasty, in respect of its authority.

It is clear that this dynasty can no longer exercise authority on the basis of an old discredited Treaty. During my trial for sedition in the "Quit Kashmir" movement, I had clarified the attitude of my party when I said:

> "The future constitutional set-up in the State of Jammu and Kashmir cannot derive authority from the old source of relationship which was expiring and was bound to end soon. The set-up could only rest on the active will of the people of the State, conferring on the head of the State the title and authority drawn from the true and abiding source of sovereignty, that is the people".

On this occasion, in 1946, I had also indicated the basis on which an individual could be entrusted by the people with the symbolic authority of a Constitutional Head:

> "The State and its Head represent the constitutional circumference and the centre of this sovereignty respectively, the Head of the State being the symbol of the authority with which the people may invest him for the realisation of their aspirations and the maintenance of their rights".

In consonance with these principles, and in supreme fulfilment of the people's aspirations, it follows that a Constitutional Head of the State will have to be chosen to exercise the function which this Assembly may chose to entrust to him.

So far as my Party is concerned, we are convinced that the institution of monarchy is incompatible with the spirit and needs of modern times which demand an egalitarian relationship between one citizen and another. The supreme test of a democracy is the measure of equality of opportunity that it affords to its citizens to rise to the highest point of authority and position. In consequence monarchies are fast disappearing from the world picture, as something in the nature of feudal anachronisms. In India, too, where before the partition, six hundred and odd Princes exercised rights and privileges of rulership, the process of democratisation has been taken up and at present hardly ten of them exercise the limited authority of constitutional heads of States.

After the attainment of complete power by the people, it would have been an appropriate gesture of good will to recognise Maharaja Hari Singh as the first constitutional Head of the State. But I must say with regret that he has completely forfeited the confidence of every section of the people. His in capacity to adjust himself to changed conditions and his antiquated views on vital problems constitute positive disqualifications for him to hold the high office of a democratic Head of the State. Moreover, his past actions as a ruler have proved that he is not capable of conducting himself with dignity, responsibility and impartiality. The people still remember with pain and regret his failure to stand by them in times of crisis, and his incapacity to afford protection to a section of his people in Jammu.

Finally we come to the issue which has made Kashmir an object of world interest, and has brought her before the forum of the United Nations. This simple issue has become so involved that people have begun to ask themselves after three and a half years of tense expectancy. "Is there any solution ?" Our answer is in the affirmative. Everything hinges round the genuineness of the will to find a solution. If we face the issue straight, the solution is simple.

The problem may be posed in this way. Firstly, was Pakistan's action in invading Kashmir in 1947 morally and legally correct, judged by any norm of international behaviour ? Sir Owen Dixon's verdict on this issue is perfectly plain. In unambiguous terms he declared Pakistan an aggressor. Secondly, was the Maharaja's accession to India legally valid or not ? The legality of the accession has not been seriously questioned by any responsible or independent person or authority.

These two answers are obviously correct. Then where is the justification of treating India and Pakistan at par in matters pertaining to Kashmir? In fact, the force of logic dictates the conclusion that the aggressor should withdraw his armed forces, and the United Nations should see that Pakistan gets out of the State.

In that event, India herself, anxious to give the people of the State a chance to express their will freely, would willingly cooperate with any sound plan of demilitarisation. They would withdraw their forces, only garrisoning enough posts to ensure against any repetition of that earlier treacherous attack from Pakistan.

These two steps would have gone a long way to bring about a new atmosphere in the State. The rehabilitation of displaced people, and the restoration of stable civic conditions would have allowed people to express their will and take the ultimate decision.

We as a Government are keen to let our people decide the future of our land in accordance with their own wishes. If these three preliminary processes were accomplished, we should be happy to have the assistance of international observes to ensure fair play and the requisite conditions for a free choice by the people.

Instead invader and defender have been put on the same plane. Under various garbs, attempts have been made to sidetrack the main issue. Sometimes against all our ideals of life and way of living attempts divide our territories have been made in the form of separation of our state religionwise, with ultimate plans of further disrupting territorial integrity.

Once an offer was made to police our country with Commonwealth forces, which threatens to bring in Imperial control by the back door. Besides the repugnance which our people have however, to the idea of bringing foreign troops on their soil, the very presence of Commonwealth troops could have created suspicions among our neighbours that we were allowing ourselves to be used as a base of possible future aggression against them. This could easily have made us into a second Korea.

The Cabinet Mission Plan has provided for three courses which may be followed by the Indian States when determining future affiliations. A State can either accede to India or accede to Pakistan, but failing to do either, it still can claim the right to remain independent. These three alternatives are naturally open to our State. While the intention of the British Government was to secure The privileges of the Princes, the representatives of the people must have the primary consideration of promoting the greatest good of the common people.

Whatever steps they take must contribute to the growth of a democratic social order wherein all invidious distinctions between groups and creeds are absent. Judged by this supreme considerations, what are the advantages and disadvantages of our State's accession to either India or Pakistan or of having and independent Status.

As a realist I am conscious that nothing is all black or all white, and there are many facts to each of the propositions before us. I shall first speak on the merits and demerits of the State's accession to India. In the final analysis, as I understand it, it is the kinship of ideals which determines the strength of ties between two States. The Indian National Congress has consistently supported the cause of the State's peoples' freedom.

The autocratic rule of the Princes has been done away with and representative government have been entrusted with the administration. Steps towards democratisation have been taken and these have raised the people's standard of living, brought about much-needed social reconstruction, and above all built up their very independence of spirit. Naturally, if we accede to India there is no danger of a revival of feudalism and autocracy. Moreover, during the last four years the Government of India has never tried to interfere in our internal autonomy this experience has strengthened our confidence in them as a democratic State.

The real character of a State is revealed in its Constitution. The Indian Constitution has set before the country the goal of secular democracy based upon justice, freedom and equality for all without distinction. This is the bedrock of modern democracy. This should meet the argument that the Muslims of Kashmir cannot have security in India, where the large majority of the population are Hindus. Any unnatural cleavage between religious groups is the legacy of Imperialism, and no modern State can afford to encourage artificial division if it is to achieve progress and prosperity. The Indian Constitution has amply and finally repudiated the concept of a religious State, which is a throw back to medievalism, by guaranteeing the equality of rights of all citizens irrespective of their religion, colour caste and class.

The national movement in our State naturally gravitates towards these principles of secular democracy. The people here will never accept a principle which seeks to favour the interests of one religion or social group against another. This affinity in political principles, as well as in past association, and our common path of suffering in the cause of freedom, must be weighed properly while deciding the future of the State.

We are also intimately concerned with the economic wellbeing of the people of this State. As I said before while referring to Constitution-building, political ideals are often meaningless unless linked with economic plans. As a State, we are concerned mainly with agriculture and trade. As you know, and I have detailed before, we have been able to put through our "land to the tiller" legislation and make of it a practical success. Land and all it means is an inestimable blessing to our peasants who have dragged along in servitude to the landlord and his allies for centuries without number. We have been able under present conditions to carry these reforms through, are we sure that in alliance with landlord-ridden Pakistan, with so many feudal privileges intact, that the economic reforms of ours will be tolerated. We have already heard that news of our Land Reforms has travelled to the peasants of the enemy-occupied area of our State, who vainly desire like status, and like benefits.

In the second place, our economic welfare is bound up with our arts and crafts. The traditional markets for these precious goods for which we are justly known all over the world, have been centred in India. The volume of our trade, in spite of the dislocation of the last few years, shows this. Industry is also highly important to us. Potentially we are rich in minerals, and in the raw materials of industry; we need help to develop our resources. India, being more highly industrialised than Pakistan, can give us equipment, technical services and materials. She can help us too in marketing. Many goods also which it would not be practical for us to produce here for instance sugar, cotton, cloth, and other essential commodities, can be got by us in large quantities from India. It is around the efficient supply of such basic necessities that the standard of the man in-the-street depends.

I shall refer now to the (alleged) disadvantages of accession to India.

To begin with, although the land frontiers of India and Kashmir are contiguous, an all-weather road-link as dependable as the one we have with Pakistan does not exist. This must necessarily hamper trade and commerce to some extent particularly during the snowy winter months. But we have studied this question, and, with improvements in modern engineering, if the State wishes to remain with India the establishment of an all-weather stable system of communication is both feasible and easy.

Similarly, the use of the State rivers as a means of timber transport is impossible if we turn to India, except in Jammu where the river Chenab still carries logs to the plains. In reply to this argument, it may be pointed out that accession to India will open up possibilities of utilising our forest wealth for industrial purposes and that, instead of lumber, finished goods, which will provide work for our carpenters and labourers, can be exported to India where there is a ready market for them. Indeed in the presence of our fleets of timber carrying trucks, river-transport is a crude system which inflicts a loss of some 20 per cent to 35 per cent, in transit.

Still another factor has to be taken into consideration. Certain tendencies have been asserting themselves in India which may in the future convert it into a religious State wherein the interests of Muslims will be jeopardised. This would happen if a communal organisation had a dominant hand in the Government, and Congress ideals of the equality of all communities were made to give way to religious intolerance. The continued accession of Kashmir to India should, however, help in defeating this tendency.

From my experience of the last four years, it is my considered judgement that the presence of Kashmir in the Union of India has been the major factor in establishing relations between the Hindus and Muslims of India. Gandhiji was not wrong when he uttered words before his death which paraphrase, "I lift up mine eyes into the hills, from whence cometh my help".

As I have said before, we must consider the question of accession with all open mind, and not let our personal prejudices stand in the way of a balanced judgement. I will now invite you to evaluate the alternative of accession to Pakistan.

The most powerful argument which can be advanced in her favour is that Pakistan is a Muslim State, and, big majority of our people being Muslims the State must accede to Pakistan. This claim of being a Muslim State is of course only a camouflage. It is a screen to dupe the common man, so that he may not see clearly that Pakistan is a feudal State in which a clique is trying by these methods to maintain itself in power. In addition to this, the appeal to religion constitutes a sentimental and a wrong approach to the question.

Sentiment has its own place in life but often it leads to irrational action. Some argue, as supposedly natural corollary to this, that on our acceding to Pakistan our annihilation or survival depends. Facts have disproved this, right-thinking men would point out that Pakistan is not an organic unity of all the Muslims in this sub-continent. It has on the contrary, caused the dispersion of the Indian Muslims for whose benefit it was claimed to have been created. There are two Pakistan at least a thousand miles apart from each other. The total population of Western Pakistan which is contiguous to our State, is hardly 15 million. While the total number of Muslims, resident in India is as many as 40 million. As one Muslim is as good as another, the Kashmiri Muslims if they are worried by such considerations should choose the forty millions living in India.

Looking at the matter too from a more modern political angle religious affinities alone do not and should not normally determine the political alliance of States. We do not find a Christian bloc, a Buddhist bloc, or even a Muslim bloc, about which there is so much talk nowadays in Pakistan. These days economic interests and a community of political ideals more appropriately influence the policies of States.

We have another important factor to consider, if the State decides to make this the predominant consideration. What will be the fate of the one million non-Muslims now in our State ? As things stand at present, there is no place for them in Pakistan. Any solution which will result in the displacement or the total subjugation of such a large number of people will not be just or fair, and it is the responsibility of this House to ensure that the decision that it takes on accession does not militate against the interests of any religious group.

As regards the economic advantages. I have mentioned before the road and river links with Pakistan. In the last analysis, we must however remember that we are not concerned only with the movement of people but also with the movement of goods and the linking up of markets. In Pakistan there is a chronic dearth of markets for our products. Neither, for that matter, can she help us with our industrialisation, being herself industrially backward.

On the debit side we have to take into account the reactionary character of her politics and State policies. In Pakistan we should remember that the lot of the States' subjects has not changed and they are still helpless and under the heel of their Rulers, who wield the same unbridled power under which we used to suffer here. This clearly runs counter to our own aspirations for freedom.

A big obstacle to a dispassionate evaluation of her policies is the lack of a Constitution in Pakistan. As it stands at present, this State enjoys the unique position of being governed by a Constitution enacted by an outside Parliament which gives no idea whatsoever of the future shape of civic and social relations. It is reasonable to argue that Pakistan cannot have the confidence of a freedom-loving and democratic people when it has failed to guarantee even fundamental rights of its citizens.

The right of self-determination for nationalities is being consistently denied and those who fought against Imperialism for this just right are being suppressed with force. We should remember Badshah Khan and his comrades who laid down their all for freedom, also Khan Abdus Samad Khan and other fighters, in Baluchistan. Our national movement in the State considers this right of self-determination inalienable, and no advantage, however great, will persuade our people to forego it.

The third course open to us has still to be discussed. We have to consider the alternative of making ourselves an Eastern Switzerland, of keeping aloof from both States but having friendly relations with them. This might seem attractive in that it would appear to pave the way out of the present deadlock. To us as a tourist country it could also have certain obvious advantages, but in considering independence we must not ignore practical considerations.

Firstly, it is not easy to protect sovereignty and independence in a small country which has not sufficient strength to defend itself on our long and difficult frontiers bordering so many countries. Secondly we must have the goodwill of all our neighbours. Can we find powerful guarantors among them to pull together always in assuring us freedom from aggression? I would like to remind you that from August 15 to October 22, 1947 our State was independent and the result was that our weakness was exploited by the neighbour with invasion. What is the guarantee that in future too we may not be victims of a singular aggression.

I have now put the pros and cons of the three alternatives before you. It should not be difficult for men of discrimination and patriotism gathered in this Assembly to weigh all these in the scales of our national good and pronounce the well being of the country lies in the future.

Statement to the Constituent Assembly on Delhi Agreement

[11th August, 1952]

I crave permission to mace a statement before the House in regard to the constitutional relationship between the Jammu and Kashmir State and the Indian Union. As the Hon'ble Members are aware, during the last session of the Constituent Assembly, the Basic Principles Committee had submitted a report making certain specific recommendations about the future Head of the State. The

House, while accepting these recommendations, had charged the Drafting Committee to present for the consideration of the Assembly, a draft resolution incorporating the proposed principles for the election of the Head of the State. The Drafting Committee will, no doubt, submit its report to the House during this session.

Since the changes proposed by this Assembly involved corresponding adjustments in the Indian Constitution, the Government of India desired that it should have time to discuss with our representatives other matters pertaining to the constitutional relationship of our State with the Union. During the last stage of these discussions, it became necessary for me and some of my other colleagues in the Government to participate in the talks. I am now in a position to inform the House that certain broad principles have been laid down and certain decisions have been tentatively arrived at between the two Governments.

The basis of our relationship with India is the Instrument of Accession which enabled our State to enter into a lemon with India. In accordance with the terms of the Instrument, certain powers were transferred to the Centre. The principal matters specified for this purpose in respect to which the Dominion Legislature could make laws for this State were:

- Defence,
- External Affairs, and
- Communications.

This arrangement involved a division of sovereignty which is the normal feature of a Federation. Beyond the powers transferred by it to the Dominion, the State enjoyed complete residuary sovereignty.

These terms of the association of our State with the Dominion of India were maintained; and, subsequently, when the Constituent Assembly of India was charged with the task of framing a Constitution, this overriding consideration was kept m view in determining the position of this State in the proposed Constitution Earlier to this, it had been agreed between the two Governments that "in view of the special problems arising in respect of this State and the fact that the Government of India have assured its people that they would themselves finally determine their political future", a special position should be accorded to Jammu and Kashmir in the future Constitution so that a limited field of the Union Powers over the State is ensured. Dour representatives were nominated from the Jammu and Kashmir State to the Constituent Assembly of India] These representatives participated in the deliberations of the Constituent Assembly of India at a time when the bulk of the Indian Constitution had already been adopted.

It was at this stage that the constitutional position of this State was determined in the Constitution of India. The representatives of the Jammu and Kashmir State reiterated their view that our association with India should be based on the terms of the Instrument of Accession.

It was at this stage that the constitutional position of the State was determined in the Constitution of India. Lithe representatives of the Jammu and Kashmir State reiterated their view that our association with India should be based on the terms of the Instrument of Accession. It was also made clear that while the accession of the Jammu and Kashmir State with India was complete in fact and law to the extent of the subjects enumerated in this Instrument the autonomy of the State with regard to all oilier subjects outside the ambit of the Instrument of accession should be preserved.

Evince a good deal of confused thinking and uninformed criticism is indulged in by some interested people. I would like to point out here that the Constitution has confined the scope and jurisdiction of the Union powers to the terms of the Instrument of accession with the proviso that they may be extended to such other matters also as the President may by order specify with the concurrence of the Jammu and Kashmir Constituent Assembly. The special problems facing the State were thus taken into account and under the Constitution the relationship approximated to that subsisting under the Instrument of accession.

The Constitution of the Indian Union, therefore, clearly envisaged the convening of a Constituent Assembly for the Jammu and Kashmir State which would be finally competent to determine the ultimate position of the State in respect of the sphere of its accession which would be incorporated as in the shape of permanent provisions of the Constitution.

The Hon'ble Members are aware that as the leader of the National Conference party, I indicated in my inaugural address the scope of the decisions which I felt the Constituent Assembly would have to take. I listed the four main issues as pertaining to the main functions of the Assembly, viz., the future of the Ruling Dynasty, payment of compensation for the land transferred to cultivators under the Big Landed Estates Act, Ratification of the State's Accession to India as well as the framing of a Constitution for the State. While discussing these issues in my address to this House, I had given clear indications of my party's views in regard to them. I had also an occasion to place my point of view on these issues before the representatives of the Government of India and I had the satisfaction that they approved of it.

When Constituent Assembly commenced its labours, it had to tackle these issues in course of time. It took decisions m regard to payment of compensation to landlords and it came to the conclusion that no compensation was justified.

The Constituent Assembly has, at present, under its consideration the future of the Ruling Dynasty. In this connection the Basic Principles Committee recommended that the institution of hereditary rulership in the State should be abolished and in future the office of the Head of State should be elective. While accepting the recommendations of the Basic Principles Committee, this Assembly charged the Drafting Committee to place before this House appropriate proposals for the implementation of these recommendations.

As I said in the beginning of my statement, such a fundamental decision involved corresponding adjustments in the Indian Constitution and in order to finalist the position in respect of this issue and other matters pertinent to it, I and my colleagues had discussions with the representatives of the Government of India as a result of which we arrived at some tentative agreement, tile details of which I wish to place before the House.

The Government of India held the view that the fact that the Jammu and Kashmir State was constituent unit of the Union of

India led inevitably to certain consequences in regard to some important matters, namely:

- Residuary Powers,
- Citizenship,
- Fundamental Rights,
- Supreme Court of India
- National Flag,
- The President of India,
- The Headship of the State
- Financial Integration,
- Emergency Provisions, and
- Conduct of elections to Houses of Parliament.

Permit me, Mr. President now to deal with each one of these Items and also the agreement, arrived at between the Jammu and Kashmir Government and the Government of India in relation to them.

Residuary Powers

It was agreed that while under the present Indian Constitution, the Residuary Powers vested in the Centre in respect of all the States other than Jammu and Kashmir, in the case of our State, they rested in the State itself. This position is compatible with Article 370 of the Indian Constitution and the instrument of Accession on which this article is based.

We have always held that the ultimate source of sovereignty resides in the people. It is, therefore, from the people that all powers can flow. Under these circumstances, it is upto the people of Kashmir through this Assembly to transfer more powers for mutual advantage to the custody of the Union Centre.

Citizenship: It was agreed that in accordance with Article 5 of the Indian Constitution persons who have their domicile in the Jammu and Kashmir State shall be the citizens of India. It was further agreed that the State legislature shall have power to define and regulate the rights and privileges of the permanent residents of the State, more especially in regard to acquisition of immovable property, appointments to services and like matters. Till then the existing State law would apply. It was also agreed that special provision should be made in the laws governing citizenship to provide for the return of those permanent residents of Jammu and Kashmir State, who went to Pakistan in connection with the disturbances of 1947 or in fear of them as well as of those who had left for Pakistan earlier but could not return. If they returned, they should be entitled to the rights, and privileges and obligations of citizenship.

There are historic reasons which necessitate such constitutional safeguards as for centuries past, the people of the State have been victims of exploitation at the hands of their well to- do neighbours. The Hon'ble Members are perhaps aware that in the late twenties, the people of Jammu and Kashmir agitated for the protection of their bona fide rights against the superior competing interests of the non-residents of the State.

It was in response to this popular demand that the Government of the day promulgated a Notification in 1927 by which a strict definition of the term "State Subject" was provided. I am glad to say that the Government of India appreciated the need for such a safeguard. No definition of the special rights and privileges of the residents of the State can afford to remain static. The need may arise at one stage or the other to liberalise such a definition. The importance of the fact that State Legislature shall retain powers to be able to effect such modifications becomes obvious in this context.

There is yet another class of State Subjects whose interests had to be safeguarded. The Hon'ble Members of this House are aware that on account of the disturbances of 1947 and also as a consequence of the invasion of this country by Pakistan large number of the residents of this State suffered dislocation. We have, therefore, to visualise the possibility of their return to their homes and hearths as soon as normal conditions are restored.

It has been suggested in certain quarters that this protection has been provided only for those residents of the State who are at present stranded in Pakistan I would like to make it clear, as I have stated earlier, that this protection will operate only when the conditions are normal and such conditions naturally presume that the resettlement of the dislocated population, whether Muslim or Non-Muslim cannot be one-sided or unilateral.

Fundamental Rights: It is obvious that while our Constitution is being framed the fundamental rights and duties of a citizen have necessarily got to be defined. It was agreed, however, that the Fundamental Rights, which are contained in the Constitution of India could not be conferred on the residents of the Jammu and Kashmir State in their entirety taking into account the economic, social and political character of our movement as enunciated in the New Kashmir Plan.

The need for providing suitable modifications, amendments and exceptions as the case may be in the Fundamental Rights Chapter of the Indian Constitution in order to harmonise those provisions with the pattern of our principles was admitted. Particular care would have to be taken to preserve the basic character of the decisions taken by this House on the question of land compensation as well as the laws relating to the transfer of land to the tiller and other matters; The main point to be determined is whether the Chapter of our Fundamental Rights should form a part of the Kashmir Constitution or that of the Union Constitution.

Supreme Court: It was agreed that the Supreme Court should have original jurisdiction in respect of disputes mentioned in Article 131 of the Constitution of India. It was further agreed that the Supreme Court should have jurisdiction in regard to Fundamental Rights which are agreed to by the State.

On behalf of the Government of India, it was recommended that the Advisory Board in the State, designated "His Highness's Board of Judicial Advisors" should be abolished and the jurisdiction exercised by it should be vested in the Supreme Court of India. That is to say that the Supreme Court should be the final Court of appeal in all civil and criminal matters as laid down in the Constitution of India.

We, however, felt that this would need a detailed examination and consequently it was agreed that we should have time to consider it further.

National Flag: We agreed that in view of the clarifications issued by me in my public statements while interpreting the resolution of this House according to which the old State flag was in no sense a rival of the National Flag. But for historical and other reasons connected with the freedom struggle in the State, the need for the continuance of this flag was recognised. The Union flag to which we continue our allegiance as a part of the Union will occupy the supremely distinctive place in the State.

President of India: It was agreed that the powers to grant reprieve and commute death sentences, etc. should also belong to the President of the Union.

Headship of the State: I am glad to inform this House that the Government of India have appreciated the principle proposed by the Basic Principle Committee as adopted by this Assembly in regard to the abolition of the hereditary rulership of the State. In order to accommodate this principle, the following arrangement was mutually agreed upon:

- The Head of the State shall be the person recognised by the President of the Union of the recommendation of the Legislature of the State.
- He shall hold office during the pleasure of the President.
- He may, by writing under his hand addressed to the President resign his office.
- Subject to the foregoing provisions, the Head of the State shall hold office for a term of five years from the date he enters upon his office.
- Provided that he shall, notwithstanding the expiration of his term, continue to hold the office until his successor enters upon his office.

Financial Integration: In regard to this subject, we agreed that it would be necessary to evolve some sort of financial arrangement between the State and the Indian Union. But as this involved far reaching consequences, it was felt that a detailed and objective examination of this subject would be necessary.

Emergency Powers: On behalf of the Government of India, it was stated that the application of Article 352 of the Constitution was necessary as it related to vital matters affecting the security of the State. They did not press for the application of Articles 356 or 360.

On behalf of the Kashmir Delegation, it was stated that the application of Article 352 to the State was not necessary. In the event of war or external aggression, item I in the Seventh Schedule relating to the defence of India applied and the Government of India would have full authority to take any steps in connection with defence, etc. In particular, we were averse to internal disturbance being referred to in this connection, as even some petty internal disorder might be considered sufficient for the application of Article 352.

In reply it was pointed out that Article 352 could only be applied in a state of grave emergency and not because of some small disorder or disturbance.

In order to meet our view point, it was suggested on behalf of the Government of India that Article 352 might be accepted as it is with the addition at the end of the first paragraph (1) of the following words: "but in regard to internal disturbance at the request or with the concurrence of the Government of the State".

We generally accepted this position, but wanted some time to consider the implications and consequences as laid down in Articles 353, 358 and 359 which on the whole we accepted. In regard to Article 354, we wanted to examine it further before expressing our opinion.

Conduct of Elections to Houses of Parliament: Article 324 of the Indian Constitution already applies to State in so far as it relates to elections to Parliament and to the Offices of the President and the vice-President of India.

I have put before this House the broad indications of the agreements arrived at between us and the Government of India. As the Hon'ble Members will, no doubt, observe, the attitude of the Government of India has been most helpful. A satisfactory position has emerged and we are now able to assess the basic issues of our constitutional relationship with India in clearer terms. There has been a good deal of accommodation of our respective points of view. Hotly the representatives of the Government of India and the Kashmir Delegation, have been impelled by the desire to strengthen further the existing relationship to remove all obscurity and vagueness. We . re convinced, as ever before, that we have the full support both of the Government and the people of India in the fulfilment of our democratic ideals and the realisation of our objectives.

Excerpts from the Opening Address to the J&K Constituent Assembly

[5 November 1951]

Our movement to freedom has been connected against the background of this same old struggle. We stood for the brotherhood of men of all creeds and strengthened our union on the basis of common work and sacrifice. Against us were ranged the force of religious bigotry centred in the Muslim league and its satellites, and the Hindu communalists from within and without the State. Ranged against us and often in alliance with communalism were the forces of the autocratic States backup on the Paramount Power, and on the other, by the rich landowners and other beneficiaries of Court patronage.

We must remember the our struggle for power has now reached its successful climax in the convening of this Constituent Assembly. It is for you to translate the vision of NEW KASHMIR into reality, and I would remind you and its opening words, which will inspire our labours:

> "We the people of Jammu, Kashmir and the Frontier regions, including Poonch and Chenani Illaqas - commonly known as Jammu and Kashmir States -in order to perfect our union in the fullest equality and self-determination to raise ourselves and our children for ever from the abyss of oppression and poverty darkness and ignorance into the sunlit valleys of plenty ruled by freedom, science and honest toil, in worthy participation of the historic resurgence of the peoples of the East and the working masses of the world, and

in determination to make this our country a dazzling gem on the snowy bosom of Asia do purpose and propound the following Constitution of our state".

Quit Kashmir Speech

[May, 26, 1946]

The tyranny of the Dogras has lacerated our souls. The Kashmiris are the most handsome people, yet the most wretched looking. It is time for action. To end your poverty, you must fight slavery and enter the field of Jehad as soldiers.

The fight slogan of our struggle is not only for our State but for the whole of India. India is fighting against Imperialism. The slogan was given on the banks of River Ravi... Then came the slogan of 'Quit India.' The British gained hold of India by the force of arms and by treachery.

The rulers of the Indian States who possess one-fourth of India, have always played traitors to the cause of Indian freedom. The demand that the Princely Order should quit is a logical extension of the policy of 'Quit India.' When the Indian freedom movement demands the complete withdrawal of British power, logically enough the stooges of British Imperialism also should go and restore sovereignty to its real owners - the people. When we raise the slogan of 'Quit Kashmir,' we naturally visualise that the Princes and Swabs should quit all the States. I am sure this demand applies similarly to a State like Hyderabad where the people will, I am sure, raise their voice, 'Quit Hyderabad.'

Those Hindus who think along with Mr. R.C. Kak that the Dogra rule should remain, should never forget that we are treated in Kashmir as a bought-up race without distinction of religion.

Handcuffs jingle. They do not make us afraid. God will dive us faith in victory. The voice of truth will prevail. Prophets have spoken for the truth, which has always triumphed finally.

Sovereignty is not the birthright of a ruler. Every man, woman and child will shout 'Quit Kashmir'. The Kashmiri nation has expressed its will. I ask for a plebiscite on this question.

Statement on the Ministerial Crisis in the Kashmir State

[April 22, 1945]

Recently the Jammu and Kashmir National Conference Working Committee reviewed the farcical character of the diarchic experiment and decided to withdraw Its representative from the Council of Ministers. Accordingly, Mirza Mohammed Afzal Beg resigned from the Ministership, and returned to the opposition benches.

The Prime Minister, backed by his clique of irresponsible bureaucrats, resorted to the base tactics of attempting to bribe and disrupt the ranks of the National Conference itself. In so doing they had resorted to Machiavellian ways, and Mian Ahmad Yar, the Leader of the whose appointment had taken place by direct command of the Maharaja, an Assembly Party has fallen prey to them. His representative capacity just does not exist. Thus the Maharaja has not only put an axe on the elective system of appointing popular ministers, on the lines of his diarchic experiment, but has become a party to the conspiracy against the popular movement in the Kashmir.

Such an attack on the rights of the people, and the unity of their representative organisation, has come at a time when the minds of the people of Kashmir are already exploring the new perspective opened up by the attempts at constitution making of the Cabinet Mission. The question of the treaty rights of the Princes has become a moot point between the peoples of the State, the Princely Order, and the Paramount Power. For us in Kashmir, the re-examination of this relationship is a vital matter, because a hundred years ago, in 1846 the land and people of Kashmir were sold away to the servitude of the Dogra House by the British for 75 lakhs of rupees. The then Governor of Kashmir resisted the transfer but was finally reduced to subjection with the aid of British. Thus the sale deed of 1846, misnamed the Treaty of Amritsar, had sealed the fate of the masses of Kashmir.

For the last fifteen years since the inception of our freedom Movement in 1931, we have attempted to give a fair trial to all reforms believing that readjustment of human relationships will take place with the extension of the democratic framework to all fields of our national life. Thus we believed that we could come in line with the rest of the world in the era of the Atlantic Charter and the revision of basic relationships with the dawn of the independence of nations.

But once again the last act of His Highness has exposed the continuance of tile "feudal master governing the serfs" mentality. This state of affairs cannot be allowed to last The resurgent spirit of the people challenges it in the name of human dignity.

No sale deed, however sacrosanct can condemn more than four million men and women to the servitude of an autocrat when the will to live under this rule is no longer there. The people of the Kashmir are determined to mould their own destiny, and we appeal to the members of the Cabinet Mission to recognise the Justice and strength of our cause.

Statement on Indian States

[1946]

Legal Document No 98: The Indian States' problems are closely linked up with those of British India. They are common both to British India and Indian States.

The British are well aware of the position, indicated the two lines of defence on which British Imperialism could relay. The first line of defence lies in the question of the Congress League understanding, with the implication of Hindu-Muslim unity. The second line of defence rests on the position of the Princes who, in the eye of British Imperialism, should be safeguarded.

With such a prospect before the people of India, it is necessary both for the people of British India and those of the Indian States to coordinate and merge the movements into a single channel. In order to do this, the people's organisations in the States should be strengthened.

The problem of the people in the States is primarily one of removing autocracy and establishing full responsible government. That object cannot be achieved unless a united front is offered by the people.

After the State's people's Conference at Udaipur I feel that the people in the States are now awakened more than ever before. There is now a more widespread political consciousness among them. It is true that sentiments have lately played a great part in the poetics of the Country, particularly in British India. Take the instance of the cry of Pakistan.

It was born of distress. Now it is stripped of all reasons. The question before the Muslims will be whether the realisation of Pakistan is a blessing to them. I personally think that Pakistan will not help the Muslim masses but hinder them in their struggle for political and economic emancipation. In our State this question however, does not arise, because an overwhelming majority of the people are Muslims and there is no need to fear Hindu domination.

Statement before the Sessions Court, Srinagar

I am not interested in a personal defence, and I would not have undertaken it if I had not felt that my trial for 'sedition' is something far more than a personal charge against me. It is, in effect, a trial of entire population of Jammu and Kashmir, even though some of them, being content with their transient personal interests or out of fear, may not be prepared to recognise or openly declare this.

Oppressed by the extreme poverty and lack of freedom and opportunity of the people of Jammu and Kashmir State, I and my colleagues of the Jammu and Kashmir National Conference, many of whom are behind prison bars or in exile today, have humbly sought to serve them during the past sixteen years. We have endeavoured to give faithful expression to the growing consciousness among the people of their imprescriptable rights, aspirations and desire for freedom.

This has attracted the penal and preventive provisions of law. Where law is not based on the will of the people, it can lend itself to the suppression of their aspirations. Such law has no more validity even though it may be enforced for a while. There is a law higher than that, the law that represents the people's will and secures their well-being, and their is the tribunal of human conscience, which judges the rulers and the ruled alike by standards which do not change by the arbitrary will of the most powerful. To that law I gladly submit and that tribunal I shall face with confidence and without fear, leaving it to history and posterity to pronounce their verdict on the claims I and my colleagues have made not merely on behalf of the four million people of Jammu and Kashmir but also of the ninety-three million people of all the States of India. That claim has not been conned to the people of a particular race, or religion or colour.

It applies to all, for I hold that humanity as a whole is Divisible by such barriers and human rights must always prevail. The fundamental rights of all men and women to live and act as free beings, to make laws and fashion their political, social and economic fabric, so that they may advance the cause of human freedom and progress, are inherent and cannot be denied though they may be suppressed for a while. I hold that sovereignty resides in the people, all relationships political, social and economic, derive authority from the collective will of the people.

It was clear that the old treaties with the States had to go. They represented something that had no relation to the modern world or to the India of today. They could not be reconciled with the inevitable changes in India and in the Sates. If this was clear to begin with, it become an accepted fact by the statement issued by Cabinet Delegation of 16th May last. That statement declared that paramountcy would end when the new Constitution of free India came into being.

It was an inevitable consequence that the old treaties and sanads and other engagements would go the way of paramountcy and the British Government being out of the picture, a new relationship would have to be negotiated between what is now known as British India and the States. The demand for the abrogation of the Amritsar Treaty was, in effect, disposed of by this clear decision.

The future constitutional set-up-in the State of Jammu and Kashmir cannot derive authority from the old source of relationship, which was expiring and was bound to end soon. That set-up could only rest on the active will of the people of the State, conferring on the Head of the State the title and authority drawn from the true and abiding source of sovereignty, that is the people. The "Quit Kashmir" cry symbolised and gave concrete shape to this demand for the termination of a system of Government: which was in process of dissolution all over India. The cry had nothing personal about it....

Some allegations have been made that "Quit Kashmir" and the demand for the abrogation of the Treaty of Amritsar had communal or communist inspiration. This is a travesty of fact and I deny and repudiate these allegations. The National Conference is essentially a national organisation including in its fold all people who agree with its objective, and cooperating with the All-India States People's Conference, with which it is affiliated. It stands in the All-India context for the independence and freedom of India. It stands also for social and economic changes to end privilege and to raise the masses.

Various other Statements of the Sheikh

[1958 to 1962]

Statement of Sheikh Mohammed Abdullah after His Release, Issued from New Delhi, February 17, 1958.

Since my release after 4-1/2 years' detention, I have tried to explain my viewpoint and possible solution in regard to various problems facing the political future of the State. With sufficient clarity, I hope, I have succeeded in elucidating the following points:

- So long as final decision about the future disposition of Jammu and Kashmir State is not arrived at, the political uncertainty, economic distress and other mental strain and miseries which the people of the State are facing at present, cannot terminate.
- The existing strained relations between India and Pakistan are not only a source of great danger to the solidarity of Asia, but also contribute to the ruin of the people of the State. The dispute over Kashmir is one of the main contributing factors to these strained relations.
- The ultimate decision with regard to the future affiliation of the State vests with the people and can only be achieved

> by allowing them to exercise their right of self-determination under impartial international supervision, in accordance with the universally recognised methods as has been already agreed to by the parties concerned or is otherwise acceptable to all.

I am deeply sorry that in order to befog my views from the public, interested people have resorted, right from 1953, to a campaign of falsehood and every attempt is being made at misrepresentation and distortion. These people wish to keep the Kashmir issue hanging in order to exploit it to serve their own ends in spite of the fact that the progress of their Motherland and international peace and amity insistently demand its immediate solution.

Those who are opposed to a satisfactory final settlement of this problem falsely charged me, five years ago, as having conspired with a foreign power. Now since my release a campaign has been started by these very people to depict me as a communalist for obvious reasons. As the charge of foreign conspiracy could not be substantiated, despite expiry of five years, an attempt is now being made to fabricate the charge of communalism against me so that public opinion in India and elsewhere may be deceived afresh, and the people's feeling and sympathy for me as a victim of persecution may be affected.

Another object seems a futile attempt on the part of these people to intimidate and coerce me into silence. I am conscious of the fact that these people have at their command services of the press, power, money and other resources with the help of which they are able to present falsehood as truth. On the other hand such facilities are denied to me. Even so I have no doubt in any mind that my effort to end this long-standing dispute about Kashmir can have no relation to communalism.

This effort, in fact, is a great service to all those who have been facing untold miseries during the last ten years because of this dispute having remained unsolved. Who can deny the reality that failure to end this dispute is not only a source of distress and misery to the Muslims of Jammu and Kashmir but is a cause of anxiety and uncertainty to the entire population of the State? A solution of this dispute will not only contribute to the strengthening of peace and security throughout Asia but will heal up a festering sore which has been seeping into the very vitals of India and Pakistan. It is, therefore, for any intelligent man to judge whether it is fair to equate with communalism any endeavour to help solve this dispute. I firmly believe that real secularism is the soul of democracy but I am unable to understand how the demand for the final settlement of the dispute in regard to the accession of the Jammu and Kashmir State in accordance with the wishes of the people does in any way infringe any principle of secularism.

It is not the first time that I am charged with communalism. During the last 27 years a large section of the press in North India often brought such charges against me and every time facts and events proved them false. Many incidents in the Freedom Movement of our State bear witness to the fact that in 1931 this section of the press went so far as to allege that I aspired to be the Sultan of Kashmir and that a crown was ready in the Jama Masjid, Srinagar, to be placed on any head at the opportune moment. Ultimately however, truth triumphed and the National Movement spread throughout the State.

Later, these charges were repeated during the "Quit Kashmir Movement". But when the practical test came in 1947, these were proved not only false and malicious but the world also came to appreciate that the attitude taken up by the Muslims of Kashmir in safeguarding life, honour and property of their non-Muslim brethren was unparalleled throughout the subcontinent. Today in 1958, the same disruptive elements are again at their old game, and surprisingly, they include even those whose hands were besmeared, in 1947, with the innocent blood of their neighbours and who celebrated with great joy and distribution of sweets the brutal assassination of Mahatma Gandhi.

Nevertheless, I feel sure that even this fresh attempt to malign me will also end in failure and fellow countrymen belonging to the minorities will find me, as ever, their best friend, well-wisher and protector of their legitimate rights. My past record should be a sufficient guarantee for any one to judge my future behaviour. I do not, therefore, wish to waste my time and that of my countrymen in putting up a defence against these slanderous accusations. When the dust raised by the propaganda of the interested people settles down, my fellow countrymen will view me in the light of their past experience of me and events which have now become part of history, and will refuse to fall a prey to such a nefarious propaganda.

The real secularism consists in safeguarding the legitimate rights of both the majority and minority communities. Happily the majority community in the State never considered the protection of the minorities as communalism and I hope and trust that the minority communities of this State will similarly not view the protection of the legitimate rights of the majority community as communalism.

I am being accused of break of pledge in support of the accession of the State to India. With all the force at my command, I repudiate this allegation and submit that the responsibility for the breach of the pledges rests elsewhere. A pledge is not a one-sided process; in regard to the accession of Kashmir the Governments of India and Kashmir accepted certain responsibilities and obligations but, unfortunately, the former did not fulfil their share in spite of the best endeavours of the Kashmir Government to persuade them to do so.

When the charge of the breach of faith is, therefore, levelled against me. I have a right to pose the question as to where lies the responsibility for not implementing the promises and assurances given by the Government of India to the State of Jammu and Kashmir from the date of tribal raid till my arrest in 1953.

Much propaganda is being made out of the fact that in November 1947, I pledged my support to Pandit Nehru in a mass meeting held at Lal Chowk in Srinagar. But with this, one should not forget what Panditji said a few minutes earlier. Explaining the Government of India policy, he stated that: "It must be remembered that the struggle in Kashmir is a struggle of the people of Kashmir under popular leadership against the invader. We have come to your help at this critical hour. Our forces are here simply to defend your country against the raiders and as soon as Kashmir is free from the invader, our troops will have no further necessity to remain here and you will be free to determine your future in accordance with your wishes."..

A few days before the Lal Chowk meeting, announcing the Government of India policy, Prime Minister Pandit Jawaharlal Nehru, in his broadcast from New Delhi on the 2nd November, 1947, said: "We are anxious not to finalise anything in a moment of crisis and without the fullest opportunity to be given to the people of Kashmir to have their say. It was for them ultimately to decide: And let me make it clear that it has been our policy all along that where there is a dispute about accession of a State to either Dominion, the accession must be made by the people of that State. It was in accordance with this policy that we have added a proviso to the Instrument of Accession of Kashmir".

When the Constitution of India was Finalised, the State of Jammu and Kashmir was given the status of an autonomous State in all matters except (a) Defence, (b) Foreign Affairs and (c) Communications (Section 370 of the Indian Constitution). This was an inviolable pledge.

May I ask, as to where all these promises and assurances stand 1948 and 5 January 1949, that the final disposition of the State of Jammu and Kashmir will be made in accordance with the will of the people expressed through the democratic method of a free and impartial plebiscite conducted under the auspices of the United Nations:

> "Affirming that the convening of a Constituent Assembly as recommended by the General Council of the All Jammu and Kashmir National Conference, and any action that Assembly might attempt to take to determine the future shape and affiliation of the entire State or any part thereof, would not constitute a disposition of the State in accordance with the above principle".

Pandit Jawaharlal Nehru, while answering a question on the subject in the Indian Parliament in 1955, declared the decision of the Constituent Assembly regarding the accession as unilateral and, therefore, of no consequence to resolve this international dispute on Kashmir. The decision of this Assembly cannot, moreover, be viewed in isolation and out of context of historical events that followed. The question is not about the decision but as to what were the means by which it was secured. A period of five years elapsed between the date of convening of the Consembly and taking a final decision on the accession issue. The Consembly which enjoyed popular support in 1951 on this side of the "Ceasefire Line" forfeited the confidence due to the events that took place on 9th August, 1953, and thereafter.

The front rank members of the body were put in prison and debarred from participating in the proceedings of the House. Those who were not in prison were forced into submission by threats of persecution and imprisonment and irresistible temptations were thrown in their way. Consequently, the masses lost faith in them as there was no contact between those members and their constituents.

The fact cannot be ignored that before the Constitution was finalised, the Leader of the House was arrested under a deeply-laid conspiracy and when the masses protested against this illegal and unconstitutional act, a reign of terror was let loose and hundreds of men, women and children were shot down in cold blood and this continued for months together. A period of four years was spent in making the members of the Assembly to toe the line of the *coup* stagers. Such of the members as did not submit were kept in jail and the Constitution declared passed.

Even though in detention, yet led by national interests, from time to time I tried to warn all concerned against the dangerous consequences of allowing the Constituent Assembly to be used for group conflicts of the National Conference. In telegram on 30th September, 1951, I asked the President of the Constituent Assembly to allow me to be heard by the Assembly before the "vote of confidence" in *coup* stagers was considered. Then again when the Constitution was going to be finalised, on 16th August, 1956, I wrote to him saying:

> "By 9th August action as well as by the long record of black deeds in and outside the House, the present Government and the Assembly have completely forfeited the confidence of the electorate and they no longer represent the political and economic aspiration of the people. It will be the height of treachery if such

> a body sits to frame a fundamental Jaw for the people and their future generations. Nothing can be worse betrayal of their aspirations. I feel therefore, duty-bound to ask you to desist from such a course of action."..

In view of these circumstances. I fail to understand why and how my refusal to accent these decisions of the Consembly could be taken as treasonable.

One of the most important objects underlying the entire political movement in the State has remained to secure the right of self-determination for the people of the State. Expression of the will of the people through a plebiscite is the one formula which has been agreed upon by the parties concerned and in a mass of disagreements about details, this common denominator has held the field so far. The Security Council, also, has held that a plebiscite, conducted in a fair and free atmosphere under its own auspices, is a just solution of the problem consistent with the provisions of the United Nations Charter. This commitment has repeatedly been reaffirmed by the parties concerned.

The people of the State consider the formula of plebiscite as a clear interpretation of their long cherished aspirations and as a lasting solution of the complicated problem which is facing them since 1947. Their political outlook is the product of the last 27 years' struggle whose sheet-anchor has ever remained the conviction that "sovereignty vests with the people". A State which was sold away for a cash consideration and remained in slavish subjugation for a century, naturally gave this demand the foremost importance and made the right of self-democratic set-up as its cardinal creed.

The Indian National Congress has throughout raised its voice in support of our demand and it was on the basis of this principle that the leaders, of the Congress, is general, and Pandit Nehru in particular, extended cooperation and help to the Freedom Struggle of the State from its very inception. I may refer in this connection to the resolutions passed and the speeches delivered at the Annual Session of the All Jammu and Kashmir National Conference held at Sopore in 1945, in which Pandit Jawaharlal Nehru, Maulana

Azad, Khan Abdul Ghaffar Khan, Khan Abdul Samad Khan and other top-ranking Congress leaders participated. In this session the people's demand for the right of self-determination formed the central theme of the resolutions passed.

The Congress leaders not only supported, all along, our demand for the right of self-determination, but also helped in organising me in the "Quit Kashmir Case". Pandit Jawaharlal Nehru did not only court arrest as a mark of his support to our struggle, but went to the extent of appearing as my council in the case, in collaboration with the late Mr. Asaf Ali and others.

Subsequently, when the subcontinent was partitioned and the tribal raid took place, it was again in defence of this very right of self-determination that Government of India agreed to send its armed forces to Kashmir.

Simultaneously, Government of India while accepting the Instrument of Accession signed by Maharaja Hari Singh on 26th October, 1947, laid down the condition that the accession was subject to ratification by the people.

Then came a period when Governments of India and Pakistan tried to solve the Kashmir dispute by direct negotiations. In May, 1953 we in "National Conference were asked to weigh and suggest the various alternate proposals for the solution. On 9th June the following unanimous decision was taken by a High Level Committee of the National Conference and communicated to Panditji:

"As a result of discussion held in the course of various meetings, the following proposals only emerge as possible alternatives for an honourable and peaceful solution of the Kashmir dispute between India and Pakistan:

(a) Overall plebiscite with conditions as detailed in the minutes of the meeting dated 4th June 1953;

(b) Independence of the whole State;

(c) Independence of the whole State with joint control of foreign affairs and defence; and

(d) Dixon plan with independence for the plebiscite area.

> "Bakhshi (Ghulam Mohammed) Sahib was emphatically of the opinion that the proposal (d) above should be put up as first and the only practicable, advantageous and honourable solution of the dispute. Maulana Sayeed, however, opined, that the order of preference as given above should be adhered to".

Unfortunately, the authorities at the helm of affairs could not appreciate the value of this and no further progress took place. In the meantime, events took an ugly turn and 9th August *coup* was staged, story of which need not be related here:

> It was as late as August. 1953, after my detention, that the two Prime Ministers of India and Pakistan, after deliberating for a number of days in Delhi as to how best to resolve this dispute, reiterated in a joint communique their "firm opinion that this (Kashmir Question) should be settled in accordance with the wishes of the people of that State".

Telegram to Cabinet Mission

[1946]

As President. All Jammu and Kashmir National Conference representing all communities and classes of people inhabiting Jammu and Kashmir State I welcome your visit to our state and hope that it will usher in new era of freedom both political and economic for four million state people. As Mission is at moment reviewing relationship of Princes with the Paramount Power with reference to treaty rights we wish to submit that for us in Kashmir re-examination of this relationship is vital matter because hundred years ago in 1846 land and people of Kashmir were sold away to servitude of Dogra House by British for seventy-five lakhs of Sikh rupees equivalent to fifty lakhs British Indian rupees. Then Governor of Kashmir resisted transfer, but was finally reduced to subjection with aid of British.

Thus sale deed of 1846 misnamed treaty of Amritsar sealed fate of Kashmir masses. We declare to world that this sale deed confers no privileges equivalent to those claimed by states governed by treaty rights. As such case of Kashmir stands on unique footing and people of Kashmir press on Mission their unchallengeable claims to freedom on withdrawal of British power from India.

We wish to declare that no sale deed however sacrosanct can condemn more than four million men and women to servitude of an autocrat when will to live under this rule is no longer there.

People of Kashmir are determined to mould their own destiny and we appeal to Mission to recognise justice and strength of our cause."

12

Golden Words of the Sheikh

- After all, we are not logs of wood, we are not dolls. We must have an opinion one way or the other.
- Handcuffs jingle. They do not make us afraid. God will give us faith in victory. The voice of truth will prevail. Prophets have spoken for the truth, which has always triumphed finally.
- The appeal to religion constitutes a sentimental and a wrong approach to the question. Sentiment has its own place in life but often it leads to irrational action.
- It is said that Sheikh Abdullah is a friend of Pandit Jawaharlal Nehru. Yes, I admit that. I feel honoured that such a great man claims me as his friend. And he happens to belong to my own land; he is also a Kashmiri, and blood is thicker than water. If Jawaharlal Nehru gives me that honour, I cannot help it. He is my friend.
- The Indian National Congress has throughout raised its voice in support of our demand and it was on the basis of this principle that the leaders, of the Congress, in general, and Pandit Nehru in particular, extended cooperation and help to the Freedom Struggle of the State from its very inception.

- The Congress leaders not only supported, all along, our demand for the right of self-determination, but also helped me in organising the "Quit Kashmir Case". Pandit Jawaharlal Nehru did not only court arrest as a mark of his support to our struggle, but went to the extent of appearing as my council in the case, in collaboration with the late Mr. Asaf Ali and others. Subsequently, when the subcontinent was partitioned and the tribal raid took place, it was again in defence of this very right of self-determination that Government of India agreed to send its armed forces to Kashmir.
- It was agreed that in accordance with Article 5 of the Indian Constitution, persons who have their domicile in the Jammu and Kashmir State shall be the citizens of India. It was further agreed that the State legislature shall have power to define and regulate the rights and privileges of the permanent residents of the State.
- There are historic reasons which necessitate constitutional safeguards as for centuries past, the people of the State have been victims of exploitation at the hands of their well to- do neighbours.
- Our movement to freedom has been connected against the background of the same old struggle. We stood for the brotherhood of men of all creeds and strengthened our union on the basis of common work and sacrifice.
- Against us were ranged the force of religious bigotry centred in the Muslim league and its satellites, and the Hindu communalists from within and without the State. Ranged against us and often in alliance with communalism were the forces of the autocratic States backup on the Paramount Power, and on the other, by the rich landowners and other beneficiaries of Court patronage.
- We have been told that Sheikh Abdullah must walk out because he has declared his point of view in favour of India. Therefore, he cannot be impartial. We must have some impartial man, we must have some neutral man. As I have submitted to the members of the Security Council,

Sheikh Abdullah happens to be there (it is) because the people wish it. As long as the people wish it, I shall be there. There is no power on earth which can displace me from the position which I have there. As long as the people are behind me, I will remain there.

- The basis of our relationship with India is the Instrument of Accession which enabled our State to enter into an agreement with India. In accordance with the terms of the Instrument, certain powers were transferred to the Centre. The principal matters specified for this purpose in respect to which the Dominion Legislature could make laws for this State were: (a) Defence, (b) External Affairs, and (c) Communications.

- To take our first task, that of Constitution-making, we shall naturally be guided by the highest principles of the democratic Constitutions of the world. We shall base our work on the principles of equality, liberty and social justice, which are an integral feature of all progressive Constitutions. The rule of law as understood in the democratic countries of the world should be the cornerstone of our political structure.

- You are no doubt aware of the scope of our present constitutional ties with India. We are proud to have our bonds with India, the goodwill of those people and government is available to us in unstinted and abundant measure. The Constitution of India has provided for a federal union and in the distribution of sovereign powers has treated us differently from other constituent units.

- The real character of a State is revealed in its Constitution. The Indian Constitution has set before the country the goal of secular democracy based upon justice, freedom and equality for all without distinction. This is the bedrock of modern democracy. This should meet the argument that the Muslims of Kashmir cannot have security in India, where the large majority of the population are Hindus. Any unnatural cleavage between religious groups is the legacy of Imperialism, and no modern State can afford to encourage artificial division, if it is to achieve progress and prosperity. The Indian Constitution has amply and finally repudiated the concept of a religious State, which is a throw back to medievalism, by guaranteeing the equality of rights of all citizens, irrespective of their religion, colour caste and class.

- It is not the first time that I am charged with communalism. During the last 27 years, a large section of the press in North India often brought such charges against me and every time facts and events proved them false. Many incidents in the Freedom Movement of our State bear witness to the fact that in 1931 this section of the press went so far as to allege that I aspired to be the Sultan of Kashmir and that a crown was ready in the Jama Masjid, Srinagar, to be placed on my head at the opportune moment. Ultimately however, truth triumphed and the National Movement spread throughout the State. Later, these charges were repeated during the "Quit Kashmir Movement". But when the practical test came in 1947, these were proved not only false and malicious but the world also came to appreciate that the attitude, taken up by the Muslims of Kashmir — in safeguarding life, honour and property of their non-Muslim brethren — was unparalleled throughout the subcontinent.

- The claim of being a Muslim State is of course only a camouflage. It is a screen to dupe the common man, so that he may not see clearly that Pakistan is a feudal State, in which a clique is trying by these methods to maintain itself in power.

- Another big obstacle to a dispassionate evaluation of her policies is the lack of a Constitution in Pakistan. As it stands at present, this State enjoys the unique position of being governed by a Constitution enacted by an outside Parliament which gives no idea whatsoever of the future shape of civic and social relations. It is reasonable to argue that Pakistan cannot have the confidence of a freedom-loving and democratic people when it has failed to guarantee even fundamental rights of its citizens.

13

Great Life at a Glance

1905, Dec., 5: Sheikh Abdullah was born at Soura in Kashmir.

1911: He was admitted to a primary school after receiving initial religious education in a Maktab.

1922: He passed Matriculation examinations from Punjab University.

1926: He passed F. Sc. examination from S.P. College, Srinagar.

1928: He completed B.Sc. from Islamia College, Lahore.

1930: He obtained M.Sc. degree from Aligarh Muslim University, Aligarh.

1931: He joined as a teacher in a school, for sometime.

— He organised an agitation against the Maharaja.

1932, Oct.: He founded Muslim Conference.

1933: He married Akbar Jehan, originally a European.

1934: Praja Sabha (Legislative Assembly) was established.

1938, June: He proposed to rename Muslim Conference as National Conference, to make it a secular organisation.

— *Aug.:* He was arrested and detained by State government.

1939, Feb.: He was released from prison.

— *Jun.:* Muslim Conference was officially renamed as National Conference.

1946, May: He launched Quit Kashmir agitation against the Maharaja. He was arrested and put behind the bars.

1947, Sept.: He was released from jail.

— ***Oct.:*** Pakistani tribals attacked Kashmir.

— Kashmir State was acceded to Indian Union, following the finalisation of an Instrument of Accession.

— ***Nov.:*** Sheikh Abdullah was appointed as the Head of the Emergency Administration in the State.

1948, March: He was appointed as Prime Minister of Kashmir, under a Sadre-Riyasat.

— He went to UN for representing Indian case on Kashmir.

— He became a member of Indian Constituent Assembly.

1952: Delhi Agreement was signed by Pt. Nehru, the Prime Minister of India and Sheikh Abdullah, the Premier of J&K, to formalise New Delhi – State relationship.

1953, Aug.: He was dismissed from his office and detained on charges of conspiracy.

— Bekhshi Ghulam Muhammed took over as the Prime Minister the State.

1964, April: All charges against him were dropped and he was released.

— He met Pt. Nehru in New Delhi and then went to Pakistan, to meet the President and other government leaders there.

1965: He was detained again, by the Central government.

1968: He was released by the central government.

1971: He was exiled from Kashmir for 18 months.

1974: Indira – Sheikh accord was signed.

1975: Sheikh assumed power as the Chief Minister of J&K.

1982, Sept. 8: Sheikh Abdullah died.

Appendix

Kashmir through the Ages

The Backdrop

Kashmir was one of the major centres of Sanskrit scholars. According to the Mahabharata, the Kambojas ruled Kashmir during the epic period with a Republican system of government, Later, the Panchalas are stated to have established their sway. The Mauryan emperor Ashoka was often credited with having founded the city of Srinagar. Kashmir was once also a Buddhist seat of learning.

Advent of Muslims

Shams-ud-Din Shah Mir was a ruler of Kashmir and the founder of the Shah Miri dynasty named after him. He came from Swat, the then (Tribal) territory on the borders of Afghanistan and played a notable role in subsequentive political history of the valley. Shahmir became the ruler of Kashmir and reigned for three years. He was the first ruler of Swati dynasty, which was established in 1339. Shah Mir was succeeded by his eldest son Jamshid, but he was deposed by his brother Ali Sher within few months, who ascended the throne under the name of Alauddin. In the 14th century, Islam gradually became the dominant religion in Kashmir, starting with the conversion in 1323 of the first king of the Sayyid Dynasty from Ladakh. The Muslims and Hindus of Kashmir lived in relative harmony, since the Sufi-Islamic way of life that ordinary Muslims followed in Kashmir complemented the Rishi tradition of Kashmiri Pandits. This led to a syncretic culture where Hindus and Muslims revered the same local saints and prayed at the same shrines. The famous sufi saint Bulbul Shah was able to persuade the king of the time Rinchan Shah from Ladakh to adopt the Islamic way of life, and the foundation of Sufiana composite culture was laid when Muslims, Hindus and Buddhists were co-existing. Several Kashmiri rulers, such as Sultan Zain-ul-Abidin, were tolerant of all religions in a manner comparable to Akbar. However, several Muslim rulers of Kashmir were intolerant to other religions. Sultan Sikandar Butshikan of Kashmir (AD 1389-1413) and his (former Brahmin) minister Saif ud-Din were often considered the worst of these.

Birth of Princely State

By the early 19th century, the Kashmir valley had passed from the control of the Durrani Empire of Afghanistan, and four centuries of Muslim rule under the Mughals and the Afghans, to the conquering Sikh armies. Earlier, in 1780, after the death of Ranjit Deo, the Raja of Jammu, the kingdom of Jammu (to the south of the Kashmir valley) was captured by the Sikhs under Ranjit Singh of Lahore and afterwards, until 1846, became a tributary to the Sikh power.

Ranjit Deo's grandnephew, Gulab Singh, subsequently sought service at the court of Ranjit Singh, distinguished himself in later campaigns, especially the annexation of the Kashmir valley by the Sikh army in 1819, and, for his services, was made Raja of Jammu in 1820. With the help of his officer, Zorawar Singh, Gulab Singh soon captured Ladakh and Baltistan, regions to the east and northeast of Jammu.

In 1845, the First Anglo-Sikh War broke out, and Gulab Singh "contrived to hold himself aloof till the battle of Sobraon (1846), when he appeared as a useful mediator and the trusted advisor of Sir Henry Lawrence. Two treaties were concluded. By the first the State of Lahore (*i.e.* West Punjab) handed over to the British, as equivalent for rupees one crore of indemnity and the hill countries between Beas and Indus; by the second. The British made over to Gulab Singh for Rupees 75 lakhs all the hilly or mountainous country situated to the east of Indus and west of Ravi" (*i.e.* the Vale of Kashmir). Soon after Gulab Singh's death in 1857, his son, Ranbir Singh, added the emirates of Hunza, Gilgit and Nagar to the kingdom.

The Princely State of Kashmir and Jammu was constituted between 1820 and 1858 and was "somewhat artificial in composition and it did not develop a fully coherent identity, partly as a result of its disparate origins and partly as a result of the autocratic rule which it experienced on the fringes of Empire." It combined disparate regions, religions, and ethnicities: to the east, Ladakh was ethnically and culturally Tibetan and its inhabitants practised Buddhism; to the south, Jammu had a mixed population of Hindus, Muslims and Sikhs; in the heavily populated central Kashmir valley, the population was overwhelmingly Muslim, however, there was also a small but influential Hindu minority, the Kashmiri Brahmins or pandits; to the northeast, sparsely populated Baltistan had a population ethnically related to Ladakh, but they were Muslim to the north, also sparsely populated, Gilgit Agency, was an area of diverse, mostly Muslim groups; and, to the west, Punch was Muslim, but of different ethnicity than the Kashmir valley. After the Indian Rebellion of 1857, in which Kashmir sided with the British, and the subsequent assumption of direct rule by Great Britain, the princely state of Kashmir came under the paramountcy of the British Crown.

At the Time of Independence

Ranbir Singh's grandson Hari Singh, who had ascended the throne of Kashmir in 1925, was the reigning monarch in 1947 at the conclusion of British rule of the subcontinent and the subsequent partition of the British Indian Empire into the newly independent Union of India and the Dominion of Pakistan. Rulers of Princely States were encouraged to accede their States to either Dominion - India or Pakistan, taking into account factors such as geographical contiguity and the wishes of their people. In 1947, Kashmir's population was "77% Muslim and 20% Hindu". To postpone, making a hurried decision, the Maharaja signed a "standstill" agreement with Pakistan, which ensured continuity of trade, travel, communication, and similar services between the two. Such an agreement was also pending with India. In October 1947, Pashtuns from Pakistan's North-West Frontier Province, invaded Kashmir, along with the Poonch rebels. The tribesmen engaged in looting and killing along the way. The ostensible aim of the guerilla campaign was to frighten Hari Singh into submission. Instead the Maharaja appealed to Lord Mountbatten for assistance, and the Governor-General agreed on the condition that the ruler accede to India. Once the Maharaja signed the Instrument of Accession, Indian soldiers entered Kashmir and drove the Pakistani-sponsored irregulars from all but a small section of the state. India accepted the accession.

Sheikh on Scene

Popular Kashmiri leader Sheikh Abdullah endorsed the accession was appointed head of the emergency administration. The Pakistani government immediately contested the accession. In the last days of 1948, a ceasefire was agreed under UN auspices; however, relations between India and Pakistan soured, and eventually led to three more wars over Kashmir in 1965, 1971 and 1999. India had control of more then half the area of the former princely state of Jammu and Kashmir; Pakistan controlled a third of the region, the Northern Areas, historically known as regions of Gilgit and Baltistan; and Pakistan occupied Kashmir. In 1949, the Indian government obliged Hari Singh to leave Jammu and Kashmir and yield the government to Sheikh Abdullah, the leader of a popular political party, the National Conference.

Rise and Fall of Sheikh: Sheikh Abdullah became the first Prime Minister of Jammu and Kashmir, following the State's accession to Indian Union. However, he was deposed in arrested and jailed in 1953. Bakhshi Ghulam Muhammed succeeded his, who in turn was succeeded by Shamsuddin G.M. Sadiq and Mir Qasim, representing National Conference, Congress and PDP. In 1975, Sheikh Abdullah returned to power as Chief Minister of the State. He remained at the hell till his death in 1982.

After Sheikh: Sheikh's son Dr. Farooq Abdullah succeed him. He was deposed several times and returned to power again and again. In between, his brother in law G.M. Shah, Mufti Saeed and Ghulam Nabi Azad occupied the seat of Chief Minister for short terms, with intervals of the Governor's role. Finally, Dr. Farooq's son Omar Abdullah assumed the leadership of National Conference and subsequently the reins of government, as the new Chief Minister of the State.

Militancy and Peace: Militancy rose in the Kashmir valley in late 80's. However, gradually, it waned and peace returned to the valley and the entire state, by and large. Currently, the State is progressing fast on the path of peace, normally and development.

The Timeline

1846: Jammu and Kashmir (J&K) State was created under the Treaty of Amritsar between the East India company and Raja Gulab Singh of Jammu who bought Kashmir Valley from the East India Company for Rs.75,00,000 and added it to Jammu and Ladakh already under his rule. Kashmir Valley was a Muslim majority region speaking the Kashmiri language and a distinct culture called Kashmiriyat.

1857: The War of independence, The Subcontinent fractured into hundreds of states.

1931: The movement against the repressive Maharaja Hari Singh began. It was brutally suppressed by the State forces. Hari Singh was part of a Hindu Dogra dynasty, ruling over a majority Muslim State. The predominantly Muslim population was kept poor, illiterate and was not adequately represented in the State's services. The Glancy Commission appointed by the Maharaja published a report in April 1932, confirming the existence of the grievances of the State's subjects and suggested recommendations providing for adequate representation of Muslims in the State's services; Maharaja accepted these recommendations but delayed implementation, leading to another agitation in 1934.

Maharaja granted a Constitution providing a Legislative Assembly for the people, but the Assembly turned out to be powerless. The 1931 protest led to the Quit Kashmir movement against the Maharaja in 1946 by the Kashmir leader Sheikh

Abdullah, and eventually to the Azad Kashmir movement which gained momentum a year later.

1940, March 23: Pakistan Resolution passed: The Pakistan Resolution was passed at Iqbal Park, Lahore. The resolution demanded the establishment of an independent state comprising all regions in which Muslims were in majority. The letter "K" in the word "Pakistan" represented Kashmir.

1946, July 26: Quit Kashmir movement gained momentum. The Muslim Conference adopted the Azad Kashmir Resolution, calling for the end of autocratic rule in the region. The resolution also claimed for Kashmiris the right to elect their own constituent assembly.

1947: An internal revolt began in the Poonch region against oppressive taxation by the Maharaja. In August, Maharaja's forces fired upon demonstrations in favour of Kashmir joining Pakistan, burned whole villages and massacred innocent people. The Poonch rebels declared an independent government of "Azad" Kashmir on 24 October.

August 14/15: Independence of the British India into India and Pakistan. Kashmir signed Standstill Agreement with Pakistan. Rulers of Princely States were encouraged to accede their States to either Dominion - India or Pakistan, taking into account factors such as geographical contiguity and the wishes of their people. The Maharaja of Kashmir delayed his decision in an effort to remain independent.

October 22: Thousands of Pashtuns from Pakistan's North West Frontier Province, recruited by the Poonch rebels, invaded Kashmir, along with the Poonch rebels, allegedly incensed by the atrocities against fellow Muslims in Poonch and Jammu. The tribesmen engaged in looting and killing along the way. Maharaja of Kashmir asked India for help.

October 26: The Maharaja of the State of Jammu and Kashmir signed the Instrument of Accession (IOA), acceding the 75% majority Muslim region to the Indian Union. India accepted the accession, regarding it provisional until such time as the will of the people could be ascertained by a plebiscite.

October 27: The Indian army entered the state to repel the invaders. Sheikh Abdullah endorsed the accession as ad-hoc which would be ultimately decided by a plebiscite and was appointed head of the emergency administration.

1947/1948: Indo-Pakistani War of 1947: Pakistan disputed that the accession was illegal and the first war over Kashmir broke out.

1948: India took the Kashmir problem to the United Nations (UN) Security Council on 1 January.

1949: On 1 January, a ceasefire between Indian and Pakistani forces left India in control of most of the valley, as well as Jammu and Ladakh, while Pakistan gained control of part of Kashmir including what Pakistan called "Azad" Kashmir and Northern territories. Pakistan claimed it was merely supporting an indigenous rebellion in "Azad" Kashmir and Northern Territories against repression, while India rightly termed that territory as POK (Pakistan Occupied Kashmir).

1949: On 5 January, UNCIP (United Nations Commission for India and Pakistan) resolution stated that the question of the accession of the State of Jammu and Kashmir to India or Pakistan would be decided through a free and impartial plebiscite. As per the 1948 and 1949 UNCIP Resolutions, both countries accepted the principle, that Pakistan secured the withdrawal of Pakistani intruders followed by withdrawal of Pakistani and Indian forces, as a basis for the formulation of a Truce agreement whose details were to be arrived at in future, followed by a plebiscite; However, both countries failed to arrive at a Truce agreement due to differences in interpretation of the procedure for and extent of demilitarisation.

1949: On 17 October, the Indian Constituent Assembly adopted Article 370 of the Constitution, ensuring a special status and internal autonomy for Jammu and Kashmir, with Indian jurisdiction in Kashmir limited to the three areas agreed in the IOA, namely, defence, foreign affairs and communications.

1951: First post-independence elections. Sheikh Abdullah won, mostly unopposed.

1947-1952: Sheikh Abdullah drifted from a position of endorsing accession to India in 1947 to insisting on the self-determination of Kashmiris in 1952. In July 1952, he signed Delhi Agreement with the Central government on Centre-State relationships, providing for autonomy of the State within India and of regions within the State.

1953-1954: In 1953, the governments of India and Pakistan agreed to appoint a Plebiscite Administrator by the end of April 1954. Abdullah procrastinated in confirming the accession of Kashmir to India. In August 1953, Abdullah was dismissed and arrested. Bakshi Ghulam Mohammed was installed in power, who then got the accession formally ratified in 1954.

1956-1957: On 30 October 1956, the state Constituent Assembly adopted a constitution for the state declaring it an integral part of the Indian Union. India's Home Minister, Pandit Govind Ballabh Pant, during his visit to Srinagar, declared that the State of Jammu and Kashmir was an integral part of India and there would be no question of a plebiscite to determine its status afresh. India would resist plebiscite efforts from then on. Kashmiri activists continued to insist on the promised self-determination.

1963-1964: On 27 December, mass upsurge occured in Kashmir Valley when the holy relic was found missing from the Hazratbal Shrine; the lost relic was recovered on 4 Jan. 1964. Protest demonstrations occured in Kashmir Valley and Pakistan held parts of the State in December against Articles 356 and 357 of the Indian Constitution being extended to the state, by virtue of which the Centre could assume the government of the State and exercise its legislative powers.

1965: Indo-Pakistan War of 1965: Pakistan took advantage of the discontent in the Valley and sent in a few thousand armed Pakistani infiltrators across the cease-fire line in August in Operation Gibraltar, and incidents of violence increased in Kashmir Valley; A full Indo-Pakistan war broke out which ended in a ceasefire on 23 September.

1966: In January, Tashkent Declaration was signed by both countries, agreeing to revert to pre-1965 position, under Russian mediation. Pakistan supported guerrilla groups in Kashmir increased their activities even after the ceasefire. Kashmiri nationalists Amanullah Khan and Maqbool Bhat formed another

Plebiscite Front with an armed wing called the National Liberation Front in Azad Kashmir, with the objective of freeing Kashmir.

December 6, 1971: Indo-Pakistan War of 1971; Secession of *East Pakistan* and birth of Bangladesh.

1972: Republic of India and Pakistan agreed to respect the cease-fire live as Line of Control. India and Pakistan signed the Simla Agreement in July, which had a clause that the final settlement of Kashmir would be decided bilaterally in future and that both the sides should respect the LOC.

1975: Sheikh Abdullah returned to power as Chief Minister of J&K, following Indira-Sheikh accord.

1976: Maqbool Bhat was arrested on his return to the Valley. Amanullah Khan moved to England and NLF became Jammu and Kashmir Liberation Front (JKLF).

1979: The USSR invaded Afghanistan. The US and Pakistan were involved in training, recruiting, arming, and unleashing the Mujahedin on Afghanistan. The mujahedin so recruited would take on their own agenda of establishing Islamic rule in Kashmir from the late 1980's.

1982: Sheikh Abdullah passed away and his son Dr. Farooq Abdullah took over.

April 13, 1984: The Indian Army took Siachen Glacier region of Kashmir. Maqbool Bhat was executed.

1987: National Conferences, Farooq Abdullah won the elections. The Muslim United Front (MUF) accused that the elections had been rigged. The insurgency in the valley increased in momentum from this point on, given the consistent failure of democracy and limited employment opportunities. The MUF candidate Mohammad Yousuf Shah, imprisoned and he later became Syed Salahuddin, chief of militant outfit Hizb-ul-Mujahedin. His election aides called the HAJY group - Abdul Hamid Shaikh, Ashfaq Majid Wani, Javed Ahmed Mir and Mohammed Yasin Malik - joined the JKLF. Amanullah Khan took refuge in Pakistan, after being deported from England and began to direct operations across the LoC. Young disaffected Kashmiris in the Valley such as the HAJY group were recruited by JKLF.

1988: Protests began in the Valley along with anti-centre demonstrations, followed by police firing and curfew.

1989: End of Soviet occupation of Afghanistan released a great deal of militant energy and weapons to Kashmir. Pakistan provided arms and training to both indigenous and foreign militants in Kashmir, thus adding fuel to the smouldering fire of discontent in the valley.

1990: In January, Jagmohan was appointed, the Governor. Farooq Abdullah resigned. On 20 January, an estimated 100 people were killed when a large group of unarmed protesters were fired upon by the troops at the Gawakadal bridge. With this incident, it became an larger insurgency. On March 1, an estimated one million took to the streets and more than forty people were killed in police firing. On 13 February, Lassa Kaul, director of Srinagar Doordarshan, was killed by the militants for implementing pro-centre media policy. Though the JKLF tried to explain that the killings of Pandits were not communal, the murders caused a scare among the minority Hindu community. The rise of new militant groups, some warnings in anonymous posters and some unexplained killings of innocent members of the community contributed to an atmosphere of insecurity for the Kashmiri Pandits. Joint reconciliation efforts by members from both Muslim and Pandit communities were actively discouraged by Jagmohan. Most of the Hindus in the Valley, including the entire Kashmiri Pandit community, fled the Valley in March.

After 1990: An officially estimated 10,000 desperate Kashmiri youth crossed over to Pakistan for training and procurement of arms, indigenous and foreign militant groups besides pro-India renegade militants proliferate through the nineties with an estimated half a million central security forces deployed in the Kashmir Valley since the nineties with increasing violence and human right violations by all sides leading to tens of thousands of civilian casualties.

1996: Farooq Abdullah returned to power, after winning elections.

1999: Kargil War.

2001, July 14–16: General Pervez Musharraf and Atal Behari Vajpayee met for peace talks.

2001, October: Kashmir assembly in Srinagar attacked, 38 people dead.

2001, December: Attack on Indian parliament in New Delhi.

2002: Dr. Farooq's son Omar Abdullah took over the reigns of National Conference.

2003, May 2: India and Pakistan restored diplomatic ties.

2003, July 11: Delhi-Lahore bus service resumed.

2004, September 24: Prime Minister Manmohan Singh and President Musharraf met in New York during UN General Assembly session.

July, 2006: Second round of Indo-Pakistan peace talks.

2007, Feb.: Samjhauta Express firebombed, 67 killed.

2009: Omar Abdullah sworn in as the Chief Minister of the State.

2010, June: Following the killing of a young Kashmiri Tufail Ahmad Mattoo, protest demonstrations continued in Kashmir for months. However, peace prevailed in the valley at last.

Bibliography

A. Q. Rafiqi: *History of the Freedom Struggle in Jammu & Kashmir*, Light & Life, New Delhi, 1980.

Abdullah, Sheikh: *Atish-e-Chinar (URDU)*, Shaukat Publications, Srinagar, 1985.

Balraj, Puri: *Kashmir: Towards Insurgency*, New Delhi 1993.

Chandra, Bipan: *India after Independence 1947-2000*, New Penguin Books, Delhi, 2000.

D. A. Wilkinson: *International Law and Political Crisis: An Analytic Casebook*, Little Brown, Boston, 1968.

E. P. Menon: *A Report on the Kashmir Problem; an Appeal for Rethinking on the India-Kashmir-Pakistan Relationship*, Dehradun, 1966.

Koithara, Verghese: *Crafting Peace in Kashmir: Through a Realist Lens*, Sage, Thousand Oaks, 2004.

Lakhanpal, P. L.: *Essential Documents and Notes on Kashmir Dispute*, International Books, Delhi, 1965.

Lamb, A.: *Birth of a Tragedy: Kashmir 1947*, Roxford Books, Hertingfordbury, 1994.

Lengyel, E.: *Jawaharlal Nehru; the Brahman from Kashmir*, F. Watts, New York, 1968.

Madhok, B.: *A story of Bungling in Kashmir*, Young Asia Publications, New Delhi, 1972.

Mather, B.: *The Pass Beyond Kashmir*, Collins, London, 1960.

Mattoo, A. M.: *Kashmir under the Mughals, 1586-1752*, Golden Horde Enterprises, Srinagar, 1988.

Misri, M. L. and M. S. Bhat: *Poverty, Planning, and Economic Change in Jammu and Kashmir*, Vikas Pub. House, New Delhi, 1994.

Mohinder, S.: *Raja Ram Singh : the Forgotten Prince and his Times, 1861-1899*, Gujral Printers, Jammu, 1990.

Morison, M. C.: *A Lonely Summer in Kashmir*, Duckworth, London, 1904.

Nair, K. and G. Karring: *Kashmir Today: Background Study for the Jarring Report*, Indian Council of World Affairs, New Delhi, 1957.

Nath, Prem Bazaz: *Democracy Through Intimidation and Terror*, Heritage Publishers, New Delhi, 1978.

Nehru, J.: *Kashmir, 1947-1956*, Information Service of India, New Delhi, 1956.

Neve, A.: *Thirty Years in Kashmir*, Asian Publications, Lucknow, 1984.

Neve, E.: *English-Kashmiri: A Vocabulary of the Kashmiri Language*, Jay Kay Book House, Jammu, 1993 .

Nisar, A.: *Agricultural Development and Income Distribution*, Rima Publication House, New Delhi, 1985.

Noorani, A. G.: *The Kashmir Question*, Manaktalas, Bombay, 1964.

Parkash, D. R.: *Fight for Kashmir*, Tagore Memorial Publications, New Delhi, 1948.

Parmu, R. K.: *A history of Muslim rule in Kashmir, 1320-1819*, People's Publication House, Delhi, New Delhi, 1948.

Pirie, P.: *Kashmir; the Land of Streams and Solitudes*, J. Lane, London, 1909.

Rabbani, G. M.: *Ancient Kashmir : A Historical Perspective*, Gulshan Publishers, Srinagar, 1981.

Rahmatullah, K.: *Kashmir and the United Nations*, Vikas Publications, Delhi, 1969.

Raina, D. N.: *Unhappy Kashmir : The Hidden Story*, Reliance Publication House, New Delhi, 1990.

Rastogi, G.: *Our Kashmir*, Suruchi Prakashan, New Delhi, 1991.

Roy, A. C.: *The Second Kashmir War as Seen from Different Angles*, Lake Publishers, Calcutta, 1969.

Roy, Chaudhury B.: *Folk Tales of Kashmir*, Sterling Publishers, Delhi, 1969.

Sandeep, Bamzai: *Bonfire of Kashmiryat*, Rupa & Co., New Delhi, 2006.

Saxena, H. L.: *The Tragedy of Kashmir*, Nationalist Publishers, New Delhi, 1975.

Saxena, K. S.: *Political History of Kashmir, B.C. 300-A.D.-A. D. 1200*, Upper India Publication House, Lucknow, 1974.

Sender, H. M.: *The Kashmiri Pandits : A Study of Cultural Choice in North India*, Oxford University Press,New York, 1988.

Shali, S. L.: *Kashmir : History and Archaeology Through the Ages*, Indus Publication Co., New Delhi, 1993.

Sharma, B. L.: *The Kashmir story*, Asia Pub. House, London, 1967.

Sharma, D.: *Education and socialization among the tribes : with special reference to Gujjars of Kashmir*, Commonwealth Publishers, New Delhi, 1965.

Sharma, P. N.: Inside Pak occupied Kashmir, Delhi Press, New Delhi, 1958.

Sharma, S. and Y. Mishra: *Kashmir, Tourism to Terrorism*, Sane Publications, Delhi, 1995.

Singh, R.: *Kashmir : Garden of the Himalayas*, New York, Thames and Hudson, NY, 1983.

Sinha, A.: *Farooq Abdullah, Kashmir's Prodigal Son: A Biography*, UBS Publishers' Distributors, New Delhi, 1996.

Sufi, G. M.: *Islamic Culture in Kashmir*, Light & Life Publishers, New Delhi, 1979.

Syed, Taffazull Hussain: *Sheikh Abdullah-A biography*, Wordclay, 2008.

Tariq, Ali: *The Clash Of Fundamentalism*, Verso Books, London, 2003.

Vashishth, S.: *Sheikh Abdullah, then and Now,* Maulik Sahitya Prakashan, Delhi, 1968.

Vidya, B.: *State politics and government: Jammu and Kashmir,* Jammu Tawi, Jay Kay Book House, J & K, 1985.

Walli, D. N.: *Kashmir Water Colour Paintings* Badiyar Srinagar, Walli, Kashmir, 1970.

Wani, G. M.: Kashmir: *From Autonomy to Azadi,* Srinagar, Valley Book House, 1996.

Wilson, H. H. and Kalhana: *The Hindu History of Kashmir,* Susil Gupta, Calcutta, 1960.

Wirsing, R.: *India, Pakistan, and the Kashmir Dispute : on Regional Conflict and its Resolution,* St. Martin's Press, New York, 1994.

Yasin, M. and M. Yasin: *Mysteries and Glimpses of Kashmir,* Raj Publications, Delhi, 1996.

Yasin, M.: *Rauzabal and other Mysteries of Kashmir,* Srinagar, Kesar Publishers, 1972.

Younghusband, F. E.: *The Northern Frontier of Kashmir,* Oriental Publishers, Delhi, 1973.

Yusuf Saraf, M.: *Kashmiris Fight-for Freedom,* Lahore, Pakistan, Ferozsons, 1977.

Zaheer, H.: *The Times and Trial of the Rawalpindi Conspiracy*: the first coup attempt in Pakistan, Oxford University Press, New York, 1998.

Zahur ud, D.: *Development of Urdu Language and Literature in the Jammu Region,* Gulshan Publishers, Srinagar, 1985.

Zohra, K.: *Muslim Saints and their Shrines,* Jay Kay Book House, Jammu, 1990.

Zutshi, N. K.: *Sultan Zain-ul-Abidin of Kashmir : An Age of Enlightenment,* Nupur Prakashan, Jammmu, 1976.

Zutshi, U. K.: *Emergence of Political Awakening in Kashmir,* Manohar Publications, New Delhi, 1986.

Index

A

B

C

D

E

F

G

H

I

J

K

L

M

N

O

P

□□□